P9-CKY-288

In this major new study of Henry James's classic text of cultural criticism, *The American Scene,* Beverly Haviland shows how James confronted the vexing problem of making sense of the past. In this record of his 1904–5 return to America and in his unfinished novels, *The Sense of the Past* and *The Ivory Tower,* he interpreted the social conflicts that seemed to be paralyzing relations between men and women, between black and white Americans, between "natives" and "aliens," between defenders of taste and censors of waste. Although James has been represented as conservative by liberal critics, it is just such simplifying oppositions that his method of interpretation works to transform. Haviland's method follows James's interpretative practice by bringing historical and theoretical readings of these texts into conversation with each other.

HENRY JAMES'S LAST ROMANCE

CAMBRIDGE STUDIES IN AMERICAN LITERATURE AND CULTURE

Editor

Eric Sundquist, *University of California, Los Angeles*

Founding Editor

Albert Gelpi, *Stanford University*

Advisory Board

Nina Baym, *University of Illinois, Urbana–Champaign*
Sacvan Bercovitch, *Harvard University*
Albert Gelpi, *Stanford University*
Myra Jehlen, *Rutgers University*
Carolyn Porter, *University of California, Berkeley*
Robert Stepto, *Yale University*
Tony Tanner, *King's College, Cambridge University*

Books in the series

Continued on page following Index

HENRY JAMES'S LAST ROMANCE

MAKING SENSE OF THE PAST AND THE AMERICAN SCENE

BEVERLY HAVILAND

State University of New York, Stony Brook

CAMBRIDGE UNIVERSITY PRESS

PS2127
H5
H38
1997

PUBLISHED BY THE PRESS SYNDICATE OF THE UNIVERSITY OF CAMBRIDGE
The Pitt Building, Trumpington Street, Cambridge CB2 1RP, United Kingdom

CAMBRIDGE UNIVERSITY PRESS
The Edinburgh Building, Cambridge CB2 2RU, United Kingdom
40 West 20th Street, New York, NY 10011-4211, USA
10 Stamford Road, Oakleigh, Melbourne 3166, Australia

© Cambridge University Press 1997

This book is in copyright. Subject to statutory exception
and to the provisions of relevant collective licensing agreements,
no reproduction of any part may take place without
the written permission of Cambridge University Press.

First published 1997

Printed in the United States of America

Typeset in Baskerville

Library of Congress Cataloging-in-Publication Data
Haviland, Beverly.
Henry James's last romance : making sense of the past and the American scene /
Beverly Haviland.
p. cm. – (Cambridge studies in American literature and culture)
Includes bibliographical references (p.   ) and index.
ISBN 0-521-56338-0 (hc)
1. James, Henry, 1843–1916 – Knowledge – History.   2. James, Henry,
1843–1916 – Knowledge – America.   3. Literature and history – United
States – History – 20th century.   4. James, Henry, 1843–1916. Sense
of the past.   5. James, Henry, 1843–1916. American scene.
6. James, Henry, 1843–1916. Ivory tower.   7. Atlantic States –
Historiography.   8. United States – Historiography.   9. United
States – In literature.   10. Culture in literature.   I. Title.
II. Series.
PS2127.H5H38   1997
813'.4 – dc20   96-43683
                                                                CIP

A catalog record for this book is available from the British Library.

ISBN 0 521 56338 0 hardback

ALBERTSON COLLEGE
CALDWELL. ID 83605

With love to
Louise Allen Haviland
1911–1991
Dancer – Social Worker – Mother

CONTENTS

Part Three
Patrimony and Matrimony:
The Ivory Tower

ACKNOWLEDGMENTS

One of the advantages of this book having been in the works for such a long time is that I now have the occasion to make sense of the past years as they are represented by the many, many people who have helped me along the way.

Recalling one of my earliest debts brings me immediately to the most vivid of all possible illustrations that the past cannot be revisited as it was. I can, however, commemorate my teacher, James M. Zito, whose premature death deprived the students at Sarah Lawrence College of the inspiration that he gave to so many of us. I am also grateful to Parker Barnum, who brought me to Mr. Zito's class, which changed the direction of my life when I read the first sentence of *The Portrait of a Lady*.

To professors from my graduate school days at Princeton I can, happily, continue to be obliged for their support. I am indebted to Emory Elliott for his encouraging this project from its earliest stages and, more recently, for expressing regret that I had to compress so much of the Swedenborg material from my dissertation on Balzac and James to make it serve this book. Joseph Frank has given a model for my work that would have been overwhelming had it not been for his modesty, his peerless devotion to teaching and to scholarship, and his great kindness. His faith in the value of my line of thinking about James sustained me as I foraged among the discourses to find a way to say what I knew we had understood together about social values in James's art.

In the process of composing this work, I have been fortunate in finding readers who were willing to share with me their knowledge of particular topics: Sidney Plotkin on Veblen; Giles Gunn on Henry James Senior; Ann E. Berthoff on C. S. Peirce; Catherine Clinton and Elizabeth Fox-Genovese on the South at the turn of the century. From my colleagues at Vassar with whom I team-taught in the American Culture Program – Clyde Griffen, James Merrell, Miriam Cohen – I learned the multidisciplinary methods I would need to construct this interpretation of James in his historical context.

I've had the opportunity to present parts of this book at conferences, and I would like particularly to thank the Interdisciplinary Center for the Humanities at the University of California, Santa Barbara; the Henry James–Joseph Conrad International Conference at the University of Kent, Canterbury; and Jonathan Freedman, who organized the panel on "James and Race" for the 1993 James Sesquicentennial (and who also read the entire manuscript with close attention and critical sympathy, as did William W. Stowe and Daniel Fogel). Members of the Vassar College Faculty Center Seminar on "Dilemmas of Persons and Property" – among them, Barbara Page, Mary L. Shanley, and Jesse Kalin – provided another constructively critical audience at an early stage of this work. Several other friends and colleagues deserve my special thanks for their insightful and sympathetic readings of the manuscript at various stages: Daniel Kempton, Robert Nelsen, Paul Russell, Robert DeMaria Jr., and Wendy Graham, my fellow Jamesian, who has been an invaluable cohort. I must also mention the much-appreciated work done on this manuscript by my research assistants at Vassar: Jenny Panchy, Lara Fischman, Martha Siemers, and Vi Nguyen.

Several friends have been so generous in giving their time and attention to talking with me, reading drafts, and then talking more that it is unimaginable that I could have persevered without them. Rebecca Bushnell, Shira Wolosky, Jeffrey Perl, and Jennifer Church have provided more than encouragement, however. We have shared over the years the deepest joys of friendship and the greatest pleasures of intellectual companionship.

To my readers for Cambridge University Press I owe a special debt, to Eric Sundquist and to Martha Banta, whose generous criticism suggested the ways in which the manuscript might best be revised. I am especially grateful for Martha Banta's appreciation of my reading of James and for the example of her scholarship. Whatever flaws remain, I am, of course, wholly responsible for, in spite of her best efforts and those of my diligent and tactful copyeditor, Brian MacDonald.

To Bay James, literary executor of the James estate, I am grateful for permission to quote from the manuscripts of Henry James's novel *The Sense of the Past*, held by the Houghton Library at Harvard University. The Houghton Library also kindly gave permission to quote from those manuscripts and from Theodora Bosanquet's *Original Diaries: 1898–1960*. Material in Chapter 5 was first published in *Common Knowledge* 3:3 (1994): 127–43; material from Chapters 4 and 6 was published in the *Henry James Review* 12:2 (1991): 166–74 and 16:3 (1995): 257–63; other material from Chapter 4 was published in the *International Journal of Politics, Culture and Society* 7:4 (1994): 615–37.

In this era of diminishing resources for the humanities, I am particularly thankful for the support I received in the form of a grant from the American Council of Learned Societies to study the James manuscripts and a fellowship from the National Endowment for the Humanities for a year of research and writing. Vassar College has also provided research support over the years.

The dedication of this book to my mother reflects the gratitude that I feel more deeply with each passing year. My brother Brian's wonder at my working on the same project for so many years has always cheered me. My last word is, however, to acknowledge wholeheartedly the value of a present that looks toward a future with Timmy, Maggie, and Paul Armstrong, with whom I will share infinite conversation about James and many things besides.

PROLOGUE

The problem of making sense of the past was of critical importance to James in the final texts that are the subjects of this book. This same problem is now at the center of many debates about how culture does and should work. Within the academy and beyond, disputes about the canon, multiculturalism, gender roles, and taste depend on assumptions about the relation between the past and the present. In American society, the terms of these debates have always tended to become polarized between, on the one hand, the reactionary position in which the traditional must be maintained intact and, on the other hand, the revolutionary posture in which the past is discarded wholesale, a gesture supposed to inaugurate a better world. Although James has been characterized as representing the nostalgic, conservative position – as I show in my introductory history of the reception of *The American Scene* – this hoary image of him obscures the valuable alternative offered in his very late writings to these exhausted rhetorical and political strategies. This neglected body of work makes a welcome contribution to the discussion of these critical cultural issues.

James shows how important it is for the future of society to relate the past and present so that they are, as it were, on speaking terms. His efforts in *The American Scene* to understand, for example, the New York of the Lower East Side in relation to the Washington Square of his youth are like a series of conversations in which there must be an exchange of points of view, and in *The Ivory Tower* a conversation between the New Woman and old Newport is needed in order to make sense of the changing conventions of patrimony and matrimony. The best future James ever imagines remains unwritten (for better or worse) in his last romance, his fabulous story of time travel, *The Sense of the Past*.

xiii

But the promise of a happy ending – the only one in his entire *oeuvre* – is clear in the notes he wrote for the novel. My study of the manuscripts of the 1900 and 1915 versions reveals how this issue came into focus for him as the horror of the war became known; and an unremarked upon note in his secretary Theodora Bosanquet's diary reveals the homosocial incident that reawakened his interest in what became his last romance. James's practice of making sense of the past does not produce a single "figure in the carpet" that would serve as a model for all situations; each conversation is unique, and yet there are conventions that are observed in this practice of making sense. Tracing those conventions is the work of my book.

I have experimented in this book with a methodology that illustrates one way to bridge the rift between historicist and theoretical orientations that has characterized much recent literary criticism. I consider James's texts in various kinds of relations to texts by his predecessors and contemporaries – for example, writings by Henry James Senior on the creation of gender and the meaning of marriage, Thorstein Veblen on the canons of taste, C. S. Peirce on the social nature of interpretation, W. E. B. Du Bois on the ambiguity of race, Jacob A. Riis on ethnic identity, and Sigmund Freud on the transformative value of transference.[1] But I also introduce into these historicist readings the voices of contemporary theorists so as to add another temporal dimension to this web of texts. Thus, Georges Bataille speaks to Veblen about waste, Anthony Appiah to Du Bois about race, and Jacques Lacan to James Senior about gender. In this way I hope to be practicing what I have learned from James about how to make sense of the past in relation to the present for the sake of the future. The theoretical implications of this historicist practice will become meaningful only as the examples accumulate.

This book contributes to a recent trend in literary studies in which writers who have been considered to epitomize the aesthetic are being reconstructed on historical grounds. Richard Ellmann's biography of Oscar Wilde, Alex Zwerdling's critical study of Virginia Woolf, and Joseph Frank's biography of Dostoevsky are exemplary. In James studies, the cultural work of reconstructing the much aestheticized "Master" has been inaugurated by Jonathan Freedman's *Professions of Taste: Henry James, British Aestheticism, and Commodity Culture* and Ross Posnock's *The Trial of Curiosity: Henry James, William James, and the Challenge of Modernity* and is being elaborated even as I write.[2]

As a result of this historicist trend, *The American Scene* (the focus of Part Two of my book) is currently receiving more of the critical attention it merits. It is a classic that is perennially rediscovered. *The Sense of the Past* and *The Ivory Tower* – the two unfinished novels to which Parts One and Three of my book are devoted – continue to be neglected.[3] Looking at them in relation to *The American Scene,* however, not only clarifies one important line of James's interests in those fictions but shows how James's more theoretical questions about articulating the past into the present in the nonfiction can be dramatized as recognizable and yet novel Jamesian situations. My contextualization of *The Ivory Tower* contributes in particular to the current discussion of James and gender (which is so interestingly explored in *The American Scene*) by explaining the grounds of his defense of what I call "heterosociality."

Although this project began with a simple question about the oddity of James's having abandoned *The Sense of the Past* in 1900 and taken it up again in 1914, it became unexpectedly complex and rewarding as soon as I discovered that there was a story to be told about how James's well-known passion for tracing all the possible relations of this and that to everything else had a social and historical use. His practice of making sense of the past allows the "restless analyst," as he often calls himself in *The American Scene,* to put the past and present on such speaking terms that the future seems, not some utopian vision of perfection or some apocalyptic pit of despair, but at least possible. I think of Henry James's "last romance" as referring, then, not only to his unfinished fantastic fiction but to the sense of the always possible transformation and elaboration of meaning and life and art that gave him hope for the future even in the very dark, depressed, and lonely days at the end of his life. In this book I hope to make the texts of this fourth phase of his career come to be seen as resources for us as we continue to try to make sense of our past – perhaps so that we might understand better the ground of his hope.

HENRY JAMES'S LAST ROMANCE

INTRODUCTION

AT HOME
THE RECEPTION OF HENRY JAMES

———————

Henry James's sense of the past was not the common sense of his time. Nor of ours.

So many of James's immediate predecessors and contemporaries had felt the past to be a burden, either because it was so much better or so much worse than the present. The patrician Henry Adams looked back to the reign of the Virgin as a time of harmonious beauty and intensity never to be seen again: "all these haunting nightmares of the Church are expressed as strongly by the gothic Cathedral as though it had been the cry of human suffering, and as no emotion had ever been expressed before or is likely to find expression again."[1] Speaking for the common man, Whitman warned his fellow Americans not to look back: "as long as the States continue to absorb and be dominated by the poetry of the Old World, and remain unsupplied with autochthonous song, to express, vitalize and give color to and define their material and political success, and minister to them distinctively, so long will they stop short of first-class Nationality and remain defective."[2] The farmer-poet Hamlin Garland epitomized the popular antipathy to the Old World culture when he urged his fellow writers and citizens: "Turn your back on the past . . . in justice to the future. Cease trying to be correct, and become creative. This is our day. The past is not vital. . . . Libraries do not create great poets and artists."[3]

The popular American sense of the past could trace its origins – were it so inclined – to such diverse sources as Emerson's silencing of the "courtly muses of Europe" in "The American Scholar" or Marx's proclamation in *The Eighteenth Brumaire of Louis Napoleon* that "[t]he tradition of all the dead generations weighs like a nightmare on the brain of the living."[4] The fact that Whitman cites Herder instructing the young Goethe as the

1

source for this theory of the relation of nation and song indicates, however, how easily this defense of the aboriginal can become contaminated by that which it would expel. The implications of this intellectual indebtedness remain unacknowledged if not unrecognized by the author of "A Backward Glance O'er Travel'd Roads." This stance is what distinguishes the American cultural situation at this time from being yet another round to the scholarly quarrel between *les anciens et les modernes;* the "autochthonous song" has no consciousness of tradition.[5]

James saw the progressivist, antihistoricist view as having come to dominate American culture by 1905. His latter-day jeremiad-cum-travelogue, *The American Scene,* is addressed to a once typologically driven people who have dropped the reference to the Old Testament and look only to the present as fulfillment of the providential design. Fin-de-siècle America's programmatic rejection of the past troubled James greatly in the last decade of his life. The tradition of the American historical romance that was once a means of maintaining a general cultural sense of the past and that had been dominant in the nineteenth-century literature – with Cooper, Hawthorne, and Melville – had been displaced by the various forms of realistic fiction, including, of course, the works of Henry James, who had no interest in the historical novel.[6] This is not to say that he had no interest in the past.

Deploring America's loss of a sense of connection to the past does not mean, however, that he assumed the nostalgic position taken by the other Henry. He had an alternative to these alternatives, but it was only after he had seen the consequences of this progressive attitude writ large in his native land that he realized his way of making sense of the past was very foreign to his compatriots and was likely to remain so in the future. Nevertheless, in most of his very late works (in what is now coming to be called his "fourth phase," succeeding the "major phase") he tried to explain and to illustrate in various ways just what was at stake for the culture if the sense of the past, such as had sustained him in his life and works, were to be lost. He was uniquely situated to do so as an American who was also not American and who could thus see things from a perspective – an often bewildered perspective, as it is played out in *The American Scene* – that his fellow citizens did not share.

After completing his great retrospective works – the revisions and prefaces of the New York Edition and his autobiographical volumes – he returned to a novel that he had not been able to figure out when he first attempted it in 1900. He set about making *The Sense of the Past* work out right this time. This was his only attempt at a romance of time travel to a past he had not known. As the only major works of fiction that he attempted after his 1904 visit to America, it and the also unfinished *Ivory Tower* offer the clearest representations of the way in which the spectacle of the land of the future had affected his sense of the past.

In one of the many allegorical episodes in *The American Scene* (that genre-bending record of James's 1904 return) the Spirit of Progress is personified by the restless rebuilders of the New York cityscape. The running title on this page is "The Defeat of History." The "strangeness of the moral" that James sees illustrated on the always already reconstructing streets of New York

> rings out like the crack of that lash in the sky, the play of some mighty teamster's whip, which ends by affecting you as the poor New Yorker's one association with the idea of "powers above." "No" – this is the tune to which the whip seems flourished – "there's no step at which you shall rest, no form, as I'm constantly showing you, to which, consistently with my interests, you *can*. I build you up but to tear you down, for if I were to let sentiment and sincerity once take root, were to let any tenderness of association once accumulate, or any 'love of the old' once pass unsnubbed, what would become of *us*, who have our hands on the whipstock, please? Fortunately we've learned the secret for keeping association at bay. We've learned that the great thing is not to suffer it to so much as begin. . . . It little matters, so long as we blight the superstition of rest."[7]

Without associations, without continuity, without a sense of a living and significant connection to the past, there can be no peace, no rest, no being at home in the world. The defeat of history is profoundly discomforting, a continual reenactment of some expulsion, not from paradise, but from a human world in which "tenderness of association" takes time to "accumulate," and a culture takes time to become meaningful.

The importance of the accumulation of associations to the state of one's mind is also represented by an image of a city in the work of another interpreter of the past's nightmares, who wrote in *Civilization and Its Discontents* that "We can only hold fast to the fact that it is rather the rule than the exception for the past to be preserved in mental life." The example Freud uses to illustrate this principle is an analogy between mental life and the cityscape of Rome, in which "nothing that has once come into existence will have passed away and all the earlier phases of development continue to exist alongside the latest one." Although it is not physically possible that the whole edifice of Agrippa's Pantheon could exist on the same ground as Hadrian's, this comparison illustrates Freud's sense that, barring physical damage to the brain, "such a preservation of all the earlier stages alongside of the final form is possible" in, and only in, the mind.[8] This is not to say that the preserved past is ever perfectly accessible to consciousness: only various kinds of symbolic transformations of past experiences – be they dreams, symptoms, or memories – are. From them the process of interpretation begins, and there it ends, insofar as interpretation is a conscious, symbolic, semiotic activity. But the preservation of some form of the past is essential to beginning the process of interpreting the present. And, as the process of psychoanalytic therapy demonstrates, it is only when knowledge of the past is transformed consciously and unconsciously that the analysand is able not to be driven into repeating its dissatisfactions.

The Americans Henry James beheld in 1904 seemed determined to prove themselves exceptions to Freud's rule and were engaged in repressing, when not completely destroying, signs of the past on an unprecedented scale. The analogy between the psyche of the individual and the life of a culture is, in my instance as in Freud's, not to be pressed too far, as he acknowledged. Nevertheless, Freud's image of the Eternal City suggests a way of living with signs of the past that was quite foreign to the New World. The modern City on the Hill seemed to live not for any idea of eternity or even of yesterday – but for this moment alone.

A Geometry of His Own

Although James sees Manhattan's restlessness and self-destructiveness as the immediate consequence of the real-estate mogul's greed, this perpetual renovation can be understood as an aggravated version of the tendency to reject the past in favor of the present that some would say characterizes modernity as such. Our belief is, as David Lowenthal put it in the title of his book, that *The Past Is a Foreign Country*. *The Estrangement of the Past*, as Anthony Kemp calls his recent book, is what makes us modern and what would have been inconceivable to the premoderns.[9] Paul de Man points to the paradoxical nature of this opposition between history and the modern as itself evidence of our "modernity."[10]

Whatever moment one chooses to mark this shift in consciousness – the Renaissance, the Reformation, the American War of Independence – the assumption is that the only way to look at the past now is from this alienated and revolutionary point of view. Warner Berthoff identified the sense of perpetual revolution with the particular heretical tradition of American religion when he wrote of "the habitual antinomianism of our literature"; he implied, paradoxically, that there is an orthodox view that is not the basis of common practice.[11]

This schema of perpetual succession has meaning, of course, only because it is seen as different from other ways in which people have conceived of the relation of the past and present. The alternative is sometimes characterized as "traditional" and is said to be the view, for example, of medieval European peoples, who felt the present to be continuous with the past. "The sentiment of nostalgia," Jean Seznec explains, "which pervades the work of Poussin is the fruit, at once bitter and delicious, of the Renaissance; it means that the perspectives of the mind have changed. The notion of antiquity as a distinct historical milieu, as a period that had run its course, did not exist in the Middle Ages."[12] Although many cultures (including Homer's and Virgil's) have looked back to the past as a glorious time and a lost one, the sense of discontinuous historical distance between the present and the past is *the* salient characteristic of post-Renaissance consciousness, according to Panofsky. Whereas the Italian Renaissance was nostalgic for the irrecoverable classical world, the Carolingian and twelfth-century renascences had felt themselves to be, respectively, the legitimate or ambivalent heirs of antiquity.[13] The medieval sense of the past is of an unbroken continuity, it is said, in which the present reproduces or renovates the past. The present is part of a continuum in which all kinds of disparate things are included rather than a rupture that implies the exclusion of what is different.[14]

This "traditional" sense of historical continuity has also been said to be observable in present-day cultures uncorrupted by Western civilization. A modern person cannot, however, choose to have a traditional relationship to the past in this sense: one cannot live in the mentality of the Middle Ages or go native to that degree. When someone like Henry Adams is characterized as being traditional or reactionary or nostalgic, it is with the clear understanding that he or she is, for better or worse, seeing this desired past through the modern, alienated point of view and that this desire for some earlier world can never be satisfied. Any invocation of tradition is always already and inescapably modern, whether it be the antiauthoritarian position of a Descartes or the humanists' claim to continuity with the Greeks. It is the longing rather than the enjoyment that is, for modern people, the mark of the traditional.

There are alternatives, however, to the opposed stories about the shape and course of history told by Frederick Jackson Turner or Henry Adams.[15] Henry James offers one such alternative. Clearly he was not a believer in the progressivist, Turnerian "whig interpretation of history," as Herbert Butterfield calls it,[16] in which the new thing is self-evidently the better thing toward which all history has been leading. Therefore, he has been assumed to be party to a traditional, Adamsian, even a reactionary view of the past. (Of course, not all conservatives would admit him to their ranks.)[17] This is an understandable conclusion if one pays attention only to those few occasions on which he remarks on the " 'love of the old' " (although he does put it in quotation marks!) and he writes in a rare epigrammatic outburst: "Houses of the best taste are like clothes of the best tailors – it takes their age to show us how good they are."[18] But judging only by this opposition between progressive and traditional (or liberal and conservative), choosing, moralistically, between a better and a worse time in human history, creates an impoverished sense of the alternatives.

Butterfield argues that making moral judgments about history is the consequence of the way in which the whig chooses to tell history. The whig historian looks to the past for the sake of understanding the present and explaining how the present came to its fuller realization of human liberty (16). (Logically, it seems to me, that this method of selective, teleological history telling could just as easily lend itself to the opposite view of the course of history, namely, that there has been degeneration, not progress. This virtual reversibility shows how the liberal–conservative binary opposition as it is generally understood fails to exhaust the possibilities for conceiving of either how causality might work in human history or, more to James's point, of how we make sense of our experience of history.) Although there may be more skepticism about Progress now than when Butterfield wrote his book in 1931, the paradigmatic methodology of the whig historian has not been as easily displaced as have progressivism's ideological claims, at least among literary critics. Recognizing the narrative frameworks that determine the telos of history, as Hayden White has done, is not the same as forswearing them, invaluable as this self-consciousness may be eventually to a change in method.[19]

Butterfield complained about the selectivity of whig methodology because of its consequences with respect to an understanding of causality, the necessary relation of past to present. Certain events from the past are selected for study because of their similarity to a present situation and the line drawn imaginatively and rhetorically between these two moments comes, by a process of inference, to be mistaken for a causal relation. Thus Luther's rebellion against the pope is the origin of the colonial revolt against George III. Similarity signifies causality in this kind of history making, and the attraction to this kind of explanation may be particularly strong among literary critics.

Roman Jakobson's speculation that poetics is more highly developed than prosaics because critics tend to suffer from contiguity disorders might usefully be recalled here.[20] That New Historicism operates by selective analogy rather than by thick description is a observation that has been made by several critics.[21] It has also been said that the "New Historicists" prefer synecdoche and chiasmus as the master tropes of their "cultural poetics."[22] Both of these tropes function by means of similarity, or, to use Jakobson's famous distinctions, on the "axis of metaphor." Thus, privileging of metaphorical construction makes good poetry, but poor history.

The antidote to this kind of reasoning and history is the kind of research that has been carried on by Butterfield's direct descendants, J. G. A. Pocock (who discerned the toryism of his teacher and strives, instead, to write counterpartisan history)[23] and Quentin Skinner (together the "Cambridge school" of "contextualists"); by certain strains of the Annales school in France (Fernand Braudel, Georges Duby, and Jacques Le Goff); and by, at its best, the work of Natalie Zemon Davis in America. Although this European tradition of historical scholarship has been important to some American scholars of early modern (a.k.a. Renaissance) literature and culture, it has made precious little impression on Americanist literary studies, which have otherwise borrowed much of value from European structuralists and poststructuralists in recent decades (the former "school of theory," of course, being another instance of privileging the construction of similarities and synchronicity). Only the historical work of Foucault has been widely influential in these literary circles, and it is often reduced to a few paradigmatic insights into the technology of power that serve his followers as axioms rather than the grounds of investigation.[24] Lee Patterson has shown how, ironically, the overt leftist social agendas of some of Foucault's followers have found themselves inadvertently reaching conservative political conclusions because of the way that Foucault's web of power/knowledge seems to preclude any possibility of resistance or change.[25]

It is now worth our while to consider this other tradition of historicist practice as a resource for literary studies because Butterfield's critique offers terms in which we might redescribe James's conception of the relations between the past and the present, and moreover, it suggests a method of approach to James's work. This passage from *The Whig Interpretation of History* could easily be mistaken for James's description of his own practice of composition:

> It is nothing less than the whole of the past, with its complexity of movement, its entanglement of issues, and its intricate interactions, which produced the whole of the complex present; and this, which is itself an assumption and not a conclusion of historical study, is the only safe piece of causation that a historian can put his hand upon, the only thing which he can positively assert about the relationship between past and present. When the need arises to sort and disentangle from the present one fact or feature that is required to be traced back into history, the historian is faced with more unravelling than a mind can do, and finds the network of interactions so intricate, that it is impossible to point to any one thing in the sixteenth century as the cause of any one thing in the twentieth. It is as much as the historian can do to trace with some probability the sequence of events from one generation to another, without seeking to draw the incalculably complex diagram of causes and effects for ever interlacing down to the third and fourth generations. Any action which any man has ever taken is part of the whole set of circumstances which at a given moment conditions the whole mass of things that are to happen next. To understand that action is to recover the thousand threads that connect it with other things, to establish it in a system of relations; in other words to place it in its historical context. But it is not easy to work out its consequences, for they are merged in the results of every-

thing else that was conspiring to produce change at that moment. (19–20)

Of course, the historian, like the artist, must choose some threads of this intricate network in order to tell the story at all (thus all history is whiggish to some degree). But the pattern must suggest what must be left unsaid. Butterfield sounds even more Jamesian when he claims: "Indeed the historian is never more himself than when he is searching his mind for a general statement that shall in itself give the hint of its own underlying complexity" (101–2).

Henry James is, of course, the master of the art of telling the story so it that suggests more than it can say, of weaving "the complex figure in a Persian carpet" that cannot be extracted from the whole and yet whose difference from the whole defines them both.[26] He famously explained this relation between the complexity of reality and the work that art does in theoretical terms in the preface to *Roderick Hudson:*

> Really, universally, relations stop nowhere, and the exquisite problem of the artist is eternally but to draw, by a geometry of his own, the circle within which they shall happily *appear* to do so. He is in the perpetual predicament that the continuity of things is the whole matter, for him, of comedy and tragedy; that this continuity is never, by the space of an instant or an inch, broken, and that, to do anything at all, he has at once intensely to consult and intensely to ignore it.[27]

James strove to make sense of the past as he made sense of all relations, namely, by charting those incremental, infinitesimal dislocations in continuous relations that finally did make a meaningful difference. Butterfield calls these kinds of differences "mediations" to distinguish them from radical "changes." There is no way to predict what *the* crucial difference might be: there are simply – that is to say, complexly – too many variables. Just so, there is little sense of the inevitable in James's fiction, as any novice reader of *The Portrait of a Lady* will confess. The contingency of events is more likely to be felt when the description of them is "thick" enough so that contradictions and incoherences can be seen along with similarities.[28] Thin description would create a stronger sense of inevitability, of necessary connections, a sense that there is in history some "poetic justice."

Butterfield warns against this fallacy: "Perhaps the greatest of all the lessons of history is this demonstration of the complexity of human change and the unpredictable character of the ultimate consequences of any given act or decision of men; and on the face of it this is a lesson that can only be learned in detail" (21). Overdetermination would be an appropriate designation for this description of causality because it carries with it the notion of the multiplicity of causes, each with its own coherent explanation, as well as the inexhaustibility of explanation, or overinterpretation. Freud's image of "the dream's navel" that "reaches down into the unknown" and must "be left obscure" even in a well-analyzed dream is another image for that "hint of . . . underlying complexity."[29]

James provides these hints for his readers in the detail of his fiction and his various autobiographical and critical writings. Butterfield's description of a method for writing history helps us to see how James himself conceived of his relation to the past, namely, as a maker of complex, artful, highly differentiated signifying webs. It is possible to suggest how a particular situation might have come about without claiming that there is a pattern thereby revealed that could be applied elsewhere as predictive. I would suggest that we might think of this as metonymical criticism, as opposed to the metaphorical criticism exemplified by the practice of the New Historicists, because contiguity and difference, not similarity, rule its associations. The kinds of associations that characterize metonymy are, of course, notoriously various and hard to pin down. This does not mean that they cannot be analyzed in any particular instance, as I propose to do in the course of my readings of the late texts by James.

As I will show in numerous contexts, James devotes himself to showing how the intricate play of associated, contiguous differences is crucial to the development of an interesting culture and, especially, that this play of differences is necessary to making sense of the past. That there be recognizable differences is more important than the particular characteristics of any of the terms in play. When James complains about the way in which Americans obliterate the sense of the past, he again and again explains that it is impossible to have any sense of anything unless there are significant differences that are recognized as such by particular participants in the culture. We take such a claim as self-evident in the wake of the linguistic turn; but this was not the theoretical construct for thinking about how meaning is made in James's day, although, as I will argue in Chapter 3, "Making Signs of the Past," James and C. S. Peirce had a common context in which they each developed their ideas about interpretation and signs – and the importance of difference to semiotics.

This important topic provides an example of the way in which it is impossible to escape being whiggish to some degree. What the past and present mean to us is always being modified by the relations of the terms that we use in order to interpret them: the relations of the past and present to each other are changed by the terms. James's contemporaries would not have had a theoretical discourse in which to analyze his semiotics; we do, and I will not hesitate to make use of it, although I hope that this conjunction will be to the end of increasing our sense of James's connected-ness to his own time as well as to ours. I must recognize the historical nature of my own choices of associations. My attention to the various ways that James theorizes difference without re-course to a fixed hierarchy, for example, is clearly informed by the contemporary scene of literary theory, however few references to Derrida I make outside of Chapter 2, "Genre Trouble." Never-theless, I hope that the method of the whole book is a tonic for the whiggish tendencies of some of its parts. An alternative to letting the present determine the representation of the past in too simple a fashion is, I believe, to multiply the kinds of associa-tions any one point has so that one line of connection does not dominate all others. It is not, for example, always difference in a Derridian sense that I mean when I describe its importance to James; sometimes it is Peircean difference; sometimes it is James-ian difference.

If such a "metonymical" method of reading is more persuasive to us now than is the method of the various "metaphorical" critical practices, it may be that it speaks to a common need at this time to feel more rather than fewer connections to the signs of our past. It makes sense to me that we can make more sense of the past and of the present when we have more, rather than fewer, terms in play, be the play harmonious or discordant. An attempt to explain why a change in critical tastes favoring forms of historicism should have come about now is, happily, beyond the scope of this present work.

I should add that I do not claim that my practice here will lend itself to the making of a new theory of historicist literary criticism. I would echo Eric Sundquist in his introduction to *To Wake the Nations* and offer my work as "a demonstration of historicist theory rather than an articulation of it."[30] The pitfalls of "grand theory" for the humanities seem to become ever more apparent. Stephen Toulmin has recently argued against applying the claims of Kuhn and Feyerabend about the theory-laden nature of science to the humanities on the grounds that this translation conflates the kinds of knowledge that Aristotle distinguishes as *episteme* and *phronesis,* the theoretical knowledge of geometrician, for example, as opposed to the practical knowledge of the physician. He suggests that "the basic knowledge we rely on in the humanities springs, not from reflecting on the theoretical ramifications of abstract ideas, but from concrete experience of actual cases and circumstances."[31] (Thus, I will refrain from speculating about contingency in James and chaos theory as I was once tempted to do.)

This is not to deny that theory has *any* part to place in deepening our grasp of the humanities: it does. But this part is not universal or foundational; it is local, occasional, and limited. There will be times in this book when I move from being historical to being theoretical. But I do not believe that a single theory unifies all of the readings I offer here of these complex, late works as I ask again and again how James makes sense of the past, and why it matters so much to him that he can make culture work to make new meanings of past and present experience. This is not an apology.

Jacobophobia

The history of the reception of *The American Scene* is a local instance of the unfortunate consequences for American cultural life of interpreting the past only in the terms of its similarity to the present (in whig fashion) rather than contextualizing it by articulating a variety of its contiguous connections to the past and the present (in Jamesian fashion). By letting metaphoric constructions based on similarities displace metonymic ones based on associated differences, this perpetual presentism has the odd consequence of paralyzing critical judgment. As I studied this *Rezeptionsgeschichte,* I was particularly struck by the repetitiveness of the complaints about James's political views and took this to be a sign of the limitations of the critical framework rather than those of any particular critic.[32] This is not to say that there were not some exceptions to this trend in critical practice, but Lionel Trilling's 1957 essay written to show that James was au courant with socialist theory of the 1870s did not spawn a school of James criticism.[33] The reception given Quentin Anderson's effort in 1957 to show that James was influenced by the religious ideas of his father might, indeed, discourage scholars from attempting to ground James's beliefs in anything other than the liberal humanist tradition.[34]

I am not, however, the first to remark on the limited range of criticism of *The American Scene*. The point had already been made by a critic writing in 1907 and was repeated by another writing in 1979.[35] Here is the paradox: although each critic of *The American Scene* speaks in the vocabulary of his or her own historical era, the judgments are surprisingly similar in reviews of 1907 and 1967 and 1987 because they share a common presentist perspective that simplifies the scheme by which James's social views are judged. Irving Howe's remark in the introduction to his 1967 edition of *The American Scene* illustrates this way of reading the book in the political terms of Howe's time:

> No, *The American Scene,* for all its brave recognitions of change, is a conservative book. In motivation, if not always perspective, it is often elegiac, a journey of the imagination backward in time, where all is fixed and irrevocable, beyond the blur of fashion.[36]

His regret at surrendering James to the enemy – the "conservative" – is minimal, despite his interest in the book. By categorizing James in terms appropriate to the poltical discourse of 1967 Howe cannot conceptualize James's method for making sense of the past, a method in which nothing is fixed and everything is always subject to acquiring a new meaning because it (whatever it is) is always coming into new and different relations with other things of all kinds.

The critical tradition's insistence that every time James refers to the past he means to privilege it obscures the important processes of discrimination and interpretation that mark his cultural work, particularly as it is elaborated in *The American Scene*. Critics who are perfectly eager to appreciate James's methods of articulating the nuances of related values in his fiction and who praise his subtlety, complexity, and brilliance in that literary realm are ready to suspect that his marking of any such differences in the social realm between the past and present must be invidious. The uneasy belief that James's "aristocratic feudalism and disdain for change seem to contradict the allegiance to transcendence that . . . informs his epistemology and his moral vision" is understandable so long as the critic relies on the construction of the liberal–conservative axis to analyze James's relation to the past, seeing it as a "wish to freeze the flow of history."[37]

On the contrary, one of the valuable consequences of James's way of making sense of the past by reference to a variety of associated differences is that it is not possible to maintain easy hierarchies as a way to organize the final value of the thing under consideration. This is not to say that values become relative in some indeterminate way but that the complexities and sometimes the contradictions of a specific situation are taken into account, even if that means (as it not infrequently does in *The American Scene*) that no clear conclusion can be reached at that particular time. On a number of occasions James acknowledges that he does not know how such an unprecedented thing as the "ethnic synthesis" of America is going to work out. That is not the same thing as nostalgia for the pattern of the past that can only be seen because it is the past. James is not elegiac; he is sometimes bewildered, just as are his characters (and his readers) upon occasion.

When so much has changed in literary criticism generally and in James studies specifically, it is notable that this way of reading James's political and social views has not. For instance, most critics today would no longer accept F. O. Mattheissen's claim that the true meaning of things can be perceived and that the way to truth is through the aesthetic: "Yet James saw the object as it really was whenever his disciplined eye alone could serve him, and in particular, therefore, whenever he was confronted with American works of art."[38] These are notions that the literary critical community now generally considers itself to have first demystified, then deconstructed, as the belief in progress, the telos, and the transcendental signified have been radically critiqued and revised. Yet Matthiessen's characterization of James as elitist and racist is confirmed by critics from Trachtenberg to Habegger (who adds "sexist" and repressor of free speech to the charges).[39]

Of course, not all paradigms shift together, and as Hayden White points out, "even those intellectual historians enlivened to the implications of modern language studies for the field have not yet fully assimilated the Saussurian theory of language as a sign system." White believes that, when sign theory is assimilated, it will offer "the best immediate prospects for a fruitful revision of the central problem of intellectual history, the problem of ideology."[40] The repetitiveness in the criticism of James's "politics" may well be an indication of a gap or lack of dialogue between the discourses of critics schooled in semiotics and those concerned with "ideology," although, as I will suggest in a later chapter, Peircean semiotics is more relevant to James than Saussurian, and I would prefer the term "social" to "ideological" as more appropriate to James's critical vocabulary. Finding ways to make semiotics and cultural criticism speak to each another is one of the purposes of this book.

Repetition may also, however, be a sign, psychoanalytically speaking, of some unresolved and unconscious conflict. The vehemence of some of James's attackers – from Maxwell Geismar, who accuses James not merely of being anti-American, but an anti-Semite only surpassed by Hitler himself, to Mark Seltzer, who turns James's criticism of the "criminal continuity" of the corporations against James qua artist – is another sign that this criticism might be motivated by something other than critical intelligence.[41] As is always true with James, some pique might be generated by mere irritation with his style. His brother William spoke for many when he wrote of *The American Scene:*

> In this crowded and hurried reading age, pages that require such close attention remain unread and neglected. You can't skip a word if you are to get the effect, and 19 out of 20 worthy readers grow intolerant. The method seems perverse: "Say it *out,* for God's sake," they say, "and have done with it."

Not all of those readers would have agreed with William's qualifying conclusion: "there are pages surely doomed to be immortal."[42]

But another of James's contemporaries points to the deeper reason for the reader's impatience. It is irritating not to know how to designate something that is unfamiliar, and the critical frameworks of the last century have not provided an adequate vocabulary for talking about James's political and social views. It is, however, possible to be conscious of the fact that the framework does not fit. In 1907 H. G. Dwight noted that "the resentment he [James] seems so curiously capable of arousing" is in part provoked by the impossibility of categorizing him: "he will not tell you whether he is Guelf or Ghibelline – though he will sometimes leave you a horrid suspicion that he is neither."[43] And this variety of difference is not tolerable to the partisan view that characterizes American literary politics.

As Philip Rahv, editor of the *Partisan Review,* drew the line in 1939, there were palefaces and there were redskins. And James has been a paleface ever since.[44] Unreliable witnesses such as Pound may have seen him primarily as a "hater of tyranny,"[45] but even the critics who generally find value in his work, like

Matthiessen or John Carlos Rowe, find the same label convenient for James's political views. Rowe can refer to "James's political conservatism" at the same time that he recognizes that "[s]exual, racial, ethnic differences are what ought to constitute a vital society, as James makes clear at several points in *The American Scene*."[46] This view of the positive value of social differences is not generally considered conservative, but Rowe, who deftly uses a multiplicity of contemporary theoretical perspectives to read James's texts, still relies on this category to situate James relative to our own framework of possible political orientations. It seems to be important to do so.

The problem with understanding the past in the terms of the present is most obvious where that tendency is most extreme. Maxwell Geismar's condemnation of James as a proto-Nazi aims transparently to destroy the "Jacobites" by staining James's reputation irremediably. Geismar's is a scorched earth policy.[47] However, Matthiessen, representing the mainstream, nay, being the fountainhead itself, of twentieth-century James criticism, also uses this strategy whenever his attention turns to James's poltical views (which, as an active socialist, he obviously did not believe he shared).[48] One example from Matthiessen's 1947 anthology *The James Family* will clarify the way that this presentism insinuates itself into his well-known judgment that Henry did not share the "militantly democratic" views of his brother and father.[49]

By 1947 there was no doubt that the scale of the Final Solution was known and that Matthiessen's words would resonate in a particular way. Referring to James's reflections in *The American Scene* on the problems that unrestricted immigration was causing for the society he had known last in 1882, Matthiessen writes:

> HJ was often at his flimsiest on the subject of politics. In contrast to the egalitarianism of both his father and his brother, he grew to take it for granted that democracy must inevitably level down; and on his late return to America he worried about the new aliens in a way that brought him dangerously near to a doctrine of Anglo-Saxon racial superiority. He was consistent within his own terms in that he carried his primary standard, his aesthetic perception of fitness, into all his judgments.[50]

The example Matthiessen gives to support his claim that James retreated to the aesthetic is, however, weirdly unsuitable. Matthiessen quotes James's response to Edmund Gosse's essay on Björnson:

Many thanks for the study of the roaring Norseman. . . .
Björnson has always been, I frankly confess, an untended
prejudice – a hostile one – of mine. . . . I don't think you
justify him, *rank* him enough – hardly quite enough for the
attention you give him. At any rate he sounds in your picture – to say nothing of looking, in his own! – like the sort
of literary fountain from which I am ever least eager to
drink: the big, splashing, blundering genius of the hit-or-
miss, the *à peu près*, family – without perfection, or the effort
toward it, without the exquisite, the love of selection: a big
superabundant and promiscuous democrat.[51]

It is possible to read this remark as Matthiessen suggests, as an
example of James's privileging of aesthetic standards; but a more
covert and serious problem with Matthiessen's verdict results
from his applying the terms of the present to the past. His remark
that James's skepticism about democracy reveals his proximity to
"a doctrine of Anglo-Saxon racial superiority" is informed by the
vocabulary of the racist doctrines of the Nazis and its use in this
context works to ally James with those views. Matthiessen glides
from James's invidious remarks about Björnson's being a "promiscuous democrat" to associating him with another aspect of the
social policies of the antidemocratic totalitarian Nazis. Being critical of democracy was associated with doctrines of racial superiority in the context of Nazi Germany, but it was not so in the context
of turn-of-the-century America. In fact, love of democracy was
specifically associated with the Scandinavians or "Norsemen,"
who were, in numerous ideologies of race that were influential in
1904, if not "Anglo-Saxon," at least "Teutonic" or "Aryan" in ways
acceptable to the interested defenders of those categories.[52] In
his 1850 book, *The Races of Man: A Philosophical Enquiry into the
Influence of Race over the Destinies of Nations*, Robert Knox claimed
that the Scandinavians were "the only race which truly compre-
hends the meaning of the word liberty." He claimed that "their
laws, manners, institutions, they brought with them from the
woods of Germany, and they have transferred them to the woods
of America."[53] It is the belief in the racial superiority of the
various blond races that was developed to nefarious extremes by
the Nazis. But there is no necessary connection between a belief
in the superiority of a particular race and being for or against
democracy.

Once we have some information about the construction of
theories of racial superiority available as a context for James's

remark, it becomes clearer that in the terms of 1904 James's remark would not have qualified as racist, whatever prejudices he might have had. If James had subscribed to any version of this doctrine of Anglo-Saxon, Teutonic, Aryan superiority, he would have had to overlook any objectionable characteristics of Björnson aesthetically speaking and to defend him on the grounds of racial brotherhood. It is hard to imagine Henry James taking such a position. A racist would be obliged to do so, not only because of Björnson's national origin, but because he embodied the very qualities – being a "big, splashing, blundering" and "superabundant and promiscuous democrat" – that were supposed at this time to be the particular virtues of the freedom-loving, independent, and aggressive Aryans who were destined to dominate the world because they were clearly so good at domination.[54]

This short *Rezeptionsgeschichte* indicates the kinds of problems that I see in the critical response to James's "politics" generally and to *The American Scene* particularly. The work of the rest of this book is to offer alternative descriptions of James's sense of the past in a variety of contexts so his views on class taste, aliens, race, and gender are not seen entirely through the perspective or in the terms of the present. But the "lesson" about how James makes sense of the past, how he makes culture work, "can only be learned in detail," as Butterfield says. So on to the details.

PART ONE

MAKING THE LAST ROMANCE:
THE SENSE OF THE PAST

1

THE SENSE OF THE PRESENT

In the summer of 1914, as ethnic and nationalist conflicts mounted in the Balkans and the Austro-Hungarian Empire sank into paralysis, Kaiser Wilhelm II's ministers reviewed the 1906 Schlieffen Plan to invade France by way of neutral Belgium – thus insuring Britain's entry into the war[1] – and Henry James began working on *The Ivory Tower*. His first novel set in America since *The Bostonians* (1886), it was a story of money corrupting values and of Europe as a possible escape from the gilded New World. As it became clear during the first few weeks of August that the Old World was threatened in ways that had been unimaginable in June and were to become increasingly so by October,[2] James abandoned work on *The Ivory Tower*. He wrote to Edith Wharton on 19 August:

> I manage myself to try to "work" – even if I *had*, after experiment, to give up trying to make certain little *fantoches* and their private adventure *tenir debout*. *They* are laid by on the shelf – the private adventure so utterly blighted by the public; but I have got hold of something else, and I find the effort of concentration to some extent an antidote.[3]

As the war dragged on, James wrote a number of articles that were directly concerned with the war effort – the relief of Belgian refugees and the American Volunteer Motor-Ambulance Corps in France[4] – but the "something else" to which he had turned on 8 August[5] seems hardly a less "private adventure" than that of his Newport puppets: he began writing *The Middle Years*, the third volume of his autobiography.

This foray into the past and into the self may seem at first glance a typically Jamesian gesture, a retreat, in this case, from a literal *Ivory Tower* into a figurative one, confirming James's reputation as an artist who "remain[ed] . . . persistently aloof from the homely realities of life,"[6] as Parrington said in 1930 and many others have believed since. But James's return to the genre of autobiography, which had played such an important role in his life and writing since the death in 1910 of his brother William, shifted in its focus in this volume from his family to recollections about his first visit to Europe as a young man by himself in 1869 – and all that that immersion in the culture of the past had meant to him. He recalls his excitement at feeling that, at last, he was a part of the great web of European civilization. One day, as the twenty-six-year-old James stood "during a renewed gape before the Bacchus and Ariadne," he recognized the man next to him who was talking vivaciously to a companion:

> I thrilled, it perfectly comes back to me, with the prodigy of this circumstance that I should be admiring Titian in the same breath with Mr. Swinburne – that is in the same breath in which *he* admired Titian and in which I also admired *him*, the whole constituting on the spot between us, for appreciation, that is for mine, a fact of intercourse, such a fact as could stamp and colour the whole passage ineffaceably, and this even though the more illustrious party to it had within the minute turned off and left me shaken.[7]

This was culture! Swinburne and Titian together! Only in Europe could an ardently artistic young man have such an experience. "I was shaken, but I was satisfied – that was the point" (570). Culture was continuous: it passed from consciousness to work of art to consciousness to work of art, being always renewed, always transformed. It was "a fact of intercourse."

Just months before the war broke out James had written to his old friend Henry Adams a letter in which he testified to his faith that it is because he is "that queer monster, the artist, an obstinate finality, an inexhaustible sensibility" that he believed he would always be able to perform the "act of life" that was necessary to sustain his faith.[8] In this Epistle to the Depressed, he claims that he will not despair because he would always continue to find his "consciousness interesting – under *cultivation* of the interest."[9] Here James preaches the lesson of his father: "Convert! convert! convert!"[10]

But the outbreak of the war made him feel that the era in which he had thrived was at its end, as he wrote to Rhoda Broughton:

Black and hideous to me is the tragedy that gathers, and I'm sick beyond cure to have lived on to see it. You and I, the ornaments of our generation, should have been spared this wreck of our belief that through the long years we have seen civilization grow and the worst become impossible. The tide that bore us along was then all the while moving to *this* as its grand Niagara – yet what a blessing we didn't know it. It seems to me to *undo* everything, everything that was ours, in the most horrible retroactive way – but I avert my face from the monstrous scene![11]

James was not alone in feeling that the world he had known was coming to an end. Others would later say goodbye to all that and see the end of the parade and write testaments of their youth, feeling mixed regret and relief that this era had ended.[12]

But what may have shocked James into feeling, as he later wrote in *Within the Rim,* that the world that followed the war would be "a world without use for the tradition so embodied . . . [in] a hundred other like touches, casually felt, extraordinary admonitions and symbols, close links of a tangible chain" was a chance homosocial encounter with a young man in the same National Gallery where he as a youth had beheld Swinburne.[13] Theodora Bosanquet recounts in her diary entry of 30 October:

H. J. also told me how on Wednesday he had been in the National Gallery, looking at the pictures brought down to fill gaps left by the removal to the vaults of the more precious treasures, and had fallen in talk with a Canadian volunteer from Toronto, who had only landed that morning and had "72 hours' " leave in which he proposed to "do" London. He showed H. J. the list he had of things to see, an interesting list, with Westminster Abbey omitted and Madame Tussaud's very much insisted on, likewise the Albert Hall! Going round the gallery he enquired of H. J. what the letters and figures "b." etc. and "d" stood for. When this had been explained he carefully noted down the dates of the artists and asked how much the pictures might be worth. H. J. made guesses, and the young man put down all that he said, though having some difficulty as to the symbol £. Finally H. J. suggested that they might meet in the afternoon, as the Canadian was quite without friends or acquaintances in London, and said he would take him to Madame Tussaud's!! They were to meet at Baker Street, the young man declaring that he could make his way "anywhere." However, he failed

to turn up, though H. J. was convinced it wasn't from any
want of eagerness. It's a pity. But what a rich treat it would
be to be anywhere near H. J. taking a raw Canadian round
Madame Tussaud's![14]

This New World innocent, as earnestly in search of culture as a
young man in a novel by Henry James, is confused by Old World
values and signs. They are not "facts[s] of intercourse" for him at
all, not "close links of a tangible chain." They are only dollars in
a foreign language.

However, for James, the young man himself was a sign, a revelation of a future that would have no sense of the past, a future that
he feared – even when it was embodied in a homosocially attractive occasion.[15] Perhaps James regretted missing an opportunity
to interpret the "raw" recruit into the "tangible chain," to make
him into a "fact of intercourse" by introducing him to more signs
of the past, even if it had to be by the intermediaries of the
cartoon figures of Madame Tussaud's. But this fleeting, chance
meeting may have started James thinking about the problem of
the relationship of the past, present, and future that had troubled
him so in *The American Scene*. The young man seemed to have
stepped right out of its pages.

It was four days after this encounter that James began the
preliminary statement on *The Sense of the Past*, a novel about a
young American coming to Europe for the first time and con-
fronting the past, not as represented in wax figures, but in the
living flesh of his ancestors. On 1 November 1914 James began
working on this novel, which he had abandoned in 1900 in order
to write *The Ambassadors*.[16] Perhaps he could see more clearly
now, after his visit to America, what he had not been able to then:
that one had to *make* sense of the past, and keep making the
sense again and again, keeping connections to the links alive by
new interpretations, by new meanings, by new signs. Making
sense of the past is a process of constant interpretation, of "conversion."[17] It is what makes culture serve human, social purposes.
It is what made a random encounter into a "fact of intercourse."
It is what makes the difference between the American culture
James had witnessed on his visit in 1904 and the Europe he had
chosen to live in. These are the lessons he learned and taught in
The American Scene, lessons that he wanted to articulate again but
differently in another genre, the romance of *The Sense of the Past*.
What is clear when the two typescripts are compared is that James
was perfectly content to build on his 1900 foundation, revising

most extensively, however, the passages concerned with the feelings the hero Ralph Pendrel has about the past.[18]

What James seemed to have feared in 1914 was that the problems that plagued American culture, that made it a thing with no sense of the past, with no sense of the future, would fracture European culture with disastrous cultural and social consequences. Writing of *The Sense of the Past*, T. S. Eliot acutely called the hero's disease "the hypertrophy . . . of a partial civilization."[19] Writing *The Middle Years* in 1914, James seems to look back on his younger self of 1869 as having suffered from a similar disease. Metaphors of illness and healing run throughout his recollection of this crucial visit:

> There was not a regular prescribed "sight" that I during those weeks neglected – I remember haunting the museums in especial . . . with a sense of duty and of excitement that I was never again to know combined in equal measure, I think, and that it might really have taken some element of personal danger to account for. There *was* the element, in a manner, to season the cup with sharpness – the danger, all the while, that my freedom might be brief and my experience broken, that I was under the menace of uncertainty and subject in fine to interruption. The fact of having been so long gravely unwell sufficed by itself to keep apprehension alive; it was our idea, or at least quite intensely mine, that what I was doing, could I but put it through, would be intimately good for me – only the putting it through was the difficulty, and I sometimes faltered by the way. (570)

James's belief that "the extraction of quintessences" of a cultural rather than a medicinal nature was a cure for whatever ailed him is a theme that is much insisted upon in this early section of this volume of his autobiography (571).

James's cure for himself might be said to be illustrated by his life's work so long as it is understood by this metaphor that there was never any absolute, normative, ideal, or permanent cure to the problems of life and art. There was always something more to say; always another way to say it, another kind of "quintessence." But an illustration of the way that he concocted a particular "extraction of quintessences" that transformed signs of the past into art of the present for the sake of the future can be seen in his solution to the generic problems that he confronts as soon as he undertakes the story of time travel in *The Sense of the Past*. Although James consciously saw this novel (according to Theo-

dora Bosanquet) as "sufficiently fantastic and divorced from present day conditions to be taken up and worked on even though
the world is 'under stress and strain, the oppression and obses-
sion' of War,"[20] its generic and thematic concerns were as close
to home as the Belgian refugees marching through the streets of
Rye. James had learned in *The American Scene* that there is no
"divorcing" the present and the past. His imaginative attempt to
do so only involved him once again in staging their complex
relations, this time in a different genre, that of the romance.

GENRE TROUBLE

James had abandoned *The Sense of the Past* in 1900 at the point in the story shortly after his modern hero, Ralph Pendrel, confronts his unnamed, but physically identical, ancestor of 1820 and is about to exchange places with him so that Ralph can fulfill his lifelong desire to know the past as it really was. Book Second ended with this recognition scene, and in Book Third Ralph recounts his extraordinary experience to the American ambassador, so that someone would know where he (Ralph) has gone, should he disappear into the past. The 1900 typescript breaks off when the ambassador asks "Is the fact of your situation that you've seen a ghost?" " 'Oh,' said Ralph Pendrel with a moment of gloom, 'I most intensely hope it wasn't that.[' "][1]

Just where James intended to go with the plot in 1900 seems to have been something of a mystery even to himself. He recalls in 1914: "the beauty of it was just that it was complicated, if it shouldn't prove too much so to become splendidly clear, that is to give out all its value of intention."[2] He then goes on to remark in a rare outburst of spleen that "the somewhat treacherous, or at least considerate, failure of further backing from Rottingdean" also contributed to his halt. "Rottingdean" (the name of a town in England that James had visited on occasion) apparently refers to William Dean Howells, who had encouraged James to do his "international ghost story" for a proposed collection that was then abandoned.[3] On 9 August 1900, James had responded more gracefully to Howells himself that, as he was "preoccupied with half a dozen things of the altogether human order now fermenting in my brain, I don't care for 'terror' (terror, that is, without 'pity') so much as I otherwise might." Since *The Ambassadors* was one of those "things of the altogether human order," one can hardly regret that he chose to be, as he put it at the time, a "Cheerful Internationalist" rather than a "Terrorist."[4]

In this letter of 1900 to Howells and in the 1914 preliminary statement James repeatedly makes the point that he imagined *The Sense of the Past* as a kind of companion piece to *The Turn of the Screw*. This comparison may not seem at first to promise illumination in view of the complications of *that* text. James insists, nevertheless, that he is out to achieve his "full kind of quasi-Turn-of-Screw effect."[5] One of the things he seems to mean by that is that he wants to succeed in pulling off a difficult generic challenge, one he congratulates himself as having managed in the case of his famous ghost story. There is a difference, he notes in the preface to *The Aspern Papers*, between the kind of fairy tale that is "short and sharp and single, charged more or less with the compactness of anecdote" and the kind that is "the long and loose, the copious, the various, the endless, where dramatically speaking, roundness is quite sacrificed." "Cinderella" is an example of the former; *Arabian Nights* of the latter. What James claims to have done in *The Turn of the Screw* is to have achieved what would seem to be the impossible and to have the advantage of the "improvisation" without losing the "great effect . . . that of [the tale] keeping on terms with itself." He boasts of its "perfect homogeneity, of [its] being to the very last grain of its virtue, all of a kind." He calls it "a study of a conceived 'tone,' the tone of suspected and felt trouble, of an inordinate and incalculable sort – the tone of tragic, yet of exquisite, mystification."[6] "Homogeneity" is not, apparently, a simple thing as James conceives it but a complex set of relations that "keep[s] on terms with itself." If this "homogeneity" is one of the characteristics that contributes to the "parenté" (349) of *The Turn of the Screw* and *The Sense of the Past*, the next question is, What "kind" of things has James put into relation in order to make the problem that is central to the latter "homogeneous"? How, in other words, is the problem of making the relation of the past and the present a fruitful, meaningful one to be represented in the plot of the story and staged by the play of the conventions of the genre James has chosen to employ?

Asking this question about this text, while keeping in mind the historical context of its second round of composition as recounted in the last chapter, can lead to several different kinds of explanation and analysis. The multiplicity of those explanations, none of which precludes or excludes or supersedes the others, will suggest something of the complexity of any attempt to make sense of the past. As I wrote in the introduction to this book, there is no single "figure in the carpet" that will explain this process – or these processes – adequately. Following Butterfield's suggestion, this method of multiple explanation seeks "to recover the thousand threads that connect [the event being studied] with other things, to establish it in a system of relations; in other words to place it in its historical context." I would differ from his suggested method, perhaps, only in that, instead of seeking to give "a general statement that shall in itself give the hint of its own underlying complexity,"[7] I will offer several kinds of general and theoretical statements – biographical, familial, literary, deconstructive, and psychoanalytic – each of which might give its own kind of hint.

The Sense of a Happy Ending

The first generic convention of the text that marks it as occupying a unique place in James's canon is that there is a very traditional happy ending promised in the notes. Already in the 1900 portion of the novel, the use of various conventions of the fairy tale is ubiquitous.[8] Most important, as in any good fairy tale, the hero and heroine, after enduring various kinds of trials, will marry and live happily ever after. Relations between the past and the present promise to become even better in the future. Although James decides that he will not represent the actual scene of the happy couple's reunion (a typically Jamesian elision of the melodramatic moment), there is no uncertainty – as there is, for example, at the end of *The Portrait of a Lady* – about what lingers beyond the threshold of the text. The very same Aurora who had made impossible conditions for Ralph Pendrel when he first asked her to marry him, now, having been through her own "psychic evolution," is his deserved and deserving mate (351).

The happy ending of the fairy tale serves a particular psychological purpose, according to Bruno Bettelheim. It gives the child hope that he or she can meet and triumph over any new trials just as the hero or heroine has triumphed in the story. The fairy tale reassures the child that happiness is achievable, and we will be better, more capable and more loving people for having successfully faced these trials. The "happily ever after" ending does not lead the child to believe in eternity, says Bettelheim, but "it does indicate that which alone can take the sting out the narrow limits of our time on this earth: forming a truly satisfying bond to another." Lewis Carroll called the fairy tale a "love-gift" to the child, and Bettelheim suggests that this description points to another important distinction between myths and fairy tales because the former make impossible (superego) demands that we can only fail, tragically, to meet, and the latter offer hope that desires can be accommodated within a recognizable, ordinary social scene.[9]

The Sense of the Past could be seen as this kind of "love-gift" from James, an effort to give hope to the Europe that had sustained him and his art for so long. In a famous letter to George Bernard Shaw about *The Saloon,* James proclaims his artistic desideratum:

> [Works of art] are capable of saying more things to man about himself than any other "works" whatever are capable of doing – and it's only by thus saying as much to him as possible, by saying, as nearly as we can, all there is, and in as many ways and on as many sides, and with a vividness of presentation that "art," and art alone, is an adequate mistress of, that we enable him to pick and choose and compare and know, enable him to arrive at any sort of synthesis that isn't through all its superficialities and vacancies, a base and illusive humbug.[10]

Hope – if it is plausible to characterize "hope" as the opposite of "humbug" – is thus given to readers by helping them, by "enabl[ing]" them to make discriminations and choices. As one critic has written of the prefaces to the New York Edition and their educational purpose as an introduction to ways of reading James rather than to the innermost secrets or origins of the texts: "It is as if James is playing a complex game with us for our benefit."[11]

If there is a need for playing, for education, for healing, for hope, it must be that there has been paralysis, ignorance, sickness, and despair. And what James represents in the plot of *The Sense of the Past* is how Ralph is enabled, after numerous trials such as are found in all fairy tales and folktales,[12] to choose the future that will make him happy. First, of course, Ralph must come to recognize that there is something unsatisfactory in his original situation. He must begin by desiring something that he does not have. But desire itself is problematic because he has an idea – expressed in his little book, "An Essay in Aid of the Reading of History" – of the relation between past and present that is paralyzing, even necrophiliac:

He was by the turn of his spirit oddly indifferent to the actual and the possible; his interest was all in the spent and the displaced, in what had been determined and composed round about him, what had been presented as a subject and a picture, by ceasing – so far as things ever cease – to bustle or even to be. It was when life was framed in death that the picture was really hung up. If his idea in fine was to recover the lost moment, to feel the stopped pulse, it was to do so as experience, in order to be again consciously the creature that *had* been, to breathe as he had breathed and feel the pressure that he had felt. (48–9)

His belief that you can get in touch with the past as it actually was is the verso of his desire to repeat the past. What he wishes in particular to reproduce is the security of his relation with his mother – whom he had stayed in America to care for even as he was yearning to go to the Old World – by marrying a woman whose only demand is that he never go the Europe. The situation is clearly impossible. At the end of their interview, he predicts that he will succeed in his suit because she will *want* to change: "It will be you – I'll be hanged! – who will come" (35). But first he must also be transformed by his changed relationship to the past as he will discover it to be. Which is not the way he thinks it will be.

Nothing has prepared him for the real complexity of the past. Its "unimaginable accidents" that he yearns to witness turn out to be just what threaten to expose him as an impostor because he had not taken account of how his own presence would change the past (49). His presence insures that the past and present are not divorced from one other, nor are they knowable on their own terms without reference to one another. He cannot know the past as it was for itself without him present, even if exactly the same events transpire. He must reinterpret the relation of past and present taking into account the "unimaginable accident" of his presence. And, as he does so, he also must reinterpret himself. His desire for the past having been frustrated, it must then be transformed and directed toward another object. And he cannot do so as an isolated subject. He must have help.

Ralph's inheritance of a London house, his encounter with the portrait of his ancestor, and the conversation with the ambassador are but further prologues to the actual moment of translation into the past, a moment that James remembers in 1914 "*having* groped for" in 1900 (292), but not having found, and so it is impossible to know what he had thought would happen once Ralph was in the past, except that he terrorizes people and becomes involved with the wrong sister.[13] Because it follows the conventional trial and triumph scenario of the fairy tale, the shape of the story is simple and clear enough – although the actual text is anything but. Readers who are distraught by the late James might despair of the posthumous.

The particular nature of Ralph's trials has been an obstacle to the appreciation (or even comprehension) of this text. Accustomed as we as readers are to various kinds of journeys to the underworld, it helps to know that there is a familiar structure that guides, for example, Dante's progression through the realms of various sinners. Imagine trying to read *The Divine Comedy* without knowing anything about Catholicism.[14] Likewise, a reader might well feel lost in this romance without knowledge of Henry James Senior's eccentric but systematic theory of psychological vastation and regeneration. It is plausible to read the particular sequence of episodes in *The Sense of the Past* by reference to this theology. Resistant as many (most) readers have been to the kind of allegorical readings of many of James's novels that Quentin Anderson suggested long ago, it is possible to interpret Ralph's course by reference to James Senior's reading of the story of Genesis as the type for the individual's spiritual and psychological development. In my discussion of *The Ivory Tower* in Part Three of this book I analyze James Senior's theory of the genesis of gender. Here I want to focus on one particular moment in this drama of the individual's psychospiritual development in order to clarify the way in which the genesis of genre in *The Sense of the Past* stages the problem of how to make sense of the past. How are past and present brought into meaningful relationships? What makes this transformation of relations possible?

Contrary to what the reader of James might think, it is not by the power of art alone. One of the surprising things in *The Sense of the Past* is that James represents taste as being of limited, and, at times, dangerous value. More than by his beautiful fiancée or her august mother, Ralph risks being seduced in the past by the character James refers to in the notes as the "little Horace Walpole man." It is Sir Cantopher Bland who both recognizes Ralph as a fellow spirit (it is as if Swinburne had turned to the young James during that fateful encounter at the National Gallery and said, "Ah, yes, you are the real thing!") and who knows – because of his impeccable taste – that Ralph does not belong in this setting. Ralph participates in it without belonging. He is the wrong kind of thing. He does not fit. And it is Sir Cantopher who makes trouble for Ralph because of the subtlety and inflexibility of his taste. If James were as sympathetic to aestheticism as was often supposed before Jonathan Freedman's historical study of James's relations to aestheticism complicated our knowledge of this ambivalent relationship, it would seem odd that he makes his "little artist man" so limited.[15] But art is no substitute for life (a lesson James also learned from his father).[16] "In life without art you can find your account; but art without life is a poor affair," James wrote in a review of *Daniel Deronda*.[17]

His devastating portrait of aestheticism as embodied in his "little Horace Walpole man" certainly shows that he saw the dangers of a connoisseurship that might be based on perfect taste, but that would nevertheless miss the secret of life. What is the good of some blue jar, when one has not reached an understanding with Nan? Sir Cantopher values in his beloved only her perfect taste. It is Ralph who recognizes that Nan, the sister of his fiancée, has "things in her world of imagination . . . which might verily have matched with some of those, the shyer, the stranger, the as yet least embodied, that confusedly peopled his own . . ." (282–3). It is not her taste that makes her special for him:

> His rejoicing gravity was at such a pitch in it that she turned, under this address, from pale to red, and that something in the expression thus produced in her, which was like a rush of some purer intelligence than he had yet touched among them all, determined in him the strangest inward cry. "Why she's modern, *modern!*" he felt he was thinking – and it seemed to launch him with one push on an extraordinary sea. (280)

Ralph and Nan will understand each other, whereas Sir Cantopher, for all his keenness will never understand – though he might threaten – either of them.

As a vision of salvation, reaching this kind of understanding may seem rather understated. Understanding is something that may be taken for granted – until it is betrayed. Ralph Pendrel may have felt frustrated when Aurora explained herself, but at least they could talk about their disagreement and arrive at an understanding that each could be trusted to be held honorable (36–7), what Paul B. Armstrong calls "non-consensual reciprocity."[18] Now Ralph is tormented because any effort to arrive at an understanding, any attempt at explanation, estranges him from his context rather than integrating him into it. He lives "in suspicion of a certain effect produced in [Mrs. Midmore] which was the very opposite of what he intented [*sic*]" (257). He feels pained when the "chill of the inevitable" (266) distance between him and the Midmores passes over him again and again. As he begins to horrify his hostess and Sir Cantopher, he perceives how desperately isolated he might become.

James wrote only about ten pages of Chapter 4 of Book Fourth – in which Nan enters the scene – but what he emphasizes in that initial meeting is how Ralph feels immediately drawn to Nan, how he recognizes in her the modernity that the others cannot interpret as he can without his actual experience of the modern. If he suddenly feels at home with her, he guesses that this is in part because she, like he, feels out of place where she is: "the light that hung during these moments about sweet Nan . . . appeared rather that of an intelligence rather at sea, or guessing free application to have been so perversely denied it" (282). He wonders, logically, how, if he seems to understand her as "modern," she can be so "without by the same stroke making *him* so" (283). "[T]his young woman's originality," moreover, encourages him to think that, if it is explanation that has bewildered the others, her difference will be proved if she is *not* turned to stone by his "free talk."

> "Modern" was she? – all the more reason then why he should be at once as explanatory as he could. . . . Was she going, sweet Nan, to be drawn to him just exactly by certain features of the play of freedom that he had felt warn the others off? . . . there was nothing to light the anomaly to any degree in his impression that he should be able to make her conceive him better simply by treating her, that is by simply looking at her even, as if she naturally would. (283–5)

The last sentence of the 1915 text promises that Ralph will not be disappointed: "He clung to his gravity, which somehow steadied him – so odd it was the sense of her understanding wouldn't be abated, which even a particular lapse, he could see . . ." (286–7). James ends on the ellipsis that foretells Ralph's salvation and regeneration by this misplaced modern girl's understanding. Her understanding means that she gives him up to the future.

One critic has dismissed this sacrifice as the "Jamesian heroine's characteristically renunciatory gesture."[19] But what looks in one context like "renunciation" can be reinterpreted in relation to other values. Here the theological foundation that James inherits from his father assigns a different value to this kind of giving. Spontaneously given love does not lead to annihilation of the self but to union with others by which the self is finally fully redeemed. In a finally evolved social order, all human beings would love one another as spontaneously as God loves us. We would love each other, that is, without regard to our intrinsic value, but simply because we recognized our bond to each other. This love, *agape* as opposed to *eros*,[20] creates value in the beloved just as God's grace makes us more valuable.

What James imagined as the transformative agent in social relationships is something very much like *agape*, a love in which the giving is asymmetrical and spontaneous. The nature of this love has been misread because readers have assumed that this kind of nonsexual relationship, such as Ralph Touchett has with Isabel Archer or Maria Gostrey has with Lambert Strether, is meant to be taken as final, as an alternative to and exclusive of erotic love.[21] This misreading of *agape* is understandable, as it is a concept for which there is no contemporary, nontheological equivalent. There is no major discourse of "beneficence" in contemporary criticism, and the agapic figures in James's fictions tend to be, like the fairy godfathers and godmothers in fairy tales, almost wholly beneficent, even if not entirely effective. (James's own generous muse is addressed simply in his notes to himself as "mon bon.")

In the second part of the preliminary statement that James dictated when he had finished reviewing the 1900 typescript, he sketches in the outlines of the rest of the plot and the crucial role played by Nan's sacrifice. This sounds vague enough and, of course, had he lived to write the rest of the novel, the nature of that sacrifice might have been clarified. In any event, he tells enough so that we know Nan is giving up the man she loves. Exactly how the magic works and how it is possible that she loves the 1820 Ralph and yet is confronted with the 1910 Ralph, who tells her that he is not the other man, are, however, confusing, not least of all to James. At one point, as he is talking to himself (while Theodora Bosanquet, his amanuensis, types), he panics because he realizes that he cannot have her already in love with Ralph unless the present action that is being narrated is a repetition of something that has happened before.

> Yet I pull up too here, in the midst of my elation – though after a little I shall straighten everything out – to see that I introduce an element of confusion in trying to work the

matter out as if anything can have *preceded* Ralph's own, Ralph's "conscious" arrival. (340–1).

James convinces himself as he paces ("solvitur ambulando" [346]) that he has solved this problem. He decides that this is possible, that the past can be repeated and yet different. And then he does not dwell on the implications of this metaphysical problem as it affects the plot or Nan's fate. Of course, this is exactly the awkwardness with any fantasy of time travel. No writer is ever comfortable rewriting history so long as a belief in the objective reality of the past lingers. But even conceiving of time travel already taints that belief. Would the past have happened in just that way if the time traveler had not shown up? Can there be two different pasts that could produce the same future? At a certain point, such speculation becomes an exercise in one's mastery of verb tenses as much as in metaphysics.

True Romance (Not)

The fairy tale *The Sense of the Past* is thus fractured at a certain point by complications introduced by the conventions of the time travel narrative. Even if the happy ending later heals that fracture, it is not a seamless text: it is marked, scarred. There is a mixing of genres in this text that calls into question the assumption that a smooth, easy, inevitable translation from the past to the present takes place just because time's arrow points in one direction. The fact that this problem comes home to James as he thinks through the issue of how Nan could love both the Ralph of 1910 and the Pendrel of 1820 suggests that it is in this most intimate context that the problem of mixing genres, mixing kinds of love, is most unsettling. But, since it is by Nan's love that Ralph is freed from the nightmare that the past has become for him, it would seem that the mixing, the impurity of the genre, of the love, is what makes it possible for the story to go on. The mixing is not something to be avoided (if that is even possible) but, on the contrary, is what changes conventional relationships so that new meanings are possible.

The point at which James runs into conceptual trouble about how the past can both be the same and yet different exposes the impossibility, the gap, the aporia of genre. That last term – aporia – will have signaled to my reader a shift in critical contexts here, namely, to the work of Derrida, here to his essay, "The Law of Genre." In this essay he performs an act familiar to students of deconstruction. He shows how there can be no pure, unmixed, originary genre to whose laws all subsequent instances conform by citation; that examples are recognizable as "participat[ing in] without belonging" to a certain genre by their characteristic "remarks"; that the examples are what define the law of genre retroactively; that no genre is ever realized in its fullness; and yet that, without that unfullfillable law, there could be no recognizable examples.[22]

James's problem of the "actual" past and a "alternate" past being folded over each other – a narrative situation that Derrida describes as "a pocket" or a "*double chiasmatic invagination of edges*" – is thus not an exceptional instance of the law of genre being violated, but an example of the impossibility of that law's adequate citation or fulfillment. Derrida asks: "And suppose for a moment that it were impossible not to mix genres. What if there were, lodged within the heart of the law itself, a law of impurity or a principle of contamination? And suppose the condition for the possibility of the law were the *a priori* of a counter-law, an axiom of impossibility that would confound its sense, order and reason?"[23]

I have been calling this text a romance – but this description assumes that there is such a definable genre. The problem of defining romance becomes nicely circular (before it invaginates itself) relative to the work of James because most critics who want to talk about the romance in American literature go to James's preface to *The American* for their definition. In that preface he uses the famous metaphor of the "balloon of experience" whose cable linking it to the earth is cut by the romancier – who, meanwhile, makes every effort to have the reader not notice that this liberation from the laws of reality has taken place. This is what James calls the "hocus-pocus," which depends upon the skill of the artist.[24] Clearly, a time travel narrative would seem to cut the cable, to qualify as "romance." But, because of the doubling of temporal frames, the liberation is not so clearly effected. The cable is and is not cut, and in this instance of "hocus-pocus" the romancier nearly hangs himself in its loops at one point.

As I have suggested, the bind in which James finds himself in *The Sense of the Past* is the same for any writer. Had James lived to write more of the story, he might have found that he could not solve this generic problem definitively by invoking the criteria of realism or those of romanticism that guide him as he works through various individual points in the story. This lack of a solution does not mean, however, that he could not have gone on writing the story to its happy end. This is not to say that the genre is "indeterminate." These distinctions are of concern to James as he composes. When he says in the notes that "I know what I mean when I say that everything altogether corresponds," he means that he wants the same amount of real time to have passed in the present and the past and wants none of the "horrid little old conceit of the dream that has only taken half an hour" to introduce a romantic element into the story at the wrong point (293); when he speaks of "the climax of the romantic hocuspocus" worked by Ralph's liberation from the past (336); or when he says that he wants to avoid the "excess of the kind of romanticism" a certain choice would allow, he clearly has in mind certain laws appropriate to each genre that must be cited only at the right time and place to maintain "that force of 'tone' which makes the thing of the parenté of the 'Screw'" (349).

But there is something more specific that can be said about the problem he faces insofar as his grappling with problems of genre stages the problem of how one knows what happened in the past. James's canonical definitions of the real and the romantic in the preface to *The American* provide the opposition with which to begin to understand why *The Sense of the Past* is so illuminating about the epistemology of historical understanding, about what it would mean to make sense of the past that cannot be known objectively:

> The real represents to my perception the things we cannot possibly *not* know, sooner or later, in one way or another; it being but one of the accidents of our hampered state, and one of the incidents of their quantity and number, that particular instances have not yet come our way. The romantic stands, on the other hand, for the things that, with all the facilities in the world, all the wealth and all the courage and all the wit and all the adventure, we never *can* directly know; the things that can reach us only through the beautiful circuit and subterfuge of our thought and our desire.[25]

Thus for all of James's definitions of romance versus realism and problematic claims about "homogeneity" in the preface to *The Turn of the Screw*[26] – which text he refers to repeatedly in the notes for *The Sense of the Past* as being most like it in "tone" – he cannot order the plausibility of his narrative so that its explanations of what is happening cite the laws of one genre or the other in any definitive manner. James remarks parenthetically: "(It is difficult, as I said above, to trace the dividing-line between the real and the romantic as to plant a milestone between north and south; but I am not sure an infallible sign of the latter is not this rank vegetation of the 'power' of bad people that good get into, or *vice versa*").[27]

What brings this problem into high relief is that this indeterminate doubling about what *really* happened and what *might* have happened following our thoughts and desires is *always* the problem in thinking about the past, not just when one is playing around with narratives of time travel. We cannot have objective knowledge of what happened in the past because such knowledge exists only as interpretation (which is always subject to our thoughts and desires), and we cannot know with exactitude what the causes of the present are (Butterfield's point).[28] It is possible – because it cannot be proved otherwise – that the same present could come about as the result of completely different past events. It is possible to provide completely different explanations of how a present event has come about. These two last sentences themselves state the same kind of possibility in two different genres of explanation – which only seem incommensurable so long as one maintains a belief, the "folly" as Quine says, that facts and interpretations can be separated by some law of genre.[29] Again, James solves his problem in the terms that matter most to him by just keeping his verb tenses comprehensible relative to one another and getting on with the story.

This impurity or mixing of genres moves into another dimension, however, in the plot of the story, at, in fact, the very point when James recognizes most anxiously that he has a problem on his hands. Not coincidentally, it is the moment in the story that is most romantic by his terms, when he is about to use "an infallible sign of the latter [romance] . . . this rank vegetation of the 'power' of bad people that good get into, or *vice versa*." When our hero finds himself homesick for the present he had so willingly abandoned when offered the extraordinary chance to see the past firsthand, he turns to Nan, and it is by means of her love that he is released (in some unspecified way) to return to the future and the woman he loves there. Here James comes face-to-face with his problem. Nan has to have *really* already loved the 1820 Pendral in order to love the 1910 Ralph: but this *same* love also has to *mean* something *different* in order for this transference of Ralph from the past to the present to take place. And what makes it mean something different for Nan, what makes everything that has happened exactly as it did in 1820 now mean something different for the whole family of Midmores, is what James calls

Ralph's "clinging taint of modernity," that which has been sensed by all the Midmores since his arrival and that has been sympathetically recognized by Nan alone because she is "worthy-herself-to-be modern" (322–3). It is impossible to separate the past and the present, to keep them pure, even if everything happens exactly the same. Nan's love – which is going to release Ralph from being stuck in the past and from repeating it, to his own intense dissatisfaction – cannot be categorized in any pure fashion as belonging to the 1820 Pendrel or the 1910 Ralph, although it participates in both (to recall Derrida's distinction). Its genre is mixed. But it does not matter for the causal effect it is going to have on the present any more than James's solution to his problem about what really happened matters as long as he can get on with his story; it does not matter that this distinction be made (impossible in any case) so long as the love does what it must for the sake of the beloved.

This kind of love – mixing the past that might have been and the present as it is felt for the sake of the future that is desired – Freud has in mind when he theorizes transference. Skepticism about the kind of spontaneous love (*agape*) by which Nan exercises her own "hocus-pocus" is made easier these days because of what Freud has taught us about the omnipresence of the erotic in psychic life, with all its violence, tensions, and conflicts. Yet psychoanalysis also provides a language with which to describe this crucial transformative relationship that moves one from past to present to a desirable future. Freud understood the need for this kind of relationship and understood that the erotic desires it might arouse in both people could not be acted on if the patient was to be cured. The patient might project all kinds of different, ambivalent affectionate and hostile feelings onto the analyst, but the analyst must play a role "for which there is no prototype in real life," neither yielding to nor discouraging the patient's love.[30] The therapeutic relationship is charged through and through with eros, but the analyst, Freud insisted, must be guided by a selfless love in which the patient's best interests are of the utmost importance. Freud did not disbelieve that good could be done in this manner. James's insistence on the necessity of this agapic relationship as a stage in one's spiritual growth can be understood, then, not as a neurotic renunciation of sexuality, but as one in which sexual relations are not appropriate and would even be malignant. They can be realized later, as they have been earlier, but it is in this relationship that the transference of *eros* from the past to the present is effected. These relationships are not thwarted romances, but the necessary interlude between the family romance and one's own.

In *The Sense of the Past* the relationship of Nan and Ralph combines erotic and agapic love much as would that between the psychoanalyst and the analysand. It may be that a happy ending was imaginable for this novel because James had arranged his story to include both kinds of love, both genres, mixed in particular ways. One need only recall the lack of erotic attraction of Isabel for her agapic Ralph to see how the crucial element in their relationship was lacking: the transference could not work in her case. The successful resolution of transference love that Freud was describing in theoretical terms in 1915, James was dramatizing in his last romance, which takes place in what Freud describes as "a kind of intermediary realm between illness and real life, through which the journey from the one to the other must be made."[31] The importance of this relationship in psychoanalysis, as Freud discovered, to his astonishment, cannot be overestimated: "The main instrument ... for curbing the patient's compulsion to repeat and for turning it into a motive for remembering consists in the handling of the transference."[32] Thus it all depends on the relationship with Nan.

Although it will not do to press the similarity between a psychoanalytic treatment and a fictional relationship too hard (this novel is, moreover, only sketched out), there are several aspects of the transference as Freud describes it that are relevant to James's portrayal of the relationship between Ralph and Nan, and tracing these similarities will allow me to show how James represents in a fictive context someone making a sense of the past that makes present and future life not only tolerable, but desirable. As Ralph took his leave of Aurora at the beginning of the story, she says that she will have him under certain conditions:

> She hesitated again but an instant. "If you come on your honour. If you come – !" But it was as if she couldn't put it.
> He tried to help her. "Without regret?"
> Ah this wasn't good enough. "If you come with desire."
> (36)

This, Freud and James would agree, is the goal of the analysis.

First and foremost in the transference is the fact that the love and hate that the patient feels for the analyst are not "real" in the sense of having a historical basis for that relationship. The feelings have nothing to do with the actual person of the analyst, as their "excess, in both character and degree, over what is rational

and justifiable" makes clear.[33] It is clear that the patient is mistaken about the nature of this passion for two reasons: the analyst
is by and large unknown to the patient (and is thus available for
the projection of some libidinally cathected prototype);[34] and
this love, rather than growing from the present relationship,
"is entirely composed of repetitions and '*rechauffés*' of earlier
reactions, including childish ones."[35]

The value of the transference is that it can effect a cure of a
debilitating neurosis and send the patient back to the social
world. This is why her or his love cannot be reciprocated by the
analyst: "The aim that he has to keep in view is that this woman,
whose capacity for love is disabled by infantile fixations, should
attain complete access over this function which is so inestimably
important for her in life, not that she should fritter it away in the
treatment, but preserve it for real life, if so be that after her cure
life makes that demand on her.[36] Or, as John Forrester describes
this series of recognitions, the founding moments of psychoanalysis, in an image informed by Lacan and Derrida's *La carte
postale:*

> Freud became an analyst, the analyst, when his desire
> crossed (as in starcrossed) that of his patient: she remained
> silent until his demand for speech became so pressing that
> she confessed that she was thinking of him, Freud, kissing
> her. Very schematically, at this moment, Breuer had fled, off
> to a *second* honeymoon, repeating so as to forget, forgetting
> so as to repeat, preferring to remain a GP and not to have
> to address this question. In his place, Breuer's place, Freud
> said: "This question, this letter is not addressed to me, it is
> addressed to another." So he readdressed it. He doubled up
> his position in the circuit of the signifier, by calling this
> moment the transference. The kiss is a repetition of some
> other scene. This scene of repetition *becomes* the analytic
> scene, by never being itself, by always being the promise (the
> bud or the echo) of some other scene. However, although
> he readdressed the letter, he did not dissuade the patient
> from believing that the letter would arrive at its destination –
> the promise of the analysis is that such letters will.[37]

And this is the foretold happy ending of *The Sense of the Past*.
Ralph, having been caught in the doubled-up, invaginated pocket
of the narrative, is then forwarded by Nan to Aurora.

As a classic case, however, Ralph believes himself to have fallen
in love with Nan; he projects his libidinally cathected prototypes

onto her, precisely because she is unknown and yet recognizable to him. She is an unforeseen value that nevertheless lends itself to interpretation because he already knows her as modern. In his scheme of desires, she thus is a sign that changes its meaning when placed in a new relation: to the 1910 Ralph rather than to the 1820. The availability of the sign to various interpretations is crucial to the process of transformative interpretation. Because more than one meaning can be made, there is the possibility of change. Ambiguity arising from the mixture of genres can be creative.

Ralph's willingness to give up his own life to stay with her in the past is not of this same order, however. This is not a transformative love like Nan's: it is a ruse to repeat the exclusive mother–son dyad that was prolonged by his own demanding mother. Aurora refused to accept his "sacrifice" of Europe, as Nan will refuse his sacrifice of his own life in the present. He desires to remain in the relative security of the past, to be loved by Nan, rather than to take a chance on the difficult future with Aurora. He is misusing the past by repeating it when he makes this offer.

Describing this resistance to change, Freud writes: "The past is the patient's armoury out of which he fetches his weapons for defending himself against the progress of the analysis, weapons which we must wrest from him one by one."[38] So long as the patient reproduces rather than remembers the past, so long as the memories remain repressed rather than becoming present to consciousness, the illness reigns. The task of the analyst is to use the transference to transform that reproduction into remembering and to make the past recognizable: "This condition of present illness is shifted bit by bit within the range and field of operation of the treatment and while the patient lives it through as something real and actual, we have to accomplish the therapeutic task, which consists chiefly in translating it back again into the terms of the past."[39] The past must be recognized so that its proper relationship to the present can be made sense of. The past must be interpreted, not reproduced or repressed.

Nan, who gets nothing but what James called "the exaltation of sacrifice," guides Ralph's interpretation into the happier future. This process is not, of course, without a struggle between them as to who will give up most, the moment that James describes as the "kind of romanticism that I don't want." This stalemate cannot be the end to which things are brought. But in the transference that takes place in a successful psychoanalysis, the patient's resistance to the therapist is as vital to the dynamics of the relationship as is the erotic attraction.[40] It is clear from James's notes that the relationship with Nan is not the end, in either a teleological or dramatic sense, of Ralph's journey. Her love transforms him so that he can be united with a woman who has gone through her own "psychic journey" and is ready to complement him. Nan's fate is, of course, unknown. She helps him, nevertheless, somehow, to "discover the repressed instinctual trends which are feeding the resistance . . . [because] only by living them through in this way will the patient be convinced of their existence and their power."[41] She will not let him "fritter [his love] away in the treatment"; she does not let him remain in the past; she helps him to make a different sense of it for the sake of his future happiness.

One longs for the whole story James would have written.

Lacking this conclusion, however, we as readers of James still are not left without resources by means of which to gain both a clearer and a more complex understanding of how this process of making sense of the past works in his writings. If, as I suggested, James's having worked on this problem in *The American Scene* gave him the means by which to attempt its solution in the context of his last romance, it is now possible to turn to that transcategorical, mixed-genre text and read from it with the promised, if unfulfilled, happy ending of *The Sense of the Past* providing a point of reference. For that text, too, is unfinished. The second volume on the journey to the West was never written. Perhaps because there was much less promise of a happy ending, in spite of James's every effort to make sense of the American past.

For the reader who would object that I am mixing up the chronology of composition and the possibility that James could have written *The American Scene* in 1907 with reference to a work that he picked up in 1914, I would offer three responses. The first is to remind ourselves that the 1914 composition was a reprise of the 1900 manuscript. The second is to remind ourselves that some kinds of interpretation are not constrained by linear time, but stage a more complex interaction of past and present, governed by other kinds of association than sequence. And, finally, and in connection with these first two responses (which I hope my reader will recognize as repetitions of the scenario I have just described as the conditions that make Ralph's translation into the present possible), it is of great interest in this context to think about *The American Scene* as the text that plays a transformative role in James's own understanding of how to make sense of the past. Between the original attempt to write *The Sense of the Past* and its reprise, something has happened to give him hope that he can now finish that story and get to the happy ending. What Nan does for Ralph, writing *The American Scene* did for Henry James with respect to his last romance.

PART TWO

CIVILIZATION AND ITS CONTENTS:
THE AMERICAN SCENE

MAKING SIGNS OF THE PAST

INTERPRETATION AND C. S. PEIRCE

When Henry James returned to America in 1904 after an absence of more than two decades, he wanted to see whether his native land had become interesting or only very wealthy. Since James's last visit in 1882, there had been many major changes in America and he was curious to see them firsthand. He also wanted, apparently, a change of scene after the rapid creation of the three novels of "the major phase." Henry wrote to William in 1903 that he planned to return to America because he felt that he needed "a general renovation of one's too monotonised grab-bag" of material and that only America, "which time, absence and change have, in a funny sort of way, made almost as romantic to me as 'Europe,' in dreams or in my earlier time here, used to be – the actual bristling (as fearfully bristling as you like) U.S.A. have the merit and the precious property that they meet and fit into my ('creative') preoccupations."[1] A romance with America was not, however, to be.

One would have expected that the writing that followed this visit would make use of the new material he had gathered. However, after publishing *The American Scene* (1907), in which he wrote of his tour, most of James's work for the next decade was retrospective and revisionary in nature. He seemed much more interested in making new sense of the old things than in beginning to work on new things.[2] From 1905 to 1909 he was engaged in revising and prefacing selected works for the New York Edition, an enterprise undertaken originally in part with the expectation that he would have, at last, a best seller but, failing that, one that could provide him with ample opportunity to reflect on the process of making a new sense of old things.[3] When William died in 1910, Henry's focus again became retrospective.[4] The first volume of his autobiography, *A Small Boy and Others,* was begun in

1911 as a memorial to William, and he followed it in 1912 with
Notes of a Son and Brother, in which the story of the James family
was continued.[5]

What James found in America did not seem to have inspired
him as the subject for a major work of fiction until he began *The
Ivory Tower* in 1914. He did write a few new tales during these
years that drew on his American experience, and he collected
them in *The Finer Grain* in 1910. Significantly, however, the most
important tale from this period, "The Jolly Corner," (which is not
included in that collection) took its *donnée* from the unfinished
Sense of the Past. Again, he was reworking old material rather than
making use of the new experiences he had had in America. "I
have an excellent little idea," he wrote to his agent on 4 August
1906, "though not having slept a wink last night *all* for thinking
of it, and must therefore at least get the advantage of striking
while the iron is hot."[6]

In "The Jolly Corner" James seems to have found a way to work
through the problems that had thwarted him in 1900 in *The Sense
of the Past* by reversing the geography of the plot (the hero returns
to an old family home in America instead of inheriting one in
England) and changing the relationship between the hero and
the preternatural "other": Spencer Brydon chases the other away
rather than trading places with him, as had Ralph Pendrel. Fantastic as Spencer Brydon's *Walpurgisnacht* might be, the story remains generically in a realm where James had succeeded before,
notably in *The Turn of the Screw.* Romance, the actual violation of
the common sense of reality that was essential to *The Sense of the
Past,* was forsworn. James could now make the confrontation
between figures representing the past and the present a conflict
of differences that could be resolved by the hero – with the help
of the third figure, Alice Staverton, who "accepted" the other "for
the interest of his difference."[7] This triadic play of differences
allows for the possibility of a meaningful future in this story. A
meaningful future in America. This was something that James
apparently had a hard time imagining.

A crucial reason for that difficulty is dramatized in James's
famous dream set in the Galerie d'Apollon of the Louvre, of
which he writes in *A Small Boy and Others.* The climax of "The
Jolly Corner" had foreshadowed what James calls "the most appalling yet most admirable nightmare of my life." He explains that
his dream passage through this treasure room represented for
him nothing less than his "cross[ing] that bridge over to Style,"
where during his "long but assured initiation" he "inhaled little

by little, that is again and again, a general sense of *glory*. The glory meant ever so many things at once, not only beauty and art and supreme design, but history and fame and power, the world in fine raised to the richest and noblest expression." "The triumph of [his] impulse" to resist the danger that the "dimly-descried figure that retreated in terror" represented to him may be interpreted as yet another attempt by James to defend his life with and by "Style." Whatever forces "the awful agent, creature or presence" embodied, clearly this battle for "glory" was not a final victory. The battle may be won, but never the war. The nightmare is a victory, however, for James because he has terrorized the "awful agent" into a retreat and, even more important, because this memory from his childhood of the Galerie d'Apollon had been "kept . . . whole, preserved . . . to this thrilling use."[8]

This kind of unforeseeable, therapeutic use of memories from James's personal past (themselves enriched by the more distant past of the Bourbons, which has been "raised to the richest and noblest expression" in works of art) is an example of how James makes sense of the past and to what ends. The end in this scene is saving his life: dramatically, in the plot of the dream, and imaginatively, in the use he makes of the memory. Making sense in this way does not mean the past makes a declarative and definitive statement. It means that the process of interpretation engages the present in a dialogue: the past is remembered, confronted, understood, and transformed to the benefit of the present and the future – thus, the uncharacteristically happy ending of "The Jolly Corner," an ending much like that projected for *The Sense of the Past.*

But this kind of beneficent relation of the past and present is not typical of James's writings on the American scene he had witnessed in 1904–5. It was not often that he could represent a situation in which the relations between the past and present pointed to a meaningful future, in spite of his efforts to interpret the American scene by his writing so that it made some kind of sense. He had seen in America the worst possible case for what could happen when a people corrupted their relations to the past. It was the verso of Ralph Pendrel's error. Ralph believed that "[i]t was when life was framed in death that the picture was really hung up";[9] the Americans didn't want any old pictures at all. They wanted no signs of the past. Having been to America in 1904–5, James no longer had to strain to imagine a romance of cultural disaster in which the relations of the past and present are fantastically confused; he had borne witness to them in his homeland. This waking nightmare had cleared the way, however, for James to understand more explicitly how the past could play the beneficent role it had in European culture as he experienced it, and why it seemed unlikely that such a culture would ever develop in America. His last attempt to write *The Sense of the Past* was for the sake of European culture threatened by the Great War, but he may not have felt compelled to make this attempt had he not seen so vividly in America the cultural consequences of not making sense of the past.

The (Blank) States of America

James had not returned to the New World expressly to find the answer to the questions that had puzzled him out of patience in 1900 when working on *The Sense of the Past*, but as he sought to understand many of the peculiarities of American culture, he found again and again that he was faced with the issue that had thwarted him in that novel. How are we to understand the relation of past and present that is productive of new and different meanings in the present? What makes it work? What makes it fail? In America, some distortion in the conception of the relations between past and present seemed to make the whole project of culture self-defeating. There is not, of course, for James some master pattern of culture to which things *should* conform, no one right way to make it interesting. It is certainly not a matter of America simply replicating the European past, filling in the blanks that were so present to James when in 1879 he wrote of the absences of Hawthorne's America.[10] Naive attempts to reproduce European culture piecemeal (more about this in the next chapter) were disastrous. The complex network of culture needs many *points d'appui* to maintain a meaningful design. And one of the necessary *points* turns out to be a sense of the past.

For example, James notes that however perfect a replica of the "Gothic" style and the Roman ritual one might produce in New England, the American church can never mean the same thing the European church (Catholic or Protestant) means because its political and social context is historically different: "to compare a simplified social order with a social order in which feudalism had once struck deep was the right way to measure the penetration of feudalism." By contrast, the American church more typically offers "the mere multiplication of the signs of theological enterprise, in the tradition and on the scale of commercial and industrial enterprise."[11] Whether a church conceived in the "tradition" of a business culture that relies on constant novelty (again, more about this in the next chapter) can offer the spiritual and social satisfactions that a church can that is connected at many points to institutions with a past is a question of compelling interest to James. What kind of spiritual life would be possible in such a church? He wanted to know whether Americans themselves were satisfied with the culture they were creating. *The American Scene* is diagnostic rather than prescriptive.

However, the diagnosis might be therapeutic if it were possible to overcome certain kinds of resistance offered by people on the American scene. These resistances were generally of two kinds. One was the refusal to make any kind of meaningful connection to the past, a trait intrinsic to American modes of cultural production, whether among the leisure, the commercial, or the working classes. But the surprisingly ubiquitous resistance was to making any kind of "discriminations" at all, "discrimination" being a word that does not carry with it for James any invidious associations:

> ... as Nature abhors a vacuum, so it is of the genius of the American land and the American people to abhor, whenever may be, a discrimination. They are reduced, together, under stress, to making discriminations, but they make them, I think, as lightly and scantily as possible. ... it was only another case of the painting with a big brush, a brush steeped in crude universal white, and of the colossal size this implement was capable of assuming. Gradation, transitions, differences of any sort, temporal, material, social, whether in man or in his environment, shrank somehow, under its sweep, to negligible items; and one had perhaps never yet seemed so to move through a vast simplified scheme. The illustration was oncemore [*sic*], in fine, of the small inherent, the small accumulated resistance, in American air, to any force that does simplify. (305–6)

The attempts of this "most brooding of analysts"[12] to engage the laconic natives in any reflection on themselves often produced incomprehension, as when he asked a Midwesterner what the conditions of social life might be there and was offered as an explanation: "Why, the same conditions as everywhere else" (42). Such a response could put an end to conversations more effectively than mere silence.[13]

With such conversational partners as these "human documents," it is no wonder that James resorts so often to the trope of prosopopeia.[14] Talking with oneself is better than having no conversation at all. James may have come home to play the role of the "pious pilgrim," to wander across the land as an "ancient, contemplative person," but faced with the blank state of American culture, the "restless analyst" found himself desperately seeking to mark the differences that make meaning possible. He asks: "*Were* there any secrets at all, or had the outward blankness, the quantity of absence, as it were, in the air, its inward equivalent as well?" (43).

The blizzard in which he found himself caught on his way to "the citronic belt" (a.k.a. Florida) figures for him the likely plight of his effort to find the answer to this question. He wants to introduce a taste for discrimination to "the human documents, deciphered from one's seat in the Pullman," readers who constitute "precious evidence" for James. But these living signs are, he thinks, unlikely to appreciate or reciprocate his attempt to find their meaning:

> The spread of this single great wash of winter from latitude to latitude struck me in fact as having its analogy in the vast vogue of some infinitely-selling novel, one of those happy volumes of which the circulation roars, periodically, from Atlantic to Pacific and from great windy State to State, in the manner, as I have heard it vividly put, of a blazing prairie fire; with as little possibility of arrest from "criticism" in the one case as from the bleating of lost sheep in the other. Everything, so to speak, was monotonized, and the whole social order might have had its nose, for the time, buried, by one levelling doom, in the pages that, after the break of the spell, it would never know itself to mention again. (306)

The wit and complexity of this conceit would introduce a differential play of values into this monochromatic scene if the reader would but notice them. The readers who prefer, however, to experience the text as a "spell" that enchants them and that proscribes any further "mention" will be left unmarked by "criticism." The master of Lamb House does more than bleat in protest against this raging insignificance, though with as little effect as the lost sheep unless the readers of *The American Scene*, after taking their noses out of its pages, notice a difference. *Its* pages will not have been blackened in vain if it sparks some "criticism." To desire such a fate for one's book is, however, to condemn it a priori to being – like the soon-to-be-lamented New York Edition – less than "infinitely-selling." Such are the paradoxes of being a fine artist in a culture that created this mass market.[15]

One consequence of this obliteration of differences is that it is impossible to make a new, different, and meaningful sense of the past in the present. Memory is replaced by mere repetition. James is amazed, for instance, by the failure of the New York nouveau riche to heed "the object-lesson supplied you, close at hand, by the queer case of Newport" (161). If New Yorkers had had these "reminder[s] . . . of the prohibited degrees of witlessness, and of the peculiarly awkward vengeances of affronted proportion and discretion" (225) before their minds' eyes, they might not have repeated the error of the Newporters, who have learned not to be "so artless and so bourgeois . . . by the rather terrible process of exhausting the list of mistakes" (162). But, James chides his fellow citizens: "No, what you are reduced to for 'importance' is the present, pure and simple squaring itself between an absent future and an absent past as solidly as it can" (161). And the present alone cannot make culture. There has to be a play of differences to make meaning. As one critic writing on the "texture of the visual" in *The American Scene* notes: "An art that eliminates history is not art."[16]

James's strenuous efforts to make the best of the "thinness" of the American scene, to celebrate "the redistribution and reconsecration of values, of representative weight, which is *the* interesting thing" sometimes leave him, however, with a sense of aesthetic malaise. He finds that the "American material is elastic . . . in the manner of some huge india-rubber cloth fashioned for 'field' use and warranted to bear inordinate stretching." But the "tension and resistance" caused by so much pulling at the same material produces a dis-ease in James regarding his interpretative practice, a fear that he might occasionally be inflating a "modest text" by his "voluminous commentary" (320–2). His efforts to make the best of this awkward situation are sometimes strained in ways he never had to imagine in his fiction and have led more than one reader to have reservations about the formal success of this text. But then Bob Assingham is a more convivial conversationalist than the average Yankee.

James's sense of aesthetic disequilibrium may, in turn, have fed his suspicion that the uniformity, repetitiveness, muteness, and blankness of phenomena as seemingly various as high society, landscapes, and commercial travelers might not be as innocent as they first appear. As James interprets the various "quaint and candid forms," it seems increasingly evident to him that American culture really is not following the path of its own unfolding in any simple way. There were forces working *against* the development

of a European-based culture at the same time that they claimed
to be patronizing, propagating, and possessing it. This is the
conflict James is attempting to trace while his subjects are just
as avidly trying to conceal its traces. An incident that confirms
his apprehension that the absence of articulation is not innocent takes place appropriately on the very steps of the nation's
Capitol:

> Though I had them [the steps] in general, for contempla-
> tion, quite to myself, I met one morning a trio of Indian
> braves, braves dispossessed of forest and prairie, but as free
> of the builded labyrinth as they had ever been of these; also
> arrayed in neat pot-hats, shoddy suits and light overcoats,
> with their pockets, I am sure, full of photographs and ciga-
> rettes: circumstances all that quickened their resemblance,
> on the much bigger scale, to Japanese celebrities, or to
> specimens, on show, of what the Government can do with
> people with whom it is supposed able to do nothing. They
> seemed just then and there, for a mind fed betimes on the
> Leatherstocking Tales, to project as in a flash an image in
> itself immense, but foreshortened and simplified – reducing
> to a single smooth stride the bloody footsteps of time. One
> rubbed one's eyes, but there, at its highest polish, shining in
> the beautiful day, was the brazen face of history, and there,
> as about one, immaculate, the printless pavements of the
> State. (363–4)

James the connoisseur of subtle texts is not fooled. The "printless
pavements" are not blank; they have been erased.

Blankness may signify that one expects to be taken at face value
and without further explanation; or it may be a sign that one has
no desire to speak of what has happened. Silence may be a sign
of confusion – not having the language to explain the problem –
or it may be a sign of willful evasion. There are many things to be
interpreted here. It is not self-evident why the Indian braves
should be wearing "shoddy suits." It is not self-evident who is
responsible for this degrading situation. What power has been
exercised to bring it to pass? What trace of a past action is
being repressed, perhaps because it is too shameful to remain
conscious? Here the quintessential paleface (to use Philip Rahv's
famous designation) speaks out on behalf of the literal (not
literary) redskins.[17]

The native Americans may have been the most abused victims
of the American tendency to wipe out the memory of past vio-

lence, but the repression of the signs of the past by effacement or repetition was typical of the American scene. What other horrors might be revealed if the blanknesses of the small towns and the vast landscapes could be deciphered as the "immaculate, printless pavements of the State" have been? When James complains that "[i]t is of the nature of many American impressions, accepted at the time as a whole of the particular story, simply to cease to be, as soon as your back is turned – to fade, to pass away, to leave not a wreck behind," he is concerned not only with the lack of "other signs of differentiation" and "fine diversities" but with the story that the "costly processes" so very much in evidence must mask. It is not possible that there is only "positive bourgeois propriety, serenely, imperturbably, massively seated and against which any experimental deviation from the bourgeois would have dashed itself in vain" (454–5). The wrecks of these deviations must be somewhere: power is not this self-effacing.

Having discovered at the Capitol a (but not the only) cause of the symptomatic American muteness and blankness, the diagnostic and therapeutic mission of the "restless analyst" then becomes to represent the "brazen face of history" to his compatriots, to dredge up the wrecks, however resistant his audience might be to this spokesman for the return of these repressed natives.[18] Making sense of the past, representing what has been effaced, may be painful, but James believes that much is to be gained thereby for the sake of the present and the future.

But in order to make sense, one must first be willing to articulate. So much of the "ugliness" that seems the "talisman for the future" in America is not the result of bad form, but of "the so complete abolition of *forms*." This welcome explanation works "positively to save the restless analyst from madness":

> He could make the absence of forms responsible, and he could thus react without bitterness – react absolutely with pity; he could judge without cruelty and condemn without despair; he could think of the case as perfectly definite and say to himself that, could forms only *be*, as a recognized accessory to manners, introduced and developed, the ugliness might begin scarcely to know itself. He could play with the fancy that the people might at last grow fairly to like them – far better, at any rate, than the class in question may in its actual ignorance suppose: the necessity would be to give it, on an adequate scale and in some lucid way, a taste of the revelation. (25)

The "taste of the revelation" that James longed to give in his *summa travelogica* was to help Americans understand for themselves the relationship between their present and their past as it was legible in forms of various kinds.

By becoming better readers of the signs of their lives, they would also become more able to create a culture that left them less baffled than they seemed to him to be about its value – and perhaps less at the mercy of those with the most power to manipulate the signs, to make the pavements appear to be "printless." Although this very late text does read like a jeremiad at times,[19] it becomes therapeutic if the reader learns from it a method of interpretation that includes signs of the past, among other things, and points to a desirable future.

Many of the phenomena that James finds formless at first become meaningful as they are interpreted. Interpretation brings them into form by bringing them into relation with other values. They begin to make more sense – that is, to expose their contradictions as well as their complexities and coherences – once they are given relations, contexts, and voices. James's animations of buildings, artifacts, and institutions are not just instances of novelistic virtuosity but the grounds for dramatic scenes in which conflicting values clash and reveal themselves dialogically.[20] Perhaps one of the reasons that some critics of this text have concluded that James failed to come to terms with the new America is that they have focused on the passages in which he confesses to bewilderment without reading on to see how he makes sense of the formless, how he shapes understanding. *The American Scene* is a dramatic dialogue of the author with himself, with his audience, and with the objects he represents, in which the meaning develops as he speaks/writes and as we read. Each time he begins his act, a different outcome is possible because one of the players is different. The apparent formlessness of New York high society and the blankness of the Confederate capitol do not mean the same thing when they are interpreted. The reader must stay through the whole act to see how the game is played each time, how the conversation begins to make sense when discriminations are made, and how connections to forms whose meaning is already known are elaborated.

One of the most remarkable of James's performances occurs at the end of *The American Scene* when he speaks from the outraged position of the native Americans whose land has been everywhere visibly ruined by the invading and exploiting white man with whom James would be supposed to identify his class interests.

This is one of the most vehement pieces of dialogue James ever wrote. The accusation with which it ends evokes the whole horrid history effaced by the "printless pavements." The oddity of Henry James speaking as and for the humiliated and furious redman leaves the reader with a sense of a play of differences in the role of writer and the role of speaker that forces a critical response. How is the reader to make sense of this bizarre identification of intersts? How is the reader, who is likely to identify with the guilty parties, to respond to James's accusation:

> You touch the great lonely land – as one feels it still to be – only to plant upon it some ugliness about which, never dreaming of the grace of apology or contrition, you then proceed to brag with a cynicism all your own. (463)

Luckily, the American readers were spared the need to make any critical discriminations about this peculiar and provocative strategy to make them reflect on the consequences of their past actions and present policies. The final chapter of James's book, in which this monologue appears, was not published in the first American edition of *The American Scene* because of confusion – or cowardice – at Harper's.[21] It was repressed. Muted. Effaced. Printless. James's text fell victim to the blight it was intended to remedy.

Signs Making Signs Making Signs

James did not, of course, invent interpretive strategies especially for *The American Scene*. Before turning to my analyses of James's explorations of how the sense of the past affects the institutions that govern taste, race, ethnicity, and gender, it would be worthwhile clarifying several of the principles by which his interpretive practice proceeds. There are certain assumptions about how meaning is made that sustain all of James's interpretive activity. His understanding of the processes of artistic creation was the starting point for his other cultural analyses. This is not because, as has been said by the New Critics, he is aestheticizing all experience. It is because all cultural experiences share certain characteristics. In his cultural analysis James anticipated the linguistically and semiotically based anthropologies of Claude Lévi-Strauss and Clifford Geertz and the semiotically based historiography of Hayden White, without, of course, ever aspiring to their systemization. We now have numerous examples of how useful sign theory can be to cultural analysis.

One of the things that allows for James's fluid passage from the semiotic to the cultural is that his sign theory has an inextricable social dimension. James proceeds along lines more like those of Peirce's triadic semiosis than like the dyadic sign theory of Saussure.[22] This semiotic gives interpretation a creative role to play in the development of social relations. Peirce called it "evolutionary love."

Peirce opposes his understanding of evolution to that of Darwin, whose theories he identifies with "The Gospel of Greed." "Evolution" is the kind of scientific paradigm that played such an important role in nineteenth-century thought that one might well be wary of introducing it into any discussion. One should keep in mind that the scientific analogies are usually just that – analogies, and not statements of fact. The historian Francis Haskell has reminded us of the dangers of using political analogies when talking of art, and the same warning applies to using scientific analogies. With hindsight, it is easy to see how a dialectical relationship and heuristic use can become positivistic and propagandistic.[23] It is now easy to see, for instance, the ways that evolutionary theory has been (mis)used to justify the survival of the fittest and the grossest forms of capitalistic exploitation. A certain interpretation of this one analogy dominated too many of the conversations of the nineteenth century. Since the days when Bishop Lawrence sermonized on the God-ordained inevitability of white domination, there have been, however, some fundamental revisions in the theory of evolution that make it available again as an analogy for a different set of social concerns. Most important for our purposes is the shift away from a teleological schema to a focus on significance generated by and within a system of relations, such as ecology.

It is on these grounds, in which social relations are integral to acts of interpretation, that we can most usefully begin a dialogue between James and Peirce that will show how central to each is the belief that the sign is always already social and that the ultimate purpose of interpretation is the fruition of rich and various human relations. This is the evolutionary fulfillment of what Peirce calls "The Law of Love" and what James would call good conversation.

The similarities between some of their beliefs about how meaning is made are so striking that if there were not evidence that James found Peirce somewhat uncongenial as a conversationalist, it would be tempting to imagine that the father of semiotics had passed on some trade secrets to the aspiring novelist during their numerous dinners together in Paris in the winter of 1875–6. Peirce was on business for the United States Coast Survey, his only steady employer, and James was frequenting the salons of Turgenev and Flaubert. It was to be expected that Peirce, who had been an intimate of William and Henry Senior in Cambridge, and James would seek each other out, but Henry Junior confessed to William that their "sympathy [was] economical rather than intellectual."[24] They seem to have found some congenial bistros. Although James wrote William that he admired Peirce's "beautiful clothes etc.," he had written his Aunt Kate that same day about his dinner companion: "I don't find him of thrilling interest, but he seems so much more gentle and urbane than I remembered him in Cambridge – that I think well of him. I should doubtless think better still if I were an astronomer or a logician."[25] In other words, James found that although Peirce "is a very good fellow, and one must appreciate his mental ability . . . he has too little social talent, too little art of making himself agreeable." One can only imagine what he talked about when James introduced him to two of the married women he knew in Paris, although he claims Peirce "took a fancy" to one.[26] William, Mrs. James had written, was "greatly amused" by this Paris "intimacy."

Peirce's ideas were clearly of the kind that T. S. Eliot claimed could not "violate" James's "fine" mind. There was obviously no direct influence of Peirce on James (or vice versa), but, as I will show later, there was a third person involved who was for Peirce, if not an influence, at least a sympathetic mind and who was, without a doubt, a major influence on James. I refer to Henry James Senior. Much has been written about the connections between the thought and art of William and Henry,[27] and without disputing the importance of that denser and more complex relation of minds and lives, I think that it is worth tracing some of the similarities between Peirce's notion of the sign and James's practice of interpretation. After reading William's *Pragmatism* in 1907, Henry had written to his brother that he was "lost in the wonder of the extent to which all my life I have (like M. Jourdain) unconsciously pragmatised."[28] I would only suggest that he had "unconsciously pragmaticised" as well.[29]

First, a sense of the past was essential to the interpretive practice and theory of both James and Peirce. Neither was in the least sympathetic to the Emersonian credo that struck such a responsive chord in many an American breast: namely, that it was possible to have an "original relation to the universe." Peirce, refuting Cartesian epistemology, explained how semiosis depends upon past knowledge:

> The Sign can only represent the Object[30] and tell about it. It cannot furnish acquaintance with or recognition of that Object; for that is what is meant in this volume by the Object of a Sign; namely, that with which it presupposes an acquaintance in order to convey some further information concerning it. No doubt there will be some readers who will say they cannot comprehend this. They think a Sign need not relate to anything otherwise known, and can make neither head nor tail of the statement that every sign must relate to such an Object. But if there be anything that conveys information and yet has absolutely no relation nor reference to anything with which the person to whom it conveys the information has, when he comprehends that information, the slightest acquaintance, direct or indirect – and a very strange sort of information that would be – the vehicle of that sort of information is not, in this volume, called a Sign.[31]

Semiosis always begins with something already known and cannot proceed in the absence of that knowledge. The problem of origins is one that Peirce acknowledges, but he does not let it stymie him.

It simply does not matter to interpretation where it all began. What matters is the continuity, or what Peirce also calls "synechism."[32] Addressing the question of how past ideas can be said to be present, Peirce rejects the idea that the past must be lost to consciousness. He explains how the past idea is present not in some vicarious way, but genuinely:

> Some minds will here jump to the conclusion that a past idea cannot in any sense be present. But that is hasty and illogical. How extravagant, too, to pronounce our whole knowledge of the past to be mere delusion! Yet it would seem that the past is as completely beyond the bounds of possible experience as a Kantian thing-in-itself.
>
> How can a past idea be present? Not vicariously. Then, only by direct perception. In other words, to be present, it must be *ipso facto* present. That is, it cannot be wholly past; it can only be going, infinitesimally past, less past than any assignable past date. We are thus brought to the conclusion

that the present is connected with the past by a series of real infinitesimal steps.[33]

And it would be possible to trace the connection of the present to the past by interpreting a whole series of present signs, even if they did not necessarily appear at first to have any obvious connection to the past. The signs must be connected and the connection continuous in the whole semiotic web for it to be meaningful.

When James writes in *The American Scene* that "for the restless analyst, there is no such thing as an unrelated fact, no such thing as a break in the chain of relations," his assertion is consonant with semiotic principles. His famous statement in the preface to *Roderick Hudson* perhaps will bear quoting one more time in this context:

> Really, universally, relations stop nowhere, and the exquisite problem of the artist is eternally but to draw, by a geometry of his own, the circle within which they shall happily *appear* to do so. He is in the perpetual predicament that the continuity of things is the whole matter, for him, of comedy and tragedy; that this continuity is never, by the space of an instant of an inch, broken, and that, to do anything at all, he has at once intensely to consult and intensely to ignore it.[34]

This continuity enriches the experience of the meaning of the present, as James explains in the preface to *The Aspern Papers* when he refers to the way he "delights" in "the palpable imaginable *visitable* past":

> nearer distances and the clearer mysteries, the marks and signs of a world we may reach over to as by making a long arm we grasp an object at the other end of our own table. The table is the one, the common expanse, and where we lean, so stretching, we find it firm and continuous. That, to my imagination, is the past fragrant of all, or of almost all, the poetry of the thing outlived and lost and gone, and yet in which the precious element of closeness, telling so of connexions but tasting so of differences, remains appreciable.[35]

Without the connections, the differences could not begin to generate meaning as both Peirce and James understand that process. And it is precisely connections between the past and present and differences between things of all kinds that are, as we have seen, effaced by the typical American people and social institutions that James encounters.

A closer look at how Peirce's semiosis works will clarify the way that various kinds of connections make meaning – and show why the ruptures of the semiotic web that distress James have such unfortunate social consequences. But Peirce's idiosyncratic terminology presents only the most obvious difficulty in understanding his semiotics. The proliferation of various kinds of triads throughout his work bespeaks a theoretical consistency and complexity that can stun a mind less agile than his. For my purposes, it will be good enough to focus only briefly on the technicalities of the logic of the sign and then move on to what is for Peirce, finally, the most important aspect of his whole philosophy, the ultimate social purpose of human life. It is his famous claim that "man himself is a sign" that explains how semiosis fulfills the evolutionary scheme of the "Law of Love."

What Peirce means by a *sign* is

> something which stands to somebody for something in some respect or capacity. It addresses somebody, that is, creates in the mind of that person an equivalent sign, or perhaps a more developed sign. That sign which it creates I call the *interpretant* of the first sign. The sign stands for something, its *object*. It stands for that object, not in all respects, but in reference to a sort of idea, which I have sometimes called the *ground* of the representamen.[36]

The three crucial terms here are "sign," "object," and "interpretant," with "ground" being a useful delimiting factor.

Perhaps the best way to clarify this conception of the way a sign acquires meaning by relations is by reference to a classic scene in the Jamesian canon, Maggie Verver's conversation with Fanny Assingham in which she reveals what she has learned by the incredible coincidence of her having bought the same golden bowl that her husband and his lover (now her father's wife) almost bought her as a wedding gift. The "gilt cup" is just a "gilt cup" until the shopkeeper who sold it to her comes to confess that it has a flaw – and then unwittingly reveals that the lovers (her husband Amerigo and her stepmother) had been to his shop together before Maggie's wedding. The process of interpretation has already begun for Maggie – and it never ends. (The same could be said for Strether, who is educated by "Parisian talk.")[37]

Translated into Peirce's terms, the golden bowl would have only the qualities of Firstness, a mere existent thing in itself,[38] until it came into connection with the Object and by that dyadic relation acquired the Secondness that made it possible for the Interpretant to bring to this relation the Thirdness that makes it representable as a Sign. The Object in this triad is the past history of Amerigo and Charlotte, which becomes known to Maggie by means of the shopkeeper; and she, by making a connection between this Sign and the Object, herself produces the Interpretant, the idea that there is a secret relation between her husband and her stepmother. The Sign (the golden bowl) is made to stand for the Object (the past history) by the Interpretant (Maggie's idea) with reference to the Ground of adultery, the particular "respect" that limits the meaning of that past history.

But James's characters are only occasionally involved in the interpretation of these kinds of material things. Much more usually it is by conversation that semiosis proceeds, and the conversation with Fanny Assingham that follows Maggie's creation of the sign of the golden bowl is an excellent example of the way signs grow, of the evolution of understanding between two people. This is not perfect understanding in the sense of some mutual transparency of selves, but an understanding that is always partial and evolving.[39]

Peirce writes that "men and words reciprocally educate each other." When he declares that "man himself is a sign," it is because "it is sufficient to say that there is no element whatever of man's consciousness which has not something corresponding to it in the word. . . . Thus my language is the sum total of myself; for the man is the thought." It is as signs – linguistic and otherwise – that we become ourselves. Peirce says that man (*sic*) is mistaken to identify himself in terms of "his will, his power over the animal organism" because "the identity of a man consists in the *consistency* of what he does and thinks, and consistency is the intellectual character of a thing; that is, is its expressing something."[40] And this expression is achieved in relation to other signs, other people. This social aspect of semiosis is always already present by the very nature of the sign. In "Logic As Semiotic," Peirce makes the continuity between the symbol and the "symbol-using mind" clear. Neither exists as unique or isolated:

A symbol, as we have seen, cannot indicate any particular thing; it denotes a kind of thing. Not only that, but it is itself a kind and not a single thing. You can write down the word

"star," but that does not make you the creator of the word,
nor if you erase it have you destroyed the word. The word
lives in the minds of those who use it. Even if they are all
asleep, it exists in their memory.[41]

Signs, words, speech, symbols – all link us to our own identities
and to other people/signs, consciously and unconsciously.

James's belief in the fundamental importance of speech to the
continuity and evolution of social relations is made clear in the
essays on American speech that he wrote at the end of his tour
and after it. He addresses himself to this topic in connection with
the relations between American men and women, and so a fuller
discussion of these essays is presented in the course of my reading
of *The Ivory Tower* in Part Three of this book; but here let me
quote a few passages from "The Question of Our Speech" to
illustrate the similarity between James's and Peirce's assumptions
about the social basis and social purposes of making meaning.

After chiding the graduating class of Bryn Mawr – to whom
these remarks are addressed – about their sloppy pronunciation,
James explains that he is not pleading on behalf of some abstract
academic standard of propriety:

> We may not be said to be able to study – and *a fortiori* do
> any of the things we study *for* – unless we are able to speak.
> All life therefore comes back to the question of our speech,
> the medium through which we communicate with each
> other; for all life comes back to the question of our relations
> with each other. These relations are made possible, are regis-
> tered, are verily constituted, by our speech, and are success-
> ful (to repeat my word) in proportion as our speech is
> worthy of its great human and social function; is developed,
> delicate, flexible, rich – an adequate accomplished fact. The
> more it suggests and expresses the more we live by it – the
> more it promotes and enhances life.[42]

Thus when Maggie Verver summons Fanny Assingham to her
following her creation of the sign of the golden bowl, it is not to
extract information from her or to blame her for anything but to
talk about the possible meanings of her life. Their talk evolves
semiotically. Peirce writes that

> Symbols grow. They come into being by development out of
> other signs, particularly from icons, or from mixed signs
> partaking of the nature of icons and symbols. We think only

in signs. These mental signs are of mixed nature; the symbol-parts of them are called concepts. If a man makes a new symbol, it is by thoughts involving concepts. So it is only out of symbols that a new symbol can grow. *Omne symbolum de symbolo.* A symbol, once in being, spreads among the peoples. In use and in experience, its meaning grows.[43]

And so the meaning of the golden bowl, what it stands for, grows as Maggie and Fanny talk, as Fanny "stood there in her comparative darkness, with her links verily still missing," only then to be able to ask the question that serves as the Object to provide Maggie with another opportunity for another idea, another Interpretant:

> "Then it all depends on the bowl? I mean your future does? That that's what it comes to, I judge."
> "What it comes to," Maggie presently returned, "is what that thing has put me, so almost miraculously, in the way of learning: how far they had originally gone together.... If there had been nothing before there might be explanations. But it makes today too much to explain. I mean to explain away," she said.[44]

It is by the difference between their interpretations of the sign that it acquires new and more meanings – the Interpretant of one triad serves as the Object of another. And so on and on: the triadic semiotic web grows. It is very important to note that the process of making meaning can be advanced as much by misunderstanding as by understanding – so long as the conversation continues. Maggie says:

> "The thing was that he made her think it would be so possible."
> Fanny again hesitated. "The Prince made her think – ?"
> Maggie stared – she had meant her father. But her vision seemed to spread. "They both made her think. She wouldn't have thought without them." (173)

Not only does she now understand how her own explanation must take account of different possible meanings, but she also sees how multiple and different from her own are the links in other people's interpretations of any given sign.

Now that we have a particular example of how conversation makes meaning, it is possible to consider for a moment the logical analysis Peirce offers of the way in which meaning grows. Peirce defines this logical process as "dialogism"[45] and contrasts it with the better-known syllogism:

> A form of reasoning in which from a single premiss a disjunctive, or alternative, proposition is concluded introducing an additional term; opposed to a syllogism, in which from a copulative proposition a proposition is inferred from which a term is eliminated.
>
> *Syllogism.*
>
> All men are animals, and all animals are mortal;
>
> ∴ All men are mortal.
>
> *Dialogism.*
>
> Some men are not mortal;
>
> ∴ Either some men are not animals, or some animals are not mortal.[46]

The introduction of the third term – in this example "animals" but in our example from *The Golden Bowl* Fanny's suggestion that "he" might refer to the Prince and not to Adam – leads to more, rather than fewer, possibilities of meaning. Semiosis is always evolving more possible meanings.

What James found in American social practices and institutions, on the other hand, seemed to defy this law of the growth of semiosis. In *The Ivory Tower* James characterizes semiotic devolution by the conversation of the lawyer, Mr. Crick: "the more he [Gray] conversed the less Gray found out what he [Mr. Crick] thought not only of Mr. Betterman's heir but of any other subject on which they touched."[47] It is as if this kind of conversation were a black hole rather than a life-giving sun (if I may introduce, anachronistically, a comparison that Peirce the astronomer would appreciate). James's further description of Mr. Crick's "conversation" gives us a clue as to another fundamental common belief that he and Peirce share about determinism and freedom.

Mr. Crick cannot have a conversation because his ability to interpret is limited by the circumscribed, predetermined grounds on which he will converse. He cannot make a fact into a symbol, he cannot generalize in order to make something representative, in order to arrive at the law that Peirce calls "Thirdness."[48] Mr. Crick cannot make connections with other series of signs and generate unexpected meanings. His conversation is thus typical of the laconic, antisemiotic Americans James encountered on his tour of the United States:

The gentleman who would, by Gray's imagination, have been acting for the executors of his uncle's will had not that precious document appeared to dispense with every superfluity, could state a fact, under any rash invitation, and endow it, as a fact, with the greatest conceivable amplitude – this too moreover not because he was garrulous or gossiping, but because those facts with which he was acquainted, the only ones on which you would have dreamed of appealing to him, seemed all perfect nests or bags of other facts, bristling or bulging thus with every intensity of the positive and leaving no room in their interstices for mere appreciation to so much as turn around. They were themselves appreciation – they became so by the simple force of their existing for Mr. Crick's arid mention, and they so covered the ground of his consciousness to the remotest edge that no breath of the air either of his own mind or of anyone's else could have pretended to circulate about them. (243–4)

Without "interstices for mere appreciation," there is no opportunity for the growth of semiosis because there is no possibility of difference, no way that some value might "turn around" and yield to other interpretations. Mr. Crick's conversation is, in other words, determined with a vengeance. Peirce complains about the "error" of this way of reasoning:

That from given premises only one conclusion can logically be drawn, is one of the false notions which have come from logicians' confining their attention to that Nantucket of thought, the logic of non-relative terms. In the logic of relatives, it does not hold good.[49]

Mr. Crick is clearly a native of this Nantucket. His conversation is a positivist's delight, and it falls into the category that Peirce called anancastic evolution, evolution that is wholly determined by mechanical necessity. He distinguishes it from tychastic evolution (or pure chance) and from agapastic evolution (or the law of love). There is little possibility for interpretation, for the play between chance and necessity, in the conversation of Mr. Crick.

There is little possibility for what Peirce calls "genuine agapasm . . . [in which] advance takes place by virtue of a positive sympathy among the created springing from continuity of mind."[50] There is in this American form of conversation little possibility for spontaneity, for love, for creativity. There is little possibility for mean-

ing, or for a culture to be defined socially, which is how Peirce
theorizes the fulfillment of the law of love:

> Thus, the very origin of the conception of reality shows that
> this conception essentially involves the notion of a COMMU-
> NITY, without definite limits, and capable of a definite in-
> crease of knowledge.[51]

For readers who are familiar with Peirce, the founder of semiotics, by means of the work of Thomas Sebeok or Umberto Eco, this
last kind of evolution might come a something of a surprise.[52] Yet
Peirce made no secret that the ultimate aim of all his philosophical, logical, and semiotic work was to understand and explain the
theological evolution of the universe as it was conceived of in
Christian terms. In the essay "Evolutionary Love" he acknowledges his "own passionate predilection" for the gospel of Christ
over the Gospel of Greed:

> Such a confession will probably shock my scientific breth-
> ren. Yet the strong feeling is in itself, I think, an argument
> of some weight in favour of the agapastic theory of evolu-
> tion, – so far as it may be presumed to bespeak the normal
> judgment of the Sensible Heart. Certainly, if it were possible
> to believe in agapasm without believing it warmly, the fact
> would be an argument against the truth of the doctrine.[53]

Just how strongly Peirce feels about the this kind of love for one's
neighbor, "the one whom we live near, not locally perhaps, but in
life and feeling," may be seen in his example of what he means
by "growth comes only from love, from – I will not say self-
sacrifice, but from the ardent impulse to fulfill another's highest
impulse."

He does not speak of loving another person here, but of caring
for "an idea that interests [him]," which he then cultivates

> as [he] would the flowers in [his] garden. The philosophy
> we draw from John's gospel is that this is the way mind
> develops; and as for the cosmos, only so far as it yet is mind,
> and so has life, is it capable of further evolution.[54]

This process of development by sympathetic transformation is
common to semiosis and to agapasm and, to recall my reading of
The Sense of the Past, to the transference of the psychoanalytic
relationship. It happens among signs, be they linguistic or human. Ralph Pendrel is transformed by this kind of sympathetic
interpretation in his conversation with Nan. The last, unfinished

sentence of that last, unfinished romance speaks of the hope and
the need for this kind of relation:

> He [Ralph] clung to his gravity, which somehow steadied
> him – so odd it was that the sense of her understanding
> wouldn't be abated, which even a particular lapse, he could
> see . . ."(286–7)

Interpretation creates fellowship by increasing relations, some of
them harmonious and some of them discordant, as when there is
a "particular lapse" of understanding. It is crucial to recognize
that these discordant differences are as integral to the semiotic
process as are the harmonies.

The idea of the creative value of difference is one that Peirce
and James may have learned of from the same source. Some of
the ideas that Peirce had heard of from his own Swedenborgian
father were probably reinforced by Henry James's father, for he
refers to "Henry James, the Swedenborgian," in glowing terms in
"Evolutionary Love." He quotes from *Substance and Shadow: An
Essay on the Physics of Creation* a passage in which James Senior
explains the creative value of difference:

> It is no doubt very tolerable finite or creaturely love to love
> one's own in another, to love another for his conformity to
> one's self: but nothing can be in more flagrant contrast with
> the creative Love, all whose tenderness *ex vi termini* must be
> reserved only for what intrinsically is most bitterly hostile
> and negative to itself.[55]

After this quotation of the idea that difference is necessary to the
development of meaning, an idea that James Senior expressed
throughout his work (as we shall have occasion to see again in
later chapters), Peirce gives the reader the source of the quotation and remarks:

> It is a pity he had not filled his pages with things like this, as
> he was able easily to do, instead of scolding at his reader
> and at people generally, until the physics of creation was
> wellnigh forgot. I must deduct, however, from what I just
> wrote: obviously no genius could make his every sentence as
> sublime as one which discloses for the problem of evil its
> everlasting solution.[56]

The sympathy of "Sensible Hearts," to use Peirce's phrase, that
shows itself here (and in Peirce's other incidental references to
James Senior)[57] and that makes conversation (such as his invalu-

able epistolary one with Victoria Lady Welby)[58] meaningful may
have been lacking during the dinners shared by James Junior and
Peirce in Paris, but in "The Question of Our Speech" James
describes this same creative, semiotic, social process that lies at
the heart of Christian love (*agape*) described by his father and
Peirce:

> A virtual consensus of the educated, of any gathered group,
> in regard to the *speech* that, among the idioms and articula-
> tions of the globe, they profess to make use of, may well
> strike us, in a given case, as a natural, an inevitable assump-
> tion. Without that consensus, to every appearance, the edu-
> cative process cannot be thought of as at all even beginning;
> we readily perceive that without it the mere imparting of a
> coherent culture would never get under way. This imparting
> of a coherent culture is a matter of communication and
> response – each of which branches of an understanding
> involves the possession of a common language, with its
> modes of employment, its usage, its authority, its beauty, in
> working form; a medium of expression, in short, organized
> and developed. So obvious is such a truth that even at these
> periods of an especially excited consciousness of your happy
> approximation to the ideal, your conquest, so far as it has
> proceeded, of the humanities, aforesaid, of the great attain-
> able amenities, you would not think of expecting that your
> not having failed to master the system of mere vocal sounds
> that renders your fruitful association with each other a
> thinkable thing should be made a topic of inquiry or of
> congratulation.[59]

Articulated, differentiated, discriminating speech makes "fruitful
association" a "thinkable thing." It brings people together and
allows them to have both a sense of continuity with the past and
the possibility of the sign – the sign that is their speech – evolving
into some different meaning in the future.

"Contact and communication, a beneficent contagion, bring
about the happy state," as James describes this evolutionary semiosis, without relying on the theological framework that seemed
indispensable to his father and to Peirce. In order to bring into
being the "happy state" of interpretation, James hopes to spread
the "beneficent contagion" by infecting the readers of *The American Scene* with a taste for "criticism." Ideally, he would spread an
epidemic of good conversation as he journeyed across America.

These semiotic processes are crucial to James's efforts to make sense of American culture, and my analysis of how he tries to make culture work relies on this conception of how meaning is made and to what social ends. I will not attempt to use Peirce's elaborate logic of the sign or illustrate my arguments with existential graphs, but the value of the past to semiosis and the social nature and purpose of meaning are principles of interpretation to which I will refer frequently throughout the remainder of this book. There is, at the least, a family resemblance between Peirce's and James's understanding of the processes and value of interpretation. Or, perhaps I should say, transforming somewhat a Peircean term, there is a logic of relatives.

WASTE MAKES TASTE

CLASSICISM, CONSPICUOUS CONSUMPTION, AND THORSTEIN VEBLEN

Not the least of the peculiarities of American culture that puzzled Henry James when he returned to America in 1904 for the first time in nearly two decades was the use to which the leisure class put its wealth. To have seen the shopping expeditions of the likes of Adam Verver, the American millionaire-hero of James's 1904 novel *The Golden Bowl*, had not prepared him for the likes of Fifth Avenue:

> This effect of certain of the manifestations of wealth in New York is, so far as I know, unique; nowhere else does pecuniary power so beat its wings in the void, and so look round it for the charity of some hint as to the possible awkwardness or possible grace of its motion, some sign of whether it be flying, for good taste, too high or too low. In the other American cities, on the one hand, the flights are as yet less numerous – though already promising no small diversion; and amid the older congregations of men, in the proportionately rich cities of Europe, on the other hand, good taste is present, for reference and comparison, in a hundred embodied and consecrated forms. Which is why, to repeat, I found myself recognizing in the New York predicament a particular character and a particular pathos. The whole costly up-town demonstration was a record, in the last analysis, of individual loneliness; whence came, precisely, its insistent testimony to waste – waste of the still wider sort than the mere game of rebuilding.[1]

Thus does the angel of the almighty dollar find itself in the consulting room of – or rather roaming the avenues with – the peripatetic "restless analyst," as James designated himself, whose speciality is interpreting the meaning that "a hundred embodied and consecrated forms" might have in and for the New World.

Thorstein Veblen was also appalled by the extravagances of the nouveau riche, as he makes abundantly clear in his 1899 *Theory of the Leisure Class*. Looking at the Gothic façades of the Fifth Avenue mansions on which vast sums had been spent, he declares that the plain back walls were "commonly the best feature of the building."[2] The economic, functional canons of taste are the most valuable to Veblen. The references to the past that seem so important to James for the formation of taste seem to Veblen signs of "conspicuous waste" because they are useless in themselves. But it is not as easy to eliminate signs of waste as Veblen would like, not even from his own sense of what is beautiful. The waste that he would exile from a rational, matter-of-fact society returns in several forms. He is most conscious of the way it haunts his own ambivalent appreciation of the classics; but, even in his own economic, functional model of society, he makes accommodations for waste, which appears in disguised, and therefore reputable, forms.

The irrepressibility of waste, even at the hands of its most acute analyst, suggests that the distinction between taste and waste might not be absolute. They are inosculated, as Veblen would say. Although both James and Veblen are interested in making this distinction serve their own aesthetic and economic purposes, respectively, neither can do so wholly. And neither offers a theoretical explanation for this compromised situation, although James is less troubled by that lack. It is possible to theorize the value of waste, however, by reference to some of Freud's and Bataille's ideas about civilization and its discontents. Focusing on the meaning of the past in James's and Veblen's analyses of the canons of taste will prepare us to appreciate the irrepressibility of waste.

The Desire for Taste

The absence in turn-of-the century America of "good taste . . . for reference and comparison" is not, at this point in history, due to the same causes of which James complained, famously, in his 1879 biography of Hawthorne. As he understood the processes by which culture grew, there had not yet been in that era enough time to accumulate the resources out of which an interesting and complex culture could develop. Now the situation was different. Something perverse figured in this former void:

That quite different admonition of the general European spectacle, the effect, in the picture of things, as of a large, consummate economy, traditionally practised, springs from the fact that old societies, old, and even new, aristocracies, are arranged exactly to supply functions, forms, the whole element of custom and perpetuity, to any massiveness of private ease, however great. Massive private ease attended with no force of assertion beyond the hour is an anomaly rarely encountered, therefore, in countries where the social arrangements strike one as undertaking, by their very nature and pretension, to make the future as interesting as the past. (159–60)

In "worlds otherwise arranged" (165), a sense of the past and a sense of the future have been necessary points of reference by which the aristocratic, hereditary leisure class created its sources of pleasure. This practice contrasts startlingly with what James comes to see as the characteristic antihistoricism of the New World leisure class generated by business: "No, what you are reduced to for 'importance' is the present, pure and simple, squaring itself between an absent future and an absent past as solidly as it can" (161).

Even after diagnosing this collective state of mind that suffers from something more like Alzheimer's disease than like amnesia, he still cannot quite believe that the leisure class is as indifferent even to its own immediate past as it feigns to be: "don't pretend, above all, with the object-lesson supplied you, close at hand, by the queer case of Newport, don't pretend, we say, not to know what we mean" (161). The problem is that this leisure class created by a particular history of capitalist development probably would *not* have the least idea what Henry James meant.[3] It was not in the habit of addressing the question of what it had made of its past or what it had made its past of and was often struck dumb by James's inquiries.

The lack of responsiveness on the part of his privileged inter-locutor does not, of course, stop James for a minute. He simply carries on both parts of the dialogue, pursuing his investigation into the oddity of the American leisure class's taste because he believes that the only way out of this confusion is to *learn* how to make sense of the past by beginning a conversation. He could not believe that this confusion was what the leisure class really wanted even if it had been weaned on the doctrine of self-reliance and fattened on the theory of the survival of the fittest. How could any people want to be so dissociated from a sense of their past as to make their present meaningless? It is too pathetic: "*There* comes in the note of loneliness on the part of these loose values – deep as the look in the eyes of dogs who plead against a change of masters" (160). These values want to belong somewhere, to be in a relationship that matters.

James recognizes that it is not for lack of effort that the leisure class has failed to realize a standard of good taste. The attempt had been made to do things well, to do them right, to create American beauty. But if the keen observer of the American scene might occasionally be momentarily beguiled into taking something "for a demonstration of taste," James warns that he or she "must remain on . . . guard, very properly":

> When once you have interpreted the admonitory sign I have just named as the inordinate *desire for taste,* a desire breaking into a greater number of quaint and candid forms, probably, than have ever been known upon earth, the air is in a manner clearer, and you know sufficiently where you are. Isn't it cleared, moreover, beyond doubt, to the positive increase of the interest, and doesn't the question then become, almost thrillingly, that of the degree to which this pathos of desire may be condemned to remain a mere heartbreak to the historic muse? . . . If with difficulties so conjured away by power, the clear vision, the creative freshness, the real thing in a word, *shall* have to continue to be represented, indefinitely, but by a gilded yearning, the inference is then irresistible that these blessings are indeed of their essence a sovereign rarity. (446–7)

The possibility that a culture such as Europe has created over the millennia might not be the inevitable result of civilization thus finally occurs to James.

He speculates that the Americans' novel attitude toward the past and the future might mark their culture as undergoing some kind of mutation that will make it a different thing altogether from the culture of "Europe." This suspicion sometimes tempts the "ancient contemplative person" to abandon his quest to understand the weird mixture of the old and the new that he found, for example, at Grant's tomb. He asks:

> Do certain impressions there represent the absolute extinction of old sensibilities, or do they represent only new forms of them? The inquiry would be doubtless easier to answer if

so many of these feelings were not mainly known to us just
by their attendant forms. At this rate, or on such a showing,
in the United States, attendant forms being, in every quarter,
remarkably scarce, it would indeed seem that the sentiments
implied *are* extinct; for it would be an abuse of ingenuity, I
fear, to try to read mere freshness of form into some of
the more rank failures of observance. There are failures of
observance that stand, at the best, for failures of sense –
whereby, however, the question grows too great. (146)

A culture that could do without forms at all would be a new thing
under the sun.

But perhaps this new thing *is* what "America" has produced,
not because it is located in a different place from "Europe," but
because a fundamental change in the way that the wealth which
sustains the leisure class is produced has taken place more thoroughly there than in Europe. Of course, capitalism was hardly an
American invention, and signs of this shift were evident to James
as he witnessed and participated in the development of the culture of the fin de siècle.[4] However, the problems of *The Princesss
Casamassima* in 1886 were not the problems of *The American
Scene*. The unhappy dead end of that novel – in which Hyacinth
Robinson (the illegitimate son of a British lord and a French
woman with revolutionary sympathies) commits suicide rather
than assassinate an aristocrat – demonstrated the way in which
James conceived of the irreconcilable dualisms of class antagonism. These oppositions no longer served as satisfactory dramatic
terms by the end of the century. In a number of shorter works,
including *The Aspern Papers* (1888), "The Real Thing" (1892),
"The Next Time" (1895), and "The Figure in the Carpet" (1896),
he focused on the ever more complicated problem of the (mis)-
appropriation of cultural property that had market value. In *The
Aspern Papers,* for example, he shows how the development of the
mass media feeds upon the romantic conception of genius to
violate personal and private human relations in numerous scan-
dalous ways. This is, of course, no longer news.

James saw that the terms of the social conflict were changing,
but what he did not see in a wholly European context was the
role that a sense of the past played in the struggle between old
and new societies. The trip to America clarified the extent to
which the "great transformation" of European society, as Polyani
has called it, was held in check by the social institutions that
protected labor, land, and money from being totally revalued as

commodities. Devastating as the Industrial Revolution was to the common people of England as the market economy expanded, there were checks: "Indeed," Polyani writes, "human society would have been annihilated but for protective countermoves which blunted the action of this self-destructive mechanism."[5] In America the force of tradition was, naturally, less. The market was thus freer to transvalue labor, land, and money – and culture – according to its needs.

James's increasing interest in these conflicts between what had seemed to be inalienable and immaterial properties of culture and a market economy makes historical as well as moral sense in the light of Thorstein Veblen's critique in *Absentee Ownership* of the "American plan or policy . . . of converting all public wealth to private gain on a plan of legalized seizure."[6] Veblen's analysis of the privatization of the common wealth of natural resources suggests an explanation for some of the abuses of cultural resources James witnesses. The opportunity for a certain kind of exploitation, be it of nature or of culture, is created by a market economy governed by rapid, almost wanton, changes of values.[7]

The stories mentioned here indicate that James had seen in England the kind of privatization and commodification of cultural property that is analogous to the seizure of common, natural resources for private profit that Veblen describes. Property can be (mis)appropriated by force, but possession can also be signified by waste. The devastation of one's property may signify possession better than its preservation in some cultures.[8] In the Old World property may well have been primarily theft; on Fifth Avenue possession is signified by waste. It would follow that those with the most property would and could make the grandest show of waste. This is what Veblen designated "conspicuous waste." Veblen would have been the ideal conversational partner for James in this inquiry into the relative values of taste and waste in turn-of-the-century America – provided, of course, that he would talk at all.

Veblen's elaboration of the "canons of taste" is precious to the critic for the distinctions it makes between such values as "economic beauty" and the "canons of reputable futility," and for the axiology that he demonstrates in *The Theory of the Leisure Class*. Rather than a taxonomy based on a series of opposed categories – such as base–superstructure or material–spiritual or mass–elite or aesthetic–pragmatic – he practices an analysis in which the heterogeneity of relative values is taken for granted. Every object can be analyzed insofar as it embodies "pecuniary," "economic," "archaic," or "aesthetic" values, and the relationships among these values are in no way predetermined. Each case exhibits a different, complex arrangement of values, even if there are some patterns that tend to form. "Economic" beauty and "pecuniary" ostentation, for example, are generally at odds with each other. Veblen's matter-of-fact canon of economic beauty, for example, presages the modernist credo of form equaling function:

> ... it happens that the requirements of beauty, simply, are for the most part best satisfied by inexpensive contrivances and structures which in a straightforward manner suggest both the office which they are to perform and the method of serving their end. ... among objects of use the simple and unadorned article is æsthetically the best. (*Leisure* 151–2)

The base metal spoon is just as efficient as the "hand-wrought spoon [that] gratifies our taste, our sense of the beautiful" (127).

In spite of his claims not to be making invidious distinctions, Veblen's own taste is demonstrated in his preference for the economic, rationalized society of the matter-of-fact. It is perhaps his animus to the antieconomic, wasteful habits of the "barbarian" society of the leisure class that makes him such an acute critic of its contradictions. Acute, but also ambivalent, for there are some characteristics of the "barbarians," whose way of life depends upon the use of "force" and "fraud" and "waste," that, it appears, cannot be fully forsworn in any society (*Leisure* 273). Of course, not all waste is the same: one can try to mark differences.

One of the ways that James tries to make a distinction between what seems to be really gratuitous, toxic, useless waste, at one extreme, and excess that might have some future, beneficent use, at the other extreme, is by gauging the relation of the particular object to its sources or tradition. What is the sense of the past that the object (or institution) exhibits? It will help to clarify James's responses to various failures and successes of leisure class culture in America to use two canons of taste that Veblen employs, even if Veblen does not consistently distinguish between the "archaic" and the "classic." The distinction that he makes between the "archaic" and the "classic" is not perfectly clear because of his ambivalence toward the "classic," to which he is, against his better judgment, attracted. The "classic" is to be reviled because it is fatally implicated in the barbarian culture of waste. The consequences of Veblen's ambivalence toward the beauty of the past will be considered more fully later in this chapter. My present purpose is to show how James understood the relation between the taste of the leisure class and the sense of the past as archaic or classic. Was the reference to the past sterile or fruitful? Was it waste or surplus?

Civilization and Its Contents

An illustrative, if perhaps ultimately trivial, instance of the way the leisure class distorts its relation to the past is found at one of the more exclusive of high cultural rituals, the opera. The most ludicrous aspect to James's eye of this display of distorted values in New York in 1904 was the ladies in their tiaras who were without correspondent gentlemen:

> The Opera, indeed, as New York enjoys it, one promptly perceives, is worthy, musically and picturesquely, of its immense function; the effect of it is splendid, but one has none the less the oddest sense of hearing it, as an institution, groan and creak, positively almost split and crack, with the extra weight thrown upon it – the weight that in worlds otherwise arranged is artfully scattered, distributed over all the ground. In default of a court-function our ladies of the tiaras and court-trains might have gone on to the opera-function, these occasions offering the only approach to the implication of the tiara known, so to speak, to the American law. Yet even here there would have been no one for them, in congruity and consistency, to curtsey to – their only possible course becoming thus, it would seem, to make obeisance, clingingly, to each other. This truth points again to the effect of a picture poor in the male presence; for to what male presence of native growth is it thinkable that the wearer of an American tiara *should* curtsey? Such a vision gives the measure of the degree in which we see the social empiricism in question putting, perforce, the cart before the horse. In worlds otherwise arranged, besides there being always plenty of subjects for genuflection, the occasion itself, with its character fully turned on, produces the tiara. In New York this symbol has, by an arduous extension of its virtue, to produce the occasion. (164–5)

One cannot expect a tiara to do what a trope by definition must. Semiotic disorder ensues.

The introduction of *the* symbol of sovereignty into a context without other signs of this semiotic system (such as crowned men) that would support and elaborate its meaning is self-defeating. The tiara appeals to the past to legitimate its significance, but these crowned heads have mistaken the degree to which the renaissance can be revived in isolation from the other cultural signs by which it can be interpreted. Without a common ground to which the interpreter can refer, without a communal and continuing tradition of meaning, the tiara is non-sense. The tiara's discontinuity from America's historical past and its isolation in the present made these references to the past archaic. Veblen uses as an example of archaism the arts and crafts movement, whose "exaltation of the defective" and whose "propaganda of crudity and wasted effort . . . reduced the matter to an absurdity" by, for example, the Kelmscott Press's "approximation to the crudities of the time when the work of book-making was a doubtful struggle with refractory materials carried on by means of insufficient appliances" (*Leisure* 162–3). The tiara in New York was no less absurd.

These artifacts made according to the conventions of an archaic canon of taste, which refers to the distant past, of course, still serve the self-interest of the leisure class because they simultaneously satisfy the pecuniary canons of taste, which are fulfilled by conspicuous waste. The tiara or the handmade book may not only appear to be venerable, but they obviously cost a lot of money and thus exhibit the possessor's ability to spend on something not necessary to sustain life. The tiara violates what Veblen calls the canon of economic beauty, that is, of good craftsmanship (or form serving function) because it serves no real human need other than signifying pecuniary power (151). Yet another canon of taste comes into play when the tiara is considered aesthetically.

What Veblen means by the aesthetic canon, as when he says, "Gold, for instance, has a high degree of sensuous beauty," is the actual physical, sensuous material, not its workmanship (which falls under the category of "economic beauty") (*Leisure* 129). It is, of course, nice work to make this distinction between the aesthetic pleasure and the archaic or classic value of the object, as Veblen discovers. Whatever the tiara's success in the terms of the archaic, pecuniary, and aesthetic canons of taste, this kind of reference to the past leads nowhere for the culture as a whole. It cannot, as it were, keep up a conversation after having offered its bon mot.

Echoing his complaint about the opera, James says of a New York dinner party that "it presented itself, on the page of New

York life, as a purple patch without a possible context – as consciously, almost painfully, unaccompanied by passages in anything like the same key" (162–3). The inappropriateness of these cultural artifacts – their not belonging where they are found – is evidence of axiological disorder and results in semiotic short circuits. Culture, as James understood it, was not like a department store from which one can pick and choose at will. Antiques become bric-a-brac used in this way. Moreover, the functional purposes for which cultural institutions existed were thwarted by their dissociation from the references that would serve to interpret as well as to create new instances of a particular kind of sign. Gentlemen's clubs, which James understood to serve a variety of purposes and clienteles in London, seemed at loose ends in New York:

> It is of extreme interest to be reminded, at many a turn of such an exhibition, that it takes an endless amount of history to make even a little tradition, and an endless amount of tradition to make even a little taste, and an endless amount of taste, by the same token, to make even a little tranquillity. Tranquillity results largely from taste tactfully applied, taste lighted above all by experience and possessed of a clue for its labyrinth. There is no such clue, for club-felicity, as some view of congruities and harmonies, completeness of correspondence between aspects and uses. A sense for that completeness is a thing of slow growth, one of the flowers of tradition precisely; of the good conservative tradition that walks apart from the extravagant use of money and the unregulated appeal to "style" – passes in fact, at its best, quite on the other side of the way. This discrimination occurs when the ground has the good fortune to be already held by some definite, some transmitted conception of the adornments and enhancements that consort and that do not consort with the presence, the habits, the tone, of lounging, gossiping, smoking, newspaper-reading, bridge-playing, cocktail-imbibing men. The club-developments of New York read here and there the lesson of the strange deserts in which the appeal to style may lose itself, may wildly and wantonly stray, without a certain light of the fine old gentlemanly prejudice to guide it. (169–70)

The "aspects and uses" of the clubs in New York do not consort: it is impossible to find a quiet room in which to write a letter, although one is conspicuously on display to the world as a member of the club. "Prejudice" provides an already formed context for meaning, which is always local to a given culture, here the culture of "gentlemen."

The context of the work makes a difference in what it means. The first thing a potential classic must do, however, is to survive the relentless renovation that characterizes the reign of American business. Survival is no easy task, as James realized when he did find a cultural artifact of "sovereign rarity."

New York's City Hall, which barely escaped demolition on a variety of occasions in the 1890s,[9] is, James writes, in "perfect taste and finish, [on its] reduced yet ample scale, [with its] harmony of parts, the just proportions, the modest classic grace, the living look of the type aimed at" (97). Even with what he calls "the pleasant promiscuous patina of time" (97) having been removed by some misguided turn-of-the-century effort at restoration,[10] it

> lives on in the delicacy of its beauty, speaking volumes again (more volumes, distinctly, than are anywhere else spoken) for the exquisite truth of the *conferred* value of interesting objects, the value derived from the social, the civilizing function for which they have happened to find their opportunity. (96)

No matter what political scandals might germinate within it, its "æsthetic character" remains "uncompromised" to "discharge[] the civilizing function ... of representing, to the community possessed of it, all the Style the community is likely to get, and of making itself responsible for the same" (97).

Thus it was not the neoclassical architecture that made this building "classic" in James's sense of the word.[11] Unlike the archaic tiara, City Hall *can* carry on a conversation: it does "speak volumes" and lends itself to a variety of interpretations. Anyone can walk into City Hall and read for himself or herself "the copious tell-tale document signed with a hundred names" that is composed by the hall of "portraits of past worthies, past celebrities and city fathers" looking out of their gilded frames "with the frankest responsibility for everything" (98–9). We may not, James concluded, "particularly desire to repeat" the events told of in some of these tales, but there they are to be read by all, "the whole array thus presenting itself as an unsurpassed demonstration of the real reasons of things" (99).

The endurance of such a place as City Hall has, thus, a positive ethical (because social) dimension. Here and there, against all odds, one might in America find something charming that has been allowed to become old so as "to show itself capable of growing up to character and authority. Houses of the best taste are like clothes of the best tailors – it takes their age to show us how good they are . . ." (113). Henry James is so rarely epigrammatic that one feels how desperately he must want to make his point absolutely clear.

But there are more serious social consequences for the culture than the distortions of taste in which the archaic and the pecuniary canons triumph at the opera. Presumably even the most credulous viewer of a Vanderbilt mansion on Fifth Avenue would not believe he had stumbled on evidence of a centuries-old aristocracy in America, which had reigned for generations in these Renaissance-style chateaux. Other misrepresentations of the American past are less easily revealed as fraudulent in the conspicuous absence of a context in which they could be variously interpreted. This absence of context left the leisure class freer to impose its own image of reality, an image almost inevitably serving its self-interest alone. Such a sign is Augustus Saint-Gaudens's 1903 statue of General Sherman.

James's critique of this work begins by emphasizing the relative positive values of various cultural constructions. In the midst of his very equivocal appraisal of Central Park, he declares:

> The best thing in the picture, obviously, is Saint-Gaudens's great group, splendid in its golden elegance and doing more for the scene (by thus giving the beholder a point of such dignity for his orientation) than all its other elements together. Strange and seductive for any lover of the reasons of things this inordinate value, on the spot, of the dauntless refinement of the Sherman image; the comparative vulgarity of the environment drinking it up, on the one side, like an insatiable sponge, and yet failing at the same time sensibly to impair its virtue. (172)

Only the " 'quiet' note" of McKim, Mead, and White's Metropolitan Club offers something other than dissonance to Saint-Gaudens's Sherman, which manages somehow to "triumphantly impose itself, and impose itself not insidiously and gradually, but immediately and with force" (172). On the one side was Central Park, across the street was the Plaza Hotel, and up and down Fifth Avenue were the millionaires' mansions that James compared to the victims of the French Revolution. The juxtaposition of these mansions (some of them built by profits made at the expense of the South's devastating postwar economic collapse) and the memory of the utter destruction wrought by Sherman (whose image faces south, as if he remained ever ready to strike again) is, perhaps only unconsciously, disconcerting.

As he continues to ponder this monument, something about its conflicting values as a civic statement and a work of art irritates him to question it further. Bewildered, he asks,

> Why does it not pay the penalty of expressing an idea and being founded on one? – such scant impunity seeming usually to be enjoyed among us, at this hour, by any artistic intention of the finer strain? But I put these questions only to give them up – for what I feel beyond anything else is that Mr. Saint-Gaudens somehow takes care of himself. (172)

James is willing to extend credit to Saint-Gaudens because he had seen the artist carry off such a task successfully before. In Boston James had seen Saint-Gaudens's bas-relief of the Massachusetts 54th Regiment (the unit of African American soldiers in which his brother served as an officer) and described it privately in letters to friends as a work of "real perfection," "extraordinarily beautiful and noble,"[12] and "altogether great."[13] In *The American Scene* he says that "[t]here are works of memorial art that may suddenly place themselves, by their operation in a given case, outside articulate criticism" (250). In his praise of Saint-Gaudens's statue of Lincoln in Chicago, he again seems to surrender the critical perspective for which he has made such a relentless plea in this book. The terms of his surrender, however, are telling: "the lesson there being simply that of a mystery exquisite, the absolute inscrutable; one of the happiest cases known to our time, known doubtless to any time, of the combination of intensity of effect with dissimulation, with deep disavowal, of process" (172–3). In this representation of the slain president who represented the principle of union at any cost, the artist's success at creating an "intensity of effect" is revealed to be possible only when combined with "dissimulation, with deep disavowal, of process." There is no unity of disparate, conflicting values without some cost to integrity. The artist's craft involves some distortion, as James confesses early in *The American Scene* when he feels almost overwhelmed by impressions: "without much foreshortening there is no representation" (13).

But there are degrees of "dissimulation" that are understandable or interpretable and then there are deceptions that are not. Here the misrepresentation of Sherman exposes the terms of the treaty between the aesthetic and the political, between the presence of the work of art and the history of the past, that can give peace of mind. The treaty that allowed a symbolic representation of Lincoln is still good; but the compromise underlying the image of Sherman does not hold up under scrutiny. Perhaps this is in part because of the differences in the two men's actions, notwithstanding the fact that they shared the same political goals.

Even if we can quibble with a tiny part of James's criticism because he confounds Nike's palm frond with an olive branch, his sense that the real historical reason for Sherman's fame is being gilded by this allegorical representation would, no doubt, have been further aggravated had he attended the dedication ceremony on 30 May 1903. Both the mayor of New York and the secretary of war seemed determined to rewrite the historic text and make the meaning absolutely clean and clear according to their own lights. The mayor referred to Sherman as "the kindly old warrior, so long a familiar figure in [New York's] streets, whose every word was full of good sense and whose wealth of experience and genial good nature made him the most delightful of companions"; the secretary of war insisted that "[e]very good and noble cause found in him encouragement and support. The simplicity and directness of his mind found a counterpart in the fearless frankness of his expression. His conversation and his life taught always the lesson of courage, of hope, of cheerfulness, and of light."[14] Not many Confederates would have seen this side of his personality. The story has it that one former rebel said when he saw this statue that it was just like a Yankee to make the lady walk. Saint-Gaudens himself may have been less than absolutely pleased with this production, for he preferred to mingle in the crowd than sit on the platform of honored guests.[15]

James begins his critique mildly enough by noting that the "idea" of the Sherman seems to have a "certain ambiguity." In the previous paragraph he has wondered why "its golden elegance" (its aesthetic/pecuniary value) is not able to overwhelm its "idea" (its functional memorial value) when the aesthetic is clearly so fine. But the "idea" refuses to be bought off. It "strikes [him] as equivocal, or more exactly as double," and becomes troubling when the context of his evaluation shifts from the aesthetic and pecuniary to the historical. His irritation is "the result doubtless of a sharp suspicion of all attempts, however glittering and golden, to confound destroyers with benefactors." Iconographically the image contradicts itself; it makes no sense.

The gilded sculpture is composed not only of General Sherman on a splendid steed – "the image being ... that of an overwhelming military advance, an irresistible march into an enemy's county – the strain forward, the very inflation of drapery with the rush, symbolizing the very breath of the Destroyer" – but also of a figure representing a "beautiful American girl," who "with an olive branch too waved in the blast and with embodied grace." The other half of the idea is "that the Destroyer is also a messenger of peace." The conjunction of images makes him uneasy, not only because this portrayal of Sherman is very much at odds with the image of him conjured up by his famous march but because the meaning suggested by this conjunction is non-sense of an insidious kind. There is a historical distortion represented here; there is also a false image of the processes of destruction and re-creation. Not only does the failure of the North to fulfill the promises of Reconstruction haunt this portrayal,[16] but the suffering involved in any trauma and healing, national or individual, is repressed:

> The military monument in the City Square responds evidently, wherever a pretext can be found for it, to a desire of men's hearts [to confound destroyers with benefactors]; but I would have it [the image] always as military as possible, and I would have the Destroyer, in intention at least, not docked of one of his bristles. I would have him deadly and terrible, and, if he be wanted beautiful, beautiful only as a war-god and crested not with peace, but with snakes. Peace is a long way round from him, and blood and ashes in between. So, with a less intimate perversity, I think, than that of Mr. Saint-Gaudens's brilliant scheme, I would have had a Sherman of the terrible march (the "immortal" march, in all abundance, if that be the needed note), not irradiating benevolence, but signifying, by every ingenious device, the misery, the ruin and the vengeance of his track. It is not one's affair to attempt to teach an artist how such horrors may be monumentally signified; it is enough that their having been perpetrated is the very ground of the monument. And monuments should always have a clean, clear meaning. (173–4)

This surprising conclusion from the author of *The Turn of the Screw* and *The Sacred Fount*, of all people, clearly presupposes a difference between monumental, memorial art and the art that he creates.

Iconographically, the image of the "beautiful American girl" leading the general who redefined "conspicuous waste" for the state of Georgia gives no indication of "the misery, the ruin and the vengeance of his track" that "is the very ground of the monument." Perhaps the representation of this figure from classical mythology seems odd also because she is such a very well feathered goddess of victory. One does begin to wonder, moreover, why, since she has these magnificent wings, she is marching like a common infantryman. The angel in the Shaw Memorial flies. But this Nike's wings seem to read as signs of conspicuous waste indicative of wifely vicarious consumption rather than as signs of her divinity. She has been domesticated by the sculptor's realism into an obliging and beautiful handmaiden and rewarded for her service with this lovely pair of twenty-four-karat wings.

Saint-Gaudens's perversion of the classical tradition does not make sense, most importantly, however, because the goddess of victory's submission to the service of the conquering hero misrepresents the hierarchical relation of their powers. The image recapitulates the myth of divinely sanctioned white male dominance, one part of which Sherman was supposedly fighting to destroy in the South, where it was represented by Negro slavery. James's rejection of this glorification of the political status quo, which vindicated the superior power of the white man and absolved Sherman of his responsibility for devastation was, however, a dissident, minority opinion. The Gilded Age adored this image of itself.[17]

The relative accuracy of the representation of historical facts is paramount in a civic memorial: it is supposed to make people remember what happened and what it meant for them. This is why the nonrepresentation, abstract, architectural memorial tomb of General/President Grant does not, perhaps, have as much aesthetic value as Saint-Gaudens's statue, but it performs its memorial function better because it does not make false claims about the also problematic hero to whom it refers.[18] Its abstraction does not arouse "suspicion."

There is, when history is composed of horrors as well as blessings, great danger in representation, yet without representation there is no meaning, no art. The statue of Lincoln, who was commander in chief but whose personal hands were unbloodied, and the bas-relief of Shaw, a noble young man meeting death in his first battle, work aesthetically and memorially. For memorial art to work, to allay "suspicion," there may be a slight distortion – "without much foreshortening there is no representation" – for

Lincoln did order death and the 54th Regiment was founded because white Northerners would not fight side by side with black volunteers. But too wanton a departure from the facts, too bold an attempt to repress the memory of ruin, and the meanings contradict each other. The whole scheme of the Sherman appears to be fraudulent because of this repression of a part of the complex meaning with which the represented event is associated. Like the lonely, archaic tiara, it becomes confused because of its dissociation from a meaningful past.

But not all aesthetic artifacts and institutions were doomed to this impasse. The Isabella Stewart Gardner collection in Boston provides an occasion for the creation of future works of art by providing to the public great works from the past. In this sense it is classic: it lends itself to various interpretations over time. This particular collection transvalues the exploitation and appropriation of material resources and the privatization of the cultural resources by transforming them back into common property.

James almost has to forswear the rare opportunity to praise a cultural act of collection in order to be consistent with his code of manners respecting privacy. But he is saved from silence because the act has not stopped prematurely at the stage of appropriation. Therefore, this act can and must and should be spoken about; the "spoils" are restored to a living tradition rather than taken out of circulation and hoarded. Isabella Stewart Gardner's fabulous collection of art, which is housed in her Venetian-inspired palace on Boston's Fenway, a collection that she opened to the public in 1903, is the best example he saw in America of a fruitful relation between the individual exercise of taste (never mind for the moment that it is largely Bernard Berenson's), inherited pecuniary resources, and collective culture. He wants to pay tribute to "the living spirit . . . and quite heroic genius of a private citizen" but is still brief about it, because

> To attempt to tell the story of the wonderfully-gathered and splendidly-lodged Gardner Collection would be to displace a little the line that separates private from public property; and yet to find no discreet word for it is to appear to fail of feeling for the complexity of conditions amid which so undaunted a devotion to a great idea (undaunted by the battle to fight, losing, alas, with State Protection of native art, and with other scarce less uncanny things) has been able consummately to flower. It is in presence of the results

magnificently attained, the energy triumphant over everything, that one feels the fine old disinterested tradition of
Boston least broken. (254–5)

That the "disinterested tradition['s]" fortune was built in part by
trading in opium is not his concern here: it is one of the things
"best done with the left hand" about which the right hand knows
nothing, as Veblen says of the slave trade that "gave rise to some
of the country's Best People. At least so they say" (*Absentee* 171n).
James's question is, What do the millionaires *do* with their inevitably somewhat ill-gotten gains once they have them? Do they do
anything that might in some way redeem the original exploitation
by serving the public? "Mrs. Jack's" collection, which is as inextricably tied to its location and its inviolable wholeness, as the
priceless collection of Mrs. Gereth in James's *Spoils of Poynton*
(1896),[19] performs a valuable cultural function not only because
it is an example of taste as a creative rather than a merely consuming act but because, even while it remains private property, it
is publicly available for others to study, to appreciate, and, perhaps, even to be inspired by.[20] This is re-creation and interpretation of cultural property on a grand scale. As a later cataloger
wrote, "[s]uch a collection is pregnant with history." This metaphor expresses the sense of creative connections to the past and
future that was so rare in 1904 America.[21]

That it is *Mrs.* Jack Gardner who did this good thing is altogether significant. It is men who create and have the money to
preserve things and women who collect. In the meanest of spirits,
we could say that all Mrs. Gardner did was decorate her house
very expensively, as a good wife should, and indeed this is how
her collecting began in the 1870s when James had first known
her on Beacon Street.[22] Typically, the businessman cannot afford
to waste much time himself acquiring genteel knowledge about
such things as the Italian Renaissance or traveling about Europe
looking for bargains (at least until his fortune is as secure as
Adam Verver's in *The Golden Bowl*). Veblen explains that the businessman's wife and other dependents are indispensable as representatives of his pecuniary reputability: they consume vicariously
for him. Mrs. Gardner has, of course, done this for the generous
and tolerant Mr. Jack, but she has also done a great deal more for
countless unknown others. She is both typical and exceptional.

The leisure class American woman is in a very peculiar position
at this moment of social evolution (more on this in the examina-

tion of *The Ivory Tower*), and Mrs. Gardner's exceptionality can only be appreciated in the context of the more typical contradiction. The typical woman is caught between being an object and a subject and thus deserves a special kind of consideration in this study of the contents of leisure class civilization. She is ambiguously the product and the producer of conspicuous waste. What James recognizes here is the dynamics of what Veblen describes as the "vicarious leisure" and "vicarious consumption of goods" performed by women for the pecuniary honor of their men (*Leisure* 66, 68).

Mrs. Jack seemed to have made an alternative to this typical dilemma of being either a subject or an object. Her choice to make her collection is informed by discriminating taste[23] (unlike, according to James, the Metropolitan, which will someday have to have a housecleaning "resembling . . . the funeral-pile of Sardanapalus") (193) and includes all viewers who would take an interest. She knows the difference between the way one discriminates among things and among people, a difference that James blames the curators of the Metropolitan for having failed to appreciate in accumulating their funeral pile:

> Here it is, no doubt, that one catches the charm of rigours that take place all in the æsthetic and the critical world. They would be invidious, would be cruel, if applied to personal interests, but they take on a high benignity as soon as the values concerned become values mainly for the mind. (192)

This sorting would be the work of the professional critic, such as Mrs. Jack's Bernard Berenson, or, in the realm of letters, James himself.[24]

By sharing her collection, she transforms her own status as a "convenience," an object, and creates a subjectivity that subverts the conventions of vicarious consumption and waste by identifying herself collectively with the art. She recycles her problematic identity as an object and creator of waste into a cultural artifact that is always renewable because always subject to reinterpretation.[25] She disperses herself from the singular "Mrs. Jack" (who made Sargent revise his 1888 portrait of her with her pearls and her rubies eight times before she was satisfied with his representation of her)[26] into "The Gardner Collection," which can always be reinterpreted, even if no work of art in it can be moved.[27]

James expressed his impression of this transformation in the privacy of his correspondence and in terms that leave no doubt as to his enjoyment of her recreation:

> You must hear from me of Mrs. Gardner, who is *de plus en plus* remarquable and whose *palais-musée* is really a great creation. Her acquisitions during the last ten years have been magnificent; her arrangement and administration of them are admirable, and her spirit soars higher still. Her spirit is immense, and proof against time and fate. It has greatly "improved" her in every way to have done a thing of so much interest and importance – and to have had to do it with such almost unaided courage, intelligence and energy. She has become really a great little personage.[28]

Here is the leisure class fulfilling its responsibilities by making the sense of the past a living presence for all who take an interest and – the unexpected dividend – by being "improved" itself spiritually.[29] The Gardner Collection should not, of course, be understood as a model for imitation (there are only so many Vermeers, after all); what should be understood is that the relationship of the various canons of taste could be reproduced more or less in other arenas with equally happy results.

What seems to be the crucial distinction is that there is no attempt to misrepresent the origins of these artifacts or force them into a context that cannot converse with them. Mrs. Gardner is not hoping to persuade the people that she was born to live in a villa or that she is a descendant of feudal aristocrats, as one could say Mr. Vanderbilt has pretended by building his reproduction. James sees numerous examples of this kind of misrepresentation of the past, and his responses to their falsity clarify the grounds for his appreciation of the "sovereign rarity" of such a thing as the conversion of Mrs. Gardner.

Not that such a metamorphosis was predictable. Having seen what is perhaps the happiest instance of how care for the future is provided by a continuing relation to the past, it is with a moralist's pleasure that I recall the first object of this series of analyses, reminding my reader that Mrs. Gardner's first interest as a collector was in pearls and that, in the Sargent portrait of her with her pearls, an elaborately figured brocade background frames her head, reading visually as both a halo and a tiara. What she and Sargent have done in this interpretation of her is to forgo the ludicrously archaic imitation of the past, such as the ladies at the opera practiced, and, instead to ground the portrait in the past in a way that lends itself to all kinds of senses. She poses herself as the ever interpretable figure in that carpet.

Waste Makes Taste

The distinction between "classic" and "archaic" that James makes (regardless of terms he uses) reveals his sense of how complex the conditions for the creation and appreciation of works of art and cultural institutions were and how much the "sovereign rarity" of a successful realization of one's "desire for taste" was to be prized. A sense of the past was intrinsic to the creation of culture and to the cultivation of taste. The continuity of classicism was more productive of a community of artists, critics, and audience than was fractured archaism, which might well remain isolated and therefore wasteful.

Yet it is not possible to say exactly where one can locate the point theoretically at which waste can be distinguished from the surplus or excess or luxury. This uncertainty about the distinction between the wasteful, the excessive, and the tasteful (or useful) plagues Veblen more than it does James.

As James sees it, there is no perfect apartheid of culture because what seems at one point to be nouveau archaic and thus wasteful might be transformed by some future, unpredictable use into a meaningful and fruitful resource. It is not possible ever to be sure that something is waste in the sense of being a dead end, meaningless once and for all. For James, redemption and conversion of the wasteful are almost always possible if the thing is allowed to retain some material existence and so become, with appropriate interpretation, someone's inherited past.

The history of taste tells of many such renaissances. The mansions on Fifth Avenue seem to him to plead for such a possibility of rebirth, "for the boon of the future, for some guarantee, or even mere hinted promise, of history and opportunity . . ." (183). Even mistakes as gross as the "white elephants" of Newport might come to serve a purpose. So long as they stand, they will, in the meantime, be a "reminder to those concerned of the prohibited degrees of witlessness, and of the peculiarly awkward vengeances of affronted proportion and discretion" (225). Today's waste might well be the source of tomorrow's taste by being, at the very least, a point of reference.

The difficulty of establishing a fixed distinction between the classic and the archaic over time is an indication of the impossibility of theorizing taste at any given moment: taste is defined not by a standard but by reference to that which is currently outside its canons: waste. On the one hand, this is just to say the old-fashioned thing: taste is relative. But on the other hand, we have learned from Derrida that differential value is not a simple matter of oppositions. A deconstruction of an instance of the taste–waste hierarchy would reveal that taste is a special and degenerate case of waste (rather than vice versa).[30] Waste may well have a value of its own in the complex process of cultural production. Furthermore, it may be a good thing that the distinction between taste and waste is not absolute, given the likelihood that the disruptive tendencies of business will not diminish in any significant way in the foreseeable future. Taste may have to make do as best it can.

For Veblen, the value of waste does seem at first a simpler matter than it is for James. The man who invented the phrase "conspicuous waste" would seem to have consigned all that does not directly serve the ultimate, rational ends of human life to the category of the perniciously (however reputably) futile. But Veblen's inconsistent use of the terms "classic" and "archaic" in his theory of leisure class taste indicates his ambivalence toward the ubiquitous vestiges of the past that play such a large role in the creation of conspicuous waste. He remains ambivalent because, although he offers compelling psychological explanations for this persistence, he resists accepting the tendency of his own argument. To do so might compromise his protest against the perpetuation of the canons of reputable futility.

Veblen's analysis of social value systems hinges on the (anthropologically based) distinction he makes between the predatory barbarian (the leisure class that lives by the work of others and cultivates an art of invidious comparison) and the quasi-peaceable savage (the industrial class that produces the necessities of life by rational, matter-of-fact means). Regardless of the historical validity of these types, the way that Veblen represents their axiologies gives a compelling image of the difference between a life organized by "the régime of status" and characterized by "ferocity, self-seeking, clannishness, and disingenuousness – a free resort to force and fraud" (*Leisure* 225) and one imbued with "that instinct of race solidarity which we call conscience, including the sense of truthfulness and equity, and the instinct of workmanship, in its naïve, non-invidious expression" (221). Veblen's diction leaves no doubt about his own opinion that the latter "archaic traits that are to be regarded as survivals from the peaceable cultural phase" are preferable to the former habits of barbaric exploit (221). These virtues of the savage are reincarnated in the community devoted to industrial efficiency:

> collective interest is best served by honesty, diligence, peacefulness, good-will, an absence of self-seeking, and an habitual recognition and apprehension of causal sequence, without admixture of animistic belief and without a sense of dependence on any preternatural intervention in the course of events. (227)

In this social order some cherished values would be displaced: "Not much is to be said for the beauty, moral excellence, or general worthiness and reputability of such a prosy human nature as these traits imply . . ." (227). And if the "prosy" is the way of the future, then the "man of the hereditary present [the barbarian] is slightly archaic as judged for the purposes of the latest exigencies of associated life" (216). With him should pass away all "disserviceable anachronisms" (394) that make the life of the barbarian, one would assume, poetic.

Obviously Veblen is using the term "archaic" in these instances to mean two different things: the first instance, "archaic traits," refers to ancient social habits and is a noninvidious use of the term; the second, "slightly archaic," means that these types are instances of "arrested spiritual development" (213), and this use is invidious. The instability in his use of the term is even more pronounced when he associates it with "classic" and implies several different categorical relations between them. Sometimes they are equivalent (399); sometimes "classic" is a "special development" of the "archaic" or "obsolete" (165); and sometimes "the classics" represent "an archaic ideal of manhood" (394); but: " 'Classic' always carries this connotation of wasteful and archaic" (398).

Technological obsolescence that makes the thing work inefficiently is the sign par excellence of the archaic for Veblen. The perversity he cites in the practices of the Kelmscott Press is also to be found in the "futile classicism" of "conventional spelling of the English language . . . it is archaic, cumbrous, and ineffective" (399). This futility does little, however, to make such conventions or affectations less appealing. This is what is so annoying about classicism.

In spite of their obvious economic uselessness, Veblen admits that "[t]here is a prevalent æsthetic and ethical predilection for the barbarian aptitudes" (263). He explains this tendency by reference to the force of habit, a most powerful psychological disposition, as C. S. Peirce would have suggested in the Johns Hopkins seminars that Veblen attended.[31] Barbarian habits go way back: "the propensity for emulation – for invidious comparison – is of ancient growth and is a pervading trait of human nature" (109). And it is not just one among many: "With the exception of the instinct of self-preservation, the propensity for emulation is probably the strongest and most alert and persistent of the economic motives proper" (110). The "barbarian aptitudes" are attractive because they have been found to be attractive in the past. This reasoning is not as circular as it might at first appear. For "canons of taste are race habits," and the longer their lineage, the more legitimate they are (392). Thus, there is no escaping certain habitual associations:

> In æsthetic theory it might be extremely difficult, if not quite impracticable, to draw a line between the canon of classicism, or regard for the archaic, and the canon of beauty. For the æsthetic purpose such a distinction need scarcely be drawn, and indeed it need not exist. For a theory of taste the expression of an accepted ideal of archaism, on whatever basis it may have been accepted, is perhaps best rated as an element of beauty; there need be no question of its legitimation. (165)

And this is as true of the "animistic superstitions and the exuberant truculence of the Homeric heroes" (392) as it is of the beauty of the lawn, which obviously appeals to this Norwegian son of the Midwest prairie:

> The lawn unquestionably has an element of sensuous beauty. . . . The close-cropped lawn is beautiful in the eyes of a people whose inherited bent it is to readily find pleasure in contemplating a well-preserved pasture or grazing land. (133–4)

Hence, also the delight in "the cattle on the grass [which] are themselves no mean addition to the beauty of the thing, as need scarcely be insisted on with any one who has once seen a well-kept pasture" (135) and who thereafter associates this spectacle with material well-being, although

> the cow as an object of taste must be avoided. Where the predilection for some grazing animal to fill out the suggestion of the pasture is too strong to be suppressed, the cow's

place is often given to some more or less inadequate substitute, such as deer, antelopes, or some such exotic beast.
These substitutes, although less beautiful to the pastoral eye
of Western man than the cow, are in such cases preferred
because of their superior expensiveness or futility, and their
consequent repute. They are not vulgarly lucrative either in
fact or in suggestion. (134–5)

The repressed returns on the hoof. On the golden California hills
of William Randolph Hearst's San Simeon, zebras stroll.

   Veblen himself is obviously not immune to the pleasures of
beauty and the classics. In a typical instance of irony indicating
his ambivalence toward the canons of classicism, Veblen argues
that college sports now have the honorific status that dead languages did formerly in institutions of higher learning and then
inserts – in Latin – a quotation foretelling the return of "old-
fashioned shame and neglected virtue."[32] Late in his life he not
only translated the Icelandic epic *The Laxdaela Saga* but continued his study of Latin hymns.[33] The futility of the classics, as he
says, "need disturb no one who has the good fortune to find
comfort and strength in the classical lore" (395). O fortunatum
nimium!

   In spite of the force of the ancient habit of emulation, Veblen
believes that the current bearer of classical, barbarian values –
the businessman – is doomed because his way of life is incompati-
ble with, although dependent on, machine industry, on the one
hand, and dynastic politics, exhibited in the predatory collusion
of military and political forces, on the other.[34] Veblen does not
say the day of doom is near, only that it must come.[35] If the
businessman becomes extinct because the values of machine
technology prevail, so may "these sentimental movements of the
human spirit [that] belong in the past" wither away.[36] Already the
institutions that embody these values are among the living dead:

   Much of the apparatus of the old order, with the good old
   way, still stands over in a state of decent repair, and the
   sentimentally reminiscent endeavors of certain spiritual
   "hold-overs" still lend this apparatus of archaism something
   of a galvanic life. But that power of aspiration that once
   surged full and hot in the cults of faith, fashion, sentiment, exploit, and honor, now at its best comes to such a
   head as it may in the concerted adulation of matter-of-fact.
   (*Learning* 9)

But this mechanistic disposition cannot, Veblen admits, satisfy "the emotional traits of human nature" (9).

Dynastic politics may yet reinstitute the reign of war, "authenticity and sacramental dignity." The "discipline of prowess" might foster a "sacramental serenity to men's outlook on the present and the future" that is now lacking (*Business* 399). But this is not a good thing as far as Veblen is concerned.

He clearly hopes that matter-of-fact habits of machine technology will prevail and will change social values – even as he recognizes that irrational, emotional human needs would not be satisfied in such an order. It is not just that Veblen is loathe to welcome the reign of barbarian fascism; the habits of thought that characterize the "pecuniary occupations" include "explanations of phenomena in terms of human relation" (*Business* 319). Presumably these explanations, too, would become meaningless in the world ordered by the matter-of-fact. And in a world that had no need of this kind of explanation, the art of Henry James, among others, would have no value.

Remembrance of Waste Past

Recognizing the uselessness of art and the futility of all that barbarian conspicuous waste simply does not make it go away. Freud, for example, also acknowledges the limits of reason when it comes to accounting for aesthetic pleasures: "Beauty has no obvious use; nor is there any clear cultural necessity for it. Yet civilization could not do without it."[37] What the experience of beauty seems to do, as Freud sees it, is induce a "mild narcosis" that can temporarily diminish "the pressure of vital needs," although "it is not strong enough to make us forget real misery" (28). Beauty can, nevertheless, be "a source of pleasure and a consolation in life" (28) because it draws its power from the "field of sexual feeling" (30), which is sublimated: "The love of beauty seems a perfect example of an impulse inhibited in its aim. 'Beauty' and 'attraction' are originally attributes of the sexual object" (30). Our quest for beauty must then follow the ways of our quest to recover the erotic satisfaction we have found in the past: "What is more natural than that we should persist in looking for happiness along the path on which we first encountered it?" (29). Indeed, Freud had earlier theorized that "all instincts tend toward the restoration of an earlier state of things."[38]

Some sense of the past is intrinsic to the experience of beauty, which gives erotic pleasure, and in these terms it is no mystery why people would want to perpetuate the sources of their experiences of beauty. One would not try to enroll undergraduates by claiming that the classics are sexy, but perhaps some of Veblen's irritation at his own enjoyment of them can be understood as ambivalence about the power of the irrational in general. There is very little that is matter-of-fact about erotic pleasure.

Freud does not theorize extensively about the pleasures of beauty, but what he says about the problem with making the pursuit of love the aim of life points to the danger of making any idea of beauty (or standard of taste) absolute:

> The weak side of this technique of living is easy to see. . . . It is that we are never so defenceless against suffering as when we love, never so helplessly unhappy as when we have lost our loved object or its love. (*Civilization* 29)

In love, if we rely on any one object to meet our needs, the chance of suffering is greater because the chance of total loss is greater.

In the quest for aesthetic pleasure, which is already protected from total devastation because it is a sublimation of desire, the chances for pleasure increase if there are numerous objects that can bring satisfaction, to a greater or less degree. And having more than one needs, is, of course, even better yet. In fact, having more than one needs, having excess, having surplus, having waste, might be what restores to one the sense of well-being that overwhelms the rational possibility of loss of the desired object. It might be that the waste is what gives the taste its undeniable allure, it piquancy, its je ne sais quoi.

The social use of this theoretical indeterminacy between taste and waste is ultimately more important for James than are its aesthetic implications. Because of this indeterminacy, discriminations in the aesthetic realm must constantly be made and remade, as the history of taste readily shows. The practice of critical discrimination in the aesthetic realm, I would suggest, fosters similar habits of negotiated and ongoing discrimination in the social realm. Likewise, the neglect of such skills might prove distressing at crucial moments in life, as when Lewis Lambert Strether, the hero of James's 1903 novel, *The Ambassadors*, returns to Woolett, Massachusetts, rather than risk the rewards of negotiating relations with Maria Gostrey in the more complex aesthetic and social world of Paris. Her offer "rested, all so firm, on selection. And what ruled selection was beauty and knowledge."[39] But Strether protests that he must instead be "right": "That, you see, is my only logic." James shows how thwarted his development has been by the culture of New England that cultivates a logic of renunciation, as Strether puts it: "Not, out of the whole affair, to have got anything for myself," even as he allows that Strether will, nevertheless, have his comforts: "There will always be something."

It is important that these constructions of value be approximate and not absolute because the psychological needs for beauty and for intimacy that they serve can never be fully satisfied, but must always make do with more or less. There is no perfect beauty; there is no perfect love. Therefore, it is best to have some ways to negotiate the approximate satisfactions that are the best one can hope for. The practice of aesthetic and social discriminations is a strategy for maximizing a pleasure that is always incomplete. While James and Veblen recognize the inescapable irrationality of these human desires, they value it in contrary ways.

Where James sees the artist working by means of "a geometry of his own,"[40] Veblen sees "invidious distinctions" that sustain the "régime of status" so contrary to a rational scheme of life. Veblen's ambivalence toward classicism can be understood as an indication of his recognition that such a canon of taste depends upon such habitual and inherited distinctions that give pleasure because they have given pleasure in the past. Thus, the very waste that he abhors as characteristic of the barbarian leisure class is a sign of the inalienable irrationality of human life that is the basis of pleasure itself.[41]

James, on the other hand, seems to assume that the leisure class, because it practices and perfects this critical and social practice of discrimination, the constant redefinition of "taste" and "manners," serves society as a whole by representing the potential value of waste conspicuously. But the leisure class would not be the sole and exclusive beneficiaries and, it could be argued, even if the day came when the leisure class passed away, the representation of the irrational would continue to be socially constructed in some public realm. In the meantime, the idle rich waste for the sake of others because they have the time and resources to do so.

Georges Bataille takes this idea many steps further, and thus clarifies this theory of the possible social value of waste, when he proposes that the economy of human life is governed by excess, not by scarcity and necessity, and "that a series of profitable operations has absolutely no other effect than the squandering of profits."[42] What appalls Veblen – "useless consumption" – is to Bataille "ebullition" (30), and the only question is "how the

wealth is to be squandered" (23). Shall it be "gloriously or cata-
strophically" (21)? Shall there be festival and art, or shall there
be war? Bataille knows that he is arguing against all prevailing
economic theories and that his theory will not satisfy those who
put justice and the concern for the individual above concern with
the well-being of the whole of human society, which, like all
organisms, makes more than it needs (38–9). But he believes that
recognizing the proper sources and use of wealth will give people
the choice of using it for pleasurable or deadly ends. The fundamental principle of his economy is that of "gift-giving," of "squandering without reciprocation" (38). The sun – solar energy – is
both literally the source of all excess and a metaphor for the
giving "without any return" that is the proper use of human
wealth (28).

The uselessness of art, idleness, and waste run counter to the
rational economic order developed to a high pitch by the de-
scendents of Calvinism because they "consum[e] without a return – without a profit – the resources that they use: They simply
satisfy us; they correspond to the *unnecessary choice* that we make
of them" (119). Religion, above all that of the Church of Rome,
has been effective at satisfying these unnecessary choices because
its material splendors "are useful on that plane [of supernatural
efficacy] precisely insofar as they are gratuitous, insofar as they
are needless consumptions of resources first and foremost"
(120). Grace bestows the ultimate gift of salvation; it cannot be
earned by any rational scheme.

The magnificent squandering of wealth is practiced by the
church, and tolerated, because it responds to an emotional need:
"Religion in general answered the desire that man always had to
find himself, to regain an intimacy that was always strangely lost"
(129). It has failed to satisfy the need, however, because "the
mistake of all religion is to always give man a contradictory answer: *an external form of intimacy*" (129). And the objects in which
religion attempts to invest the desired intimacy are always disap-
pointingly revealed to be merely things. And things, whether
represented by the Grail or as a minimum assured standard of
life or the triumph of the proletariat, are not the "solution of the
problems of life – the key to which is a man's not becoming
merely *a thing,* but of *being in a sovereign manner*" (131). It is the
freedom (a word that Bataille avoids perhaps because in 1967 it
belonged to Sartre), it is the gratuitousness of waste that makes it
satisfying. And the grander the spectacle of uselessness, the more
the "lost intimacy" is found:

The expression of intimacy in the church corresponds . . .
to the needless consumption of labor: From the start the
purpose of the edifice withdraws it from public utility, and
this first movement is accentuated in a profusion of useless
ornaments. . . . Intimacy is not expressed by a *thing* except
on one condition: that this *thing* be essentially the opposite
of a *thing*, the opposite of a product, of a commodity – a
consumption and a sacrifice. Since intimate feeling is a
consumption, it is consumption that expresses it, not a *thing*,
which is its negation. (132)

Thus, the medieval Roman Church remains an attractive image
of the "relative stability and equilibrium of a world in which man
was less estranged from himself than we are at present" (131)
because it was, as an agent of waste, so vastly superior to Protes-
tantism and its paltry descendants in the world of full-blown
capitalism. The Vanderbilts and Rockefellers would have been
surprised to hear that they were a lame excuse for a leisure class.

A Taste for Living

James's pet name for Edith Wharton, "the angel of devastation,"
resonates with all of its affectionate appreciation of the leisure
class doing its very best to squander its goods when it is read
against Bataille's hosanna to waste in the highest. But James's
most explicit recognition of the exuberant pleasures of excess are
found expressed in uncharacteristically theoretical terms in what
is undoubtedly his most metaphysical work, a 1910 essay titled "Is
There Life after Death?":

This mere fact that so small a part of one's visionary and
speculative and emotional activity has even a traceably indirect bearing on one's doings or purposes or particular desires contribute [*sic*] strangely to the luxury – which is the
magnificent waste – of thought, and strongly reminds one
that even should one cease to be in love with life it would be
difficult, on such terms, not to be in love with living.[43]

The discrepancy between what one thinks and feels and what one
does reveals a vast disproportion in favor of the thing not done,
in favor of that which is in excess, and it is on just such a basis
that one wants to live. The "magnificent waste" makes one desire,
not desire any particular things in a particular life, but desire to

go on reveling in this "luxury" of having more than one could ever use.

All human schemes of rational organization are too limited. Even those people who would seem least able to produce the "luxury – which is the magnificent waste – of thought" make their own contribution to the whole of human life:

> The probability is, in fact, that what we dimly discern as waste the wisdom of the universe may know as a very different matter. We don't think of slugs and jellyfish as the waste, but rather as the amusement, the attestation of wealth and variety, of gardens and sea-beaches; so why should we, under stress, in respect to the human scene and its discussable sequel, think differently of dull people? (603)

It is in the experience of excess, which tends toward a supernatural dimension, that it is possible to discover the satisfying "lost intimacy" that depends upon oneself being not a thing or an agent but "sovereign" in Bataille's terms – and "social" in James's:

> The truth is that to live, to this tune, intellectually, and in order to do beautiful things, with questions of being as such questions may for the man of imagination aboundingly come up, is to find one's view of one's share in it, and above all of its appeal to *be* shared, in an infinite variety, enormously enlarged. (611)

One's very self may be consumed and dispersed in an act of imagination that takes one far beyond the limits of the actual. Such is the blissful experience of doing "beautiful things."

And one of the aspects of such "beautiful things" is inevitably for James – as for Bataille, who recognizes that "[t]he spirit of rigor is thus committed to destroying the remnants of the ancient world" (139) – a sense of the past. As James writes in *The American Scene* on his return from the void of the Far West and his passage through the Hudson Valley, he had

> the absurdest sense of meeting again a ripe old civilization and travelling through a country that showed the mark of established manners. It will seem, I fear, one's perpetual refrain, but the moral was yet once more that values of a certain order are, in such conditions, all relative, and that, as some wants of the spirit *must* somehow be met, one knocks together any substitute that will fairly stay the appetite. (147)

The excess that allows one to regain the "lost intimacy" *must* necessarily carry with it some sign of that which came before, that which was loved and lost. The pleasure of having more than one needs, or imagining that one has more than one needs (does this come to the same thing?), is thus inextricably related to having a sense of the past. For there is no new pleasure except in that which recalls some earlier (erotic) pleasure. One must "make it old."

The cultivation of taste, which depends upon some notion of the past as embodied in classicism or tradition, is in the service of the pleasurable experience of waste, which also carries an (unconscious) sense of the past with it. Taste, with its practice of discrimination and its flexibility, insures that there is always something in excess. In times of scarcity, such as James experiences on his journey through the Far West, the "relative" boundary between taste and waste can be shifted so that the "wants of the spirit" do not perish in the famine. The artist will make out of the given that which surpasses it.[44] That is his creative defiance of the actual. It is the means by which he gives – freely – to others.

But this is not to say that there are not some arrangements of society, of culture, of art that will yield more satisfaction than others. As Jaroslav Pelikan argues in his vindication of tradition: "An abstract concept of parenthood is no substitute for our real parents, an abstract cosmopolitanism no substitute for our real traditions."[45] It takes time, of course, to know which traditions will turn out to have been "real." Frank Kermode has proposed that "[t]he survival of the classic must therefore depend upon its possession of a surplus of signifier; as in *King Lear* or *Wuthering Heights* this may expose [these texts] to the charge of confusion, for they must always signify more than is needed by any one interpreter or any one generation of interpreters."[46]

But that "surplus" of the great works of art will not be fruitful unless the culture has provided for their preservation even when they were out of fashion. The leisure class alone can afford this preservation of the useless. It conserves, for the society as a whole, habits of mind, archaic artifacts and paractices of culture, traditions of waste, and institutions of taste that might become useful again in times of cultural scarcity or transformation.

This conservation of the signs of collective memory is something that even Veblen must allow has its place, although he is concerned with what we might call "practical classicism." Implicit in Veblen's canon of economic beauty is the notion he makes explicit in connection with his analysis of the creative capacities of the industrial arts to "convert[] otherwise meaningless elements of physiography and mineralogy into industrial wealth" (*Absentee* 167). The state of the industrial arts is

> of the nature of a joint stock of technical knowledge and proficiency, held, worked, augmented, and carried forward in common by the population at large; indeed, by the population of the civilised world at large, not by any one class or country unaided or in isolation. It is a joint stock of technical knowledge and workmanlike habits, without the use of which the existing material wealth of the civilised nations would not be wealth. (167)

This joint stock is traditional knowledge, which is collective, continuous, cumulative, and creative. Although parts of it may be in the control of individuals at times, it is, like the gene pool, social property. This kind of surplus is as necessary a resource to the engineer as to the artist. Thus, the windmill may have been abandoned as an engine for a water pump only to be revived on California hillsides as a means to generate electricity. The technology of handwriting may have seemed on the verge of becoming obsolete in the age of computer keyboards – until devices for recognizing and translating handwriting into electronic information were created.

It is very much in these same terms that James talks about the artistic tradition to which he is an heir. When James laments Hawthorne's isolation because his work cost him twice the pains it would have if Hawthorne had been part of a community of artists or when James acknowledges his artistic debts to Balzac, Turgenev, and George Eliot, he is designating the same power of traditional knowledge and skill to create value from mere material that Veblen has in mind when he writes that:

> It is no serious stretch of language to say that this current state of the industrial arts has made America a land of abundant resources, inasmuch as these industrial arts have made these material facts of the American continent serviceable for industrial use. (*Absentee* 167)

The "joint stock" must, like a museum or a library, preserve knowledge that may not be immediately useful but might be again in the future under different material circumstances. Knowledge and techniques may become obsolete but may just as likely become the means of innovation at some unforeseeable turn of events. Thus, even the industrial habit of mind that rationalizes the material world must make allowance for some conservatorial, unpragmatic reservoir in its own best and unknowable interests. The development of culture is not determined according to an abstract pattern that would allow the elimination of some never to be useful "resources"; rather, it is contingent on many, many different kinds of causes that cannot be predicted.

Likewise, there is another kind of waste that might contribute to the world of matter-of-fact in the long run. Also flowing into that reservoir of temporarily useless practical knowledge is the runoff, if I may extend my metaphor, of the streams of useless "esoteric knowledge" that it is the function of the university to let flow whither they will. Veblen defends this mediated economy at work in the "higher learning," which is ruled by "idle curiosity" rather than immediate matter-of-fact practical knowledge. "Idle curiosity" he defines as

> a disinterested proclivity to gain a knowledge of things and to reduce this knowledge to a comprehensible system. The objective end is a theoretical organization, a logical articulation of things known, the lines of which must not be deflected by any consideration of expediency or convenience, but must run true to the canons of reality accepted at the time. (*Learning* 8)

This pursuit of knowledge for the sake of some unknowable future occupies, as the wag said, the leisure of the theoried class.

Waste or surplus or luxury or the impractical or the useless is thus no exclusive province of the barbarian leisure class, however much Veblen may wish to escape from all signs of the irrational, especially when they are embodied in the classic. Waste seems to be a normal, necessary, perhaps even glorious part of living. Waste makes taste.

"PSYCHIC MULATTO"

THE AMBIGUITY OF RACE AND W. E. B. DU BOIS

In the South, which he had never visited before, James found a different kind of misrepresentation of the past than he had in the North. He had hoped to find all kinds of interesting contrasts between the two regions, indeed, longed to find them as a relief from the monotonous dominance of business interests. He had assumed there would be legible traces of the past in the South not only because a trauma as great as the war could be expected to have left scars, but because the South had self-consciously and self-righteously revered the past and tradition in ways inconceivable to the transcendentalist or the man of business.[1]

James had looked forward to being "romantically affected" by the "vivid images, mainly beautiful and sad" of the Southern past, but he found instead that he was "wondering and a trifle mystified" by his first impressions. He asked himself:

> How was the sight of Richmond not to be a potent idea; how was the place not, presumably, to be interesting, to a restless analyst? . . . One had counted on a sort of registered consciousness of the past, and the truth was that there appeared, for the moment, on the face of the scene, no discernible consciousness, registered or unregistered, of anything. Richmond, in a word, looked to me simply blank and void – whereby it was, precisely, however, that the great emotion was to come.[2]

As soon as he realized that Richmond was not blank but "*weak –* 'adorably' weak," however, his compassionate and analytic interest was aroused:

> I can doubtless not sufficiently tell why, but there was something in my whole sense of the South that projected at

moments a vivid and painful image – that of a figure somehow blighted or stricken, discomfortably, impossibly seated
in an invalid-chair, and yet fixing one with strange eyes that
were half a defiance and half a deprecation of one's notic-
ing, and much more of one's referring to, any abnormal
sign. The deprecation, in the Southern eyes, is much greater
to-day, I think, than the old lurid challenge; but my
haunting similitude was an image of the keeping-up of appearances, and above all of the maintenance of a tone, a
historic "high" tone, in an excruciating posture. (377)

The "excruciating posture" of this invalid indicates the power of
the conflicts it is trying to repress. The "abnormal signs," the
symptoms of this conflict, are what gave the South its unique
character.

Having recognized that the blankness of Richmond was not an
absence but a disguise – "that the large, sad poorness was in itself
a reference" – James could try to trace the symptom to its cause
in the past, working through the collective amnesia, for now "a
hundred grand historic connections were on the spot, and quite
thrillingly, re-established. What was I tasting of," he asked himself
as he wandered randomly, "at that time of day, and with intensity,
but the far consequences of things, made absolutely majestic by
their weight and duration?" (371). And the cause of these "far
consequences" was

the very essence of the old Southern idea – the hugest
fallacy, as it hovered there to one's backward, one's ranging
vision, for which hundreds of thousands of men had ever
laid down their lives. I was tasting of the very bitterness
of the immense, grotesque, defeated project – the project,
extravagant, fantastic, and to-day pathetic in its folly, of a
vast Slave State (as the old term ran) artfully, savingly isolated in the world that was to contain it and trade with it.
This was what everything round me meant – that that absurdity had once flourished there; and nothing, immediately,
could have been more interesting than the lesson that such
may remain, for long years, the tell-tale face of things where
such absurdities *have* flourished. (371)

The "lesson" was that such "grotesque" versions of human society
could only develop in isolation from the culture's historical origins and contemporary connections. James was particularly apt to
recognize this twice-told tale because he had seen in his youth

how even the relatively cosmopolitan Cambridge suffered by its isolation from European culture.

The Olde South

The tale that James tells of how the culture of the South reached its miserable state was a story he had told before but never with a region as the hero. He had told the story of the consequences of isolation, for example, in *The Turn of the Screw,* and he had told it in his biography of Hawthorne. In fact, the very theme was one of his heritages from Hawthorne. What was the unpardonable sin but self-inflicted isolation from the human community? The consequences for the governess in his most famous ghost story are well known, if not easily described; the consequences for Hawthorne, as James saw it, were not fatal but at least inhibiting to his genius.

In his discussion of his predecessor's intellectual and artistic isolation, James focuses on the necessity of time to the development of "a complexity of manners and types" so vital to the novelist. What he says of Hawthorne in 1879 prefigures his diagnosis of Southern culture in 1905:

> The best things come, as a general thing, from the talents that are members of a group; every man works better when he has companions working in the same line, and yielding the stimulus of suggestion, comparison, emulation. Great things of course have been done by solitary workers; but they have usually been done with double the pains they would have cost if they had been produced in more genial circumstances. The solitary worker loses the profit of example and discussion; he is apt to make awkward experiments; he is in the nature of the case more or less of an empiric. The empiric may, as I say, be treated by the world as an expert; but the drawbacks and discomforts of empiricism remain to him, and are in fact increased by the suspicion that is mingled with his gratitude, of a want in the public taste of a sense of the proportions of things.[3]

"Poor Hawthorne" circumvented enough of these obstacles to creation, but the South had not succeeded so well and only increased its liability when it seceded. In Hawthorne's case it is the famous "absence" of things – "no Epsom nor Ascot" – that is the ghostly impediment to his partaking of the community of culture; in the case of the Old South the cultural gap is fortified by a presence in the flesh.[4] But the Old South's isolation from contemporary culture was not circumstantial in a way that New England's was. It was deliberate and self-interested.

In order to justify chattel slavery in the modern world, the South had disinherited itself from the legacy of Western thought:

> Since nothing in the Slave-scheme could be said to conform – conform, that is, to the reality of things – it was the plan of Christendom and the wisdom of the ages that would have to be altered. History, the history of everything, would be rewritten *ad usum Delphini* – the Dauphin being in this case the budding Southern mind. This meant a general and a permanent quarantine; meant the eternal bowdlerization of books and journals; meant in fine all literature and all art on an expurgatory index. It meant, still further, an active and ardent propaganda; the reorganization of the school, the college, the university, in the interest of the new criticism. (374)

The culture that grew from this was

> beyond measure queer and quaint and benighted – innocent above all; stamped with the inalienable Southern sign, the inimitable *rococo* note. We talk of the provincial, but the provinciality projected by the Confederate dream, and in which it proposed to steep the whole helpless social mass, looks to our present eyes as artlessly perverse, as untouched by any intellectual tradition of beauty or wit, as some exhibited array of the odd utensils or divinities of lone and primitive islanders. (374)

Having broken off intellectual contact with the rest of the world, culture in the Old South regresses, becomes "primitive" and "odd" because "[t]here were no *references*" (371) that would temper its eccentricities.[5]

James calls this oddity of style "rococo," but there does not seem to be anything specifically postbaroque about it.[6] He may have chosen the term to indicate simply that it is at odds with Northern style, that it is, in a word, peculiar. The Southerners themselves had often figured their cultural difference in the image of the cavalier, the aristocratic superior of the Northern roundhead. But more telling of the way in which they considered themselves as living by a different axiology from that of the North were the many strains of medievalism that informed Southern culture. The Old South had broken off connections with its actual

European origins and community (although not, obviously, the markets of that world) and substituted a distorted image of a much older social order on which to model itself. It then pretended to be the true fulfillment of Western civilization, which, it claimed, had been corrupted by Renaissance and Enlightenment values.

This kind of disconnection from the immediate past and reference to the distant past is, as I suggested in the introduction to this book, typical of the nostalgic frame of mind that is itself a product of the Renaissance. The desire to return to an authentic origin that was uncorrupted by some version of the false, the antichrist in its many forms, motivated the slaveholders, as it had Valla and Luther.[7] The difference between the Southern slaveholder's nostalgia and that of many others was that he actually lived in a social order that was an alternative to bourgeois capitalism, which otherwise dominated Atlantic societies.[8]

The situation was paradoxical. Explained in another vocabulary, that of psychoanalysis, it could be said that the Old South was engaged in something like the family romance described by Freud but on a social rather than an individual scale. It was as if someone suffering from this delusion of noble birth abused his biological parents while claiming to believe in traditional family values. Of course, real medieval societies were quite different from their Southern reincarnations.

This borrowing of a different origin by the slaveholders, which drew upon a very distorted "memory" of a feudalism that never was, thus filled the gap left by the Southerners's "bowdlerization" of the Western tradition since the Renaissance. Specifically, the Southerners needed a European model for their slave society. Although the Old Testament gave them their "divine sanction" for slavery, they could not use it as a cultural model: they were not a nomadic or Semitic people. The slaveholders may well have acquired their love and knowledge of the Middle Ages primarily from Walter Scott, whose *Ivanhoe* was the most popular book in the South before the war, but they had not fixed on this era simply because it provided an opportunity for pageants and jousts on the plantations.

Although most Southern gentlemen knew perfectly well, as Eugene Genovese argues, that "[s]laves were not serfs; slaveholders were not feudal lords; plantations were not manors," nevertheless, "this insistence upon a historical and indeed divinely sanctioned continuity between the medieval world the world of modern slavery" served their need for a model for an organic, non-market-based society.[9] It established an ideal connection to a tradition and mitigated their isolation, which condition was not sanctioned by a doctrine of individualism as it might have been in the North. The Southern gentleman venerated continuity in formulations that would have been utterly foreign to the Northern transcendentalists or the Gilded Age. "He longs to live as his fathers lived before him, in both the Old World and the New," Daniel R. Hundley wrote in 1860 in *Social Relations in Our Southern States.*[10]

For this reason, "[t]heir attempt to identify the divinely inspired, the permanent, the admirable in the medieval experience proved both intellectually powerful and politically significant."[11] Although plantation slavery clearly existed primarily for the financial benefit of the masters, the Southerners' version of medievalism brought with it, however inadvertently, a conception of human relations that had some redeeming features. The cult of medievalism, based upon organic, familial relations, Genovese argues, had some advantages over the market relations of bourgeois capitalism: "It encouraged acceptance by the masters of duties, responsibilities, and a code of conduct that made the ultimate test of a gentleman the humane and Christian treatment of his slaves."[12] The South's unique creation of a necessarily false past for itself had, in spite of itself, also provided some comfort for those it exploited most grossly, even if it was not the paradise described by George Fitzhugh in his 1857 classic defense of slavery, *Cannibals All! or, Slaves without Masters.* However biased Fitzhugh's portrayal of slavery is, his critique of the human cost of Northern market relations has merit.[13] Human relations on the plantation, in theory and sometimes in practice, were not regulated solely by market values but by "mutual if unequal rights, responsibilities, and duties."[14] The federal victory brought an end to this peculiarity.

In Black and White

The extent to which the Old South's conception of itself rested on a corrupt image of medieval, seigniorial society was revealed in the New South by the horrible state of relations between blacks and whites. The turn of the century has been described as the "nadir of the Negro."[15] During the period from approximately 1897 to 1907, in which the Southern Radicals institutionalized their vision of the retrograde and bestial Negro, the white South's taste for alienation was redirected from the North to the Negro.[16]

In many ways, racial relations were worse at the turn of the century for the blacks than they had been before the war: disenfranchisement of the Negro was programmatically effected; segregation of the races was regulated by the Jim Crow laws that mandated not only separate street cars and jury boxes but separate Bibles on which witnesses were to swear to tell the whole truth. The ideology of racism was sustained by scholarship at Northern as well as Southern universities, where the imperialist dogma of the white man's burden was the prevailing wisdom.[17]

This was also the period during which lynching flourished. However fictive on the whole the myth of the benevolent paternalism of the manor was, a slaveholder did not kill his valuable property casually. A historian of the period writes, "In the first decade of the twentieth century, a person was lynched approximately every fourth day, and nine out of ten were Black, a ratio of Black over white that held into the 1930s."[18] The nefarious effects of what James calls the South's "grotesque" scheme of social organization endured long after the war. This was the social scene on which Henry James arrived in 1904, and it makes a difference to the interpretation of his chapters on the South to read them with an awareness of their historical context.[19]

James cannot have been unaware of the situation even before he set foot in the South. His publisher, Colonel George Harvey, had written on "The New Negro Crime" in *Harper's Weekly* in January 1904, and it was to Harvey's house in New Jersey that James went upon his arrival in America.[20] Harvey's basic argument is that the lynchings would stop if Negroes would stop protecting the sexually uncontrollable rapists of white women. He had several ingenious solutions to this problem. One was to disenfranchise black men, as Mississippi had done and where there was, he said, no more "negro crime"; the other suggestion he took from that authority on the Southerner's problem, Thomas Nelson Page, who found that the British system of using a native police force seems to have worked quite well. The anxiety occasioned by the fear of "amalgamation" lurks behind these fantasies of the black man as a sexual beast, notably in Thomas Dixon's 1902 novel, *The Leopard's Spots*.[21] This fear of the loss of distance and difference might also be seen in a much less direct form in works such as W. D. Howells's 1874 novel, *A Foregone Conclusion*, in which the heroine flees in horror from the passion of a frocked priest. Intimate contact between representatives of different cultural traditions is viewed with fear and loathing.

However skeptically one might read documents such as the

recollections of former slaves gathered by the WPA, in which the circumstances of the interview might have affected their telling,[22] no less a witness to racial relations in the South in 1903 than W. E. B. Du Bois regrets the passing of some parts of the old pattern of community. With the loss of intimate daily, domestic contact between "master and man," and "mistress and maid," the best opportunities for sympathetic understanding between the races vanished and they became aliens to each other. In his 1903 classic *The Souls of Black Folk*, Du Bois laments this estrangement between the races.[23]

James received a copy of this book from his brother William, Du Bois's former teacher and life-long supporter, and he had characterized it as "the only 'Southern' book of any distinction for many a year . . . by that most accomplished of members of the negro race" (418). He makes this comment in the chapter on his visit to Charleston, following his visit to and chapter on Richmond, during another episode questioning and lamenting the absence of Southern culture. James may have put "Southern" in quotation marks here because Du Bois was, after all, a New Englander, born and raised in Great Barrington, Vermont. Du Bois's first exposure to the South came when he began college at Fisk University in Nashville, and the South was as surprising to him as was James's, on different terms, to him. While James as a Northerner was taken aback at first only by the blankness of Richmond, Du Bois's initial shock came from finding himself as an African American – regardless of his Northern bourgeois nativity or his intellectual distinction – subjected to a degree of racial prejudice for which the less brutal segregation of Vermont had not given him a precedent. He wrote in his autobiography: "No one but a Negro going into the South without previous experience of color caste can have any conception of its barbarism."[24] Because of this difference in their racial positioning, Du Bois's analysis of his experience in the South can be read fruitfully in dialogue with James's. Each of these outsiders tried to make sense of the signs of the past in order to make a different meaning of the relations between blacks and whites than the ready-made one offered to them by the New South. What each worked toward in these texts was reinterpreting those living signs in black and white that resisted understanding each other. For each, the play of double consciousness is invaluable.

Du Bois wrote about the increasing isolation of the two races from each other in a chapter entitled "Of the Sons of Masters and Men":

One thing, however, seldom occurs: the best of the whites and the best of the Negroes almost never live in anything like close proximity. It thus happens that in nearly every Southern town and city, both whites and blacks see commonly the worst of each other. This is a vast change from the situation in the past, when, through the close contact of master and house-servant in the patriarchal big house, one found the best of both races in close contact and sympathy, while at the same time the squalor and dull round of toil among the field-hands was removed from the sight and hearing of the family. (477)

Later in that same chapter Du Bois returns twice more to the contrast between the kind of relations that were possible at their best in the Old South and that are impossible now:

Now if one notices carefully one will see that between these two worlds, despite much physical contact and daily intermingling, there is almost no community of intellectual life or point of transference where the feelings of one race can come into direct contact and sympathy with the thoughts and feelings of the other. Before and directly after the war, when all the best of the Negroes were domestic servants in the best of the white families, there were bonds of intimacy, affection, and sometimes blood relationship, between the two races. They lived in the same home, shared in the family life, often attended the same church, and talked and conversed with each other. But the increasing civilization of the Negro since then has naturally meant the development of higher classes: there are increasing numbers of ministers, teachers, physicians, merchants, mechanics, and independent farmers, who by nature and training are the aristocracy and leaders of the blacks. Between them, however, and the best elements of the whites, there is little or no intellectual commerce. (488–9)

The two cultures were developing isolated from each other in ways that could only be deleterious to both. Even if the material circumstances of some blacks were improving with their professionalization, this segregation is bad for the soul:

It is hardly necessary for me to add very much in regard to the social contact between the races. Nothing has come to replace that finer sympathy and love between some masters and house servants which the radical and more uncompromising drawing of the color-line in recent years has caused almost completely to disappear. In a world where it means so much to take a man by the hand and sit beside him, to look frankly into his eyes and feel his heart beating with red blood; in a world where a social cigar or a cup of tea together means more than legislative halls and magazine articles and speeches, – one can imagine the consequences of the almost utter absence of such social amenities between estranged races, whose separation extends even to parks and street-cars. (490)

The ideal of a brotherhood of man is very much alive in Du Bois's book, but he does not confuse the actual and general conditions of slavery with what it could be at its best. He knows that the solution to the present is not a retreat to the past.

In his 1905 review of Thomas Nelson Page's *The Negro: The Southerner's Problem* (1904), Du Bois does not hesitate to use irony as a weapon against the authority whom Colonel Harvey has deferred to so willingly:

It is as inaccurate to call Southern slavery barbarous as it is to call the modern wage system ideal; but it is not inaccurate to say that Southern slavery fostered barbarism, was itself barbaric in thousands of instances, and was on the whole a system of labor so blighting to white and black that probably the only thing that saved Mr. Page's genius to the world was the Emancipation Proclamation, the very deed that allows the present reviewer the pleasure of criticising Mr. Page's book instead of hoeing his cotton.[25]

The spiritual cost of slavery was something paid by both classes, although only one, Du Bois argues, was prone to recognize it:

It is inconceivable that a laboring class placed under the complete domination of such a man should prosper; and with all the instances of kindness and affection (and there were hundreds of such instances) the net result of any such system was, and was bound to be, oppression, cruelty, concubinage, and moral retrogression.[26]

In choosing the word "retrogression," Du Bois makes clear that he is attacking the argument of the Radicals that the Negro was improved under the discipline of slavery and now has "retrogressed" to his original bestial state.

Du Bois shows that Page contradicts his belief in this fundamental principle by advocating education and opportunity for the Negro. Such a contradiction is, however, certainly preferable to the consistent logic of racism worked out by its more rigorous partisans, such as Professor William Benjamin Smith in his book, *The Color Line* (1905), which Du Bois refers to in this review. Compared with Smith and his ilk, Page, "while not a friend of the Negro race is certainly not to be counted an enemy."[27] Du Bois found it important to discriminate between Page's wrongheadedness and Smith's fanaticism, his "naked, unashamed shriek for the survival of the white race by means of the annihilation of all other races . . . [which] could easily be passed over in silence, did it not state flatly and with unnecessary barbarism a thesis that is the active belief of millions of our fellow countrymen." This extreme form of racism, which Du Bois calls the "new barbarism of the twentieth century," is "the heart and kernel of the Negro problem."[28] But this enemy – racism at its supremacist worst – was only one of the Negro's enemies, only one of the causes of terrible relations between the blacks and whites.

The Negro of 1904 was under attack from white Southerners for his very life; but he and she were also corrupted spiritually by the forces of pecuniary interest that James saw so distressingly dominant in the North. Du Bois criticizes both of these destructive forces by reference to a standard, again, of the best aspects of human nature that were known under the slave system. In "Of the Wings of Atalanta," an earlier chapter of *The Souls of Black Folk,* he writes:

> Atalanta must not lead the South to dream of material prosperity as the touchstone of all success; already the fatal might of this idea is beginning to spread; it is replacing the finer type of Southerner with vulgar money-getters; it is burying the sweeter beauties of Southern life beneath pretence and ostentation. For every social ill the panacea of Wealth has been urged, – wealth to overthrow the remains of the slave feudalism; wealth to raise the "cracker" Third Estate; wealth to employ the black serfs, and the prospect of wealth to keep them working; wealth as the end and aim of politics, and as the legal tender for law and order, and finally, instead of Truth, Beauty, and Goodness, wealth as the ideal of the Public School. . . . Hither has the temptation of Hippomenes penetrated; already in this smaller world, which now indirectly and anon directly must influence the larger for

good or ill, the habit is forming of interpreting the world in dollars. The old leaders of Negro opinion, in the little groups where there is a Negro social consciousness, are being replaced by new; neither the black preacher nor the black teacher leads as he did two decades ago. Into their places are pushing the farmers and gardeners, the well-paid porters and artisans, the business-men, – all those with property and money. And with all this change, so curiously parallel to that of the Other-world, goes too the same inevitable change in ideals. The South laments to-day the slow, steady disappearance of a certain type of Negro, – the faithful, courteous slave of other days, with his incorruptible honesty and dignified humility. He is passing away just as surely as the old type of Southern gentleman is passing, and from not dissimilar causes, – the sudden transformation of a fair far-off ideal of Freedom into the hard reality of bread-winning and the consequent deification of Bread. (417–18)

The old types, black and white, between whom some bond of compassion was possible because their relative positions within a stratified social system allowed for the possibility of benevolence (as well as exploitation), are passing away. The new system has not recuperated the benefits of the old. Where there had been organic social relations, there now were fragments which could only grind each other down.

The whole mood of the South was tense and irritable in 1904. Du Bois wrote of the discontent in the chapter of *The Souls of Black Folk* titled "Of the Black Belt:"

They are not happy, these black men whom we meet throughout this region. There is little of the joyous abandon and playfulness which we are wont to associate with the plantation Negro. At best, the natural good-nature is edged with complaint or has changed into sullenness and gloom. And now and then it blazes forth in veiled but hot anger. ... Careless ignorance and laziness here, fierce hate and vindictiveness there; – these are the extremes of the Negro problem which we met that day, and we scarce knew which we preferred. (451–2)

This profound inner conflict, which makes every effort of the blacks to improve their situation doubly hard, is the heritage of

slavery. Du Bois's most famous insight into the state of mind of
the blacks explains the ground of this tension:

> ... the Negro is a sort of seventh son, born with a veil, and
> gifted with second-sight in this American world, – a world
> which yields him no true self-consciousness, but only lets
> him see himself through the revelation of the other world.
> It is a peculiar sensation, this double-consciousness, this
> sense of always looking at one's self through the eyes of
> others, of measuring one's soul by the tape of a world that
> looks on in amused contempt and pity. One ever feels his
> two-ness, – an American, a Negro; two souls, two thoughts,
> two unreconciled strivings; two warring ideals in one dark
> body, whose dogged strength alone keeps it from being torn
> asunder.[29] (364–5)

This double consciousness was the sign of the hyphenated
"African-American" mind for Du Bois.

Yet this sense of alienation from the self was not in every way
unique to the African Americans. The sense of disconnectedness
from one's origins and oneself was, more generally, a part of the
heritage of modernity, and thus what Du Bois discovered when
he went South was that the African Americans were always already
modern in a way that the slaveholders and their descendants were
not. At least in this psychic dimension of experience, they were
not, oddly enough, isolated from the mainstream of the Republic
of Mind.

It may well have been at Harvard itself that Du Bois gained the
groundwork for understanding this experience of alienation. The
conception of a double consciousness was being explored by
various contemporary thinkers, among them, his teacher, William
James. In *The Principles of Philosophy* (1890) James wrote of the
brain that it could allow "one system to give rise to one consciousness, and those of another system to another *simultaneously* existing consciousness."[30] William's source, in turn, of this conception may well have been the fundamental premise of his father's
cosmogony, namely, that creation is composite, not simple, so
that consciousness can be created by difference.[31] According to
Henry Junior, his father illustrated this composite consciousness
in his own life experience, "there being no human predicament
he couldn't by a sympathy more *like* direct experience than any I
have ever known enter into. . . ."[32] Thus this doubleness, so clearly
a source of suffering for the African Americans Du Bois is referring to, might also be the ground making empathy possible.

Du Bois's own experience as a "psychic mulatto," as Arnold Rampersad has called him, was, however, often painful.[33] He felt the separation from the very people of color in relation to whom he had conceived his famous formulation. Here was a young man from New England who responded to the passionate music of the Southern blacks but who could not participate in this folk culture because of his own cultivation in a European-derived culture. Du Bois dramatized something like his own situation in his first novel, *The Quest of the Silver Fleece* (1911), at the moment when a rather corrupted woman says to the hero that a Yankee do-gooder "has gone and grafted a New England conscience on a tropical heart, and – dear me! – but it's a gorgeous misfit."[34] This conflict between different parts of his heritage had serious consequences throughout his life. His expatriation did not have as happy consequences as did Henry James's. The difference in how these two critics understood the best way to use the doubleness of consciousness might explain one aspect of why Henry James's way of making sense of the past allowed him to think that blacks and whites might come to understand each other.

The problem is, as might be expected, the meaning of race. Tracing the transformations of this central concept of Du Bois's life and work, Anthony Appiah shows how Du Bois's various efforts, from his earliest writings, to change the meaning of race never succeeded in discarding the basis for its definition, a biological basis that had always been used to the disadvantage of the people of African descent. In an intellectual move characteristic of what Appiah calls the classic dialectic, Du Bois seeks to change the axiology of racial differences, to show that the true relationship of the races is complementary, not hierarchical. Each race has a particular and different "message, its particular ideal, which shall help to guide the world nearer that perfection of human life for which we all long, that 'one far off Divine event.' "[35] Even as the theological grounds for Du Bois's credo diminished in the course of his life, this early statement in "The Conservation of Races" (1897) signals the essential problem. How are the races to be distinguished on these social-historical grounds? Du Bois never, Appiah concludes, found a way to do so.

So long as he held the category of race to be essential, there was no way he could rotate its axis of value so that he could discuss the variety of cultures, which was his fundamental moral concern. He did not consider the possibility, I would suggest, that the qualities in the relations between master and man that he describes in the passages quoted earlier were possible because race did not matter as much under slavery as it did later. There were other kinds of relations that held the society together, for better or worse, and so race did not function as *the* essential difference. Later race was essentialized, and because it had no real scientific or historical basis, it could never be anything but an insurmountable barrier. Henry Louis Gates Jr. writes that "Race is the ultimate trope of difference because it is so very arbitrary in its application."[36] As the whole concept of race becomes more and more biologically dubious, Appiah suggests that the conceptual work that "race" has been asked to do, work that has often been "evil," should be forsworn. The use of this "vocabulary" or "language" or "idiom" is self-defeating: it brings with it the very problems it would undo.

J. G. A. Pocock writes that one way to think about reading is as an act of translation, but that "some idioms are remarkably resistant to translation and use their impenetrability as a means of gaining ascendancy over other idioms."[37] The idiom of "race," created by those whose interest was in proving the natural superiority of the "white race," has not been effectively translated, even by those like Du Bois who devoted a lifetime to this end. There are alternative vocabularies for the questions about culture we want to ask: "What exists 'out there' in the world – communities of meaning, shading variously into each other in the rich structure of the social world – is the province not of biology but of hermeneutic understanding."[38] It is on these grounds that James habitually wanders.

In the chapter that follows James's insight into the fundamental cause of the South's repression of the signs of its past,[39] he had two major revelations about the "far consequences" – the present signs – of the Old South's isolation from the greater world of bourgeois enlightenment. Since these signs are not to be found in the aesthetic culture of Richmond, he turned to the living signs that he chanced to encounter and there read the legacy of the "Slave State" written as legibly as he could want. The "abnormal signs" that James imagined the invalided South was imploring him not to notice thus became the most conspicuous signs in the "decipherable South" (373) as soon as he realized they stood before him in black and white.

The Beast in the Paleface

James's first encounter with Southern blacks took him by surprise, and he dramatizes his reaction with a memorable trope:

I was waiting, in a cab, at the railway-station, for the delivery of my luggage after my arrival, while a group of tatterdemalion darkies lounged and sunned themselves within range. To take in with any attention two or three of these figures had surely been to feel one's self introduced at a bound to the formidable question, which rose suddenly like some beast that had sprung from the jungle. These were its far outposts; they represented the Southern black as we knew him not, and had not within the memory of man known him, at the North; and to see him there, ragged and rudimentary, yet all portentous and "in possession of his rights as a man," was to be not a little discomposed, was to be in fact very much admonished. (375)

James's figure of the beast in the jungle is crucial to understanding what he makes of these African Americans but not in the way it might at first appear.[40]

This simile may have struck many readers as an instance of the contemporary stereotypical racist depictions of the Negro as beast, such as is found in Charles Carroll's 1900 book, *The Negro, a Beast,* or in Thomas Dixon's best-selling trilogy: *The Leopard's Spots* (1902), *The Clansman* (1905) (upon which W. D. Griffith's *Birth of a Nation* [1915] was based), and *The Traitor: A Story of the Fall of the Invisible Empire* (1907). But to hear these resonances without recalling that in James's 1903 tale "The Beast in the Jungle" the hero, John Marcher, is portrayed as the man who "utterly, insanely missed" the special meaning of his life is to miss a crucial clue.

By identifying his position with that of the hero who "had justified his fear and achieved his fate; he had failed, with the last exactitude, of all he was to fail of."[41] James castigates himself for his ignorance of what should have been obvious. John Marcher failed to realize the meaning of his life by failing to understand the value of the relationship he was *already* having with someone; what Henry James had failed to do, he now realizes, was to understand what race meant in the South and to foresee that as soon as he, a white man, stepped over that border, he would *already* be defined by the South's rules.[42] No one visible escapes signifying racially in the South.

Much as James yearned in the all-too-homogenized North for the retention of some of the signs of difference that the immigrants brought from the Old World, here he saw how a simple axiology with one dominant value can be fatal for interpretation by repressing all other differences: "One understood at a glance how [the Negro] must loom, how he must count, in a community in which, in spite of the ground it might cover, there were comparatively so few other things" (375). If race is the only thing that matters, then all relationships will become distorted by the pressure to explain too much by too little.

James sensed that pressure – he felt afraid of the "black teamsters who now emphasized for me with every degree of violence that already-apprehended note of the negro really at home" (378) – and realized that it is thus that the Southern white man lives: in fear.[43] If the white man created an image of the Negro as beast, as rapist, as inhuman, it was because he knew how strong the resistance to his construction of the Negro as subordinate was. Revolt is possible at every moment: "It came to one, soon enough, by all the voices of the air, that the negro had always been, and could absolutely not fail to be, intensely 'on the nerves' of the South" (376). And on the nerves of Henry James. He finds that the Southern Negro makes, in spite of stereotypes to the contrary, a very incompetent servant. He is so aggravated by several incidents that he is moved to wonder that the planters would have gone to war to hold on to such poor service: "I could have shed tears for them at moments, reflecting that it was for *this* they had fought and fallen" (423). James's concern is that the task at hand be done well; his complaint is aesthetically, not racially, motivated.[44]

Yet if James was to understand the "abnormal signs" of the blighted figure of the South, he could only do so from the frequently uncomfortable position in which he found himself. Even a stranger at a train station seems to have recognized James's disorientation, having remarked to him, " 'I guess we manage our travelling here better than in *your* country!' " – James not having, of course, the least idea which country the man "imputed" to him (423).

Just as he does not resort in his fiction to authorial omniscience, James did not pretend to be able to understand the experience of the Southern black, to see the world from the African American's point of view.[45] He always writes from a character's necessarily limited point of view and shows how that particular consciousness comes to understand something new in relation to what he or she has known before. James is notorious as a novelist whose narrators do not, unlike Dickens's or Balzac's, step in and clear up the moral ambiguities for the reader. The ambiguity elicits interpretation and the interpretation, importantly, introduces the possibility of multiple meanings. Here James interprets the distant, intense relationship that he was already actually having with the blacks and tries to make various possible senses of his fear.

He identified his apprehension of the Negro's potential revolt with the "nerves" of the white Southerners because he finds himself marked as a possible victim in the violent South of 1905, in which one's fate was determined by one's race. In his anxiety, he does not, let us be clear, take refuge in arguments justifying white supremacy, slavery, or racism. He sees whites and blacks bound together painfully, although not identically, in the traces of the past.[46] This "thumping legacy of the intimate presence of the negro" is what the white Southerners have inherited

> and one saw them not much less imprisoned in it and overdarkened by it to-day than they had been in the time of their so fallacious presumption. The haunting consciousness thus produced is the prison of the Southern spirit; and how was one to say, as a pilgrim from afar, that with an equal exposure to the embarrassing fact one would have been more at one's ease? (375)

He does not have to work very hard to imagine the discomfort of the New England "pilgrim," however theoretically he may pose the matter of its possibility. Though he may not have partaken of the "fallacious presumption" of plantation slavery,[47] "[t]he haunting consciousness" is, he has found to his surprise, his "legacy" as well, just by the fact of his race.

When critics have written about James's chapters on the South, he generally has been characterized as an apologist for the Southern status quo or as a racist. He is said to have been willing to leave the "Negro Question" "for solution to those (in this case, white Southerners) who supposedly had the greatest understanding of the problem ... [and] he perceived no need to lecture southern whites or moralize about the southern Negro question."[48] Or he is accused of veiling "vulgar and trite prejudices" in his complex prose and betraying "his democratic American heritage."[49] What is implied, at worst, is that James was content to let Southern whites lynch their own blacks.

James tended so little to moralize or to lecture anyone at any time that these criticisms seem to overlook the characteristic style of the author as well as to ignore the man's life. If there was any lesson he had learned at his father's knee, it was that any human relation that was not the result of spontaneous love but of coer-

cion was absolutely corrupt. Henry Senior, with his habitual rhetorical gusto, had proclaimed this truth many times in many ways.
In 1861 in his Independence Day speech, he asked what social
"taint" had turned us

> from an erect sincere hopeful and loving brotherhood of
> men intent upon universal aims, into a herd of greedy luxu-
> rious swine, into a band of unscrupulous political adventur-
> ers and sharpers, the stink of whose corruption pervades the
> blue spaces of ocean, penetrates Europe, and sickens every
> struggling nascent human hope with despair?
>
> The answer leaps at the ears; it is Slavery, and Slavery
> only.[50]

James had always known that slavery was wrong;[51] but it was not
until he became conscious that he was implicated in its legacy of
racism that he discovered what he (who had not served in the
war because of a back injury)[52] had now to do about its "far
consequence."

Yet James did urge discretion on the part of the outsider,
and this plea for silence of a certain kind looks something like
complicity:

> The admonition accordingly remained, and no further ap-
> peal was required, I felt, to disabuse a tactful mind of the
> urgency of preaching, southward, a sweet reasonableness
> about him. Nothing was less contestable, of course, than
> that such a sweet reasonableness might play, in the whole
> situation, a beautiful part; but nothing, also, was on reflec-
> tion, more obvious than that the counsel of perfection, in
> such a case, would never prove oil upon the waters. The lips
> of the non-resident were, at all events, not the lips to utter
> this wisdom; the non-resident might well feel themselves
> indeed, after a little, appointed to silence, and with any
> delicacy, see their duty quite elsewhere. (375–6)

James did see his duty elsewhere and does not fail to perform it,
but his conception was subtle and has, I think, been overlooked.[53]

Rather than moralize on the injustice of race relations as they
were, James makes in his writing an effort to "disprovincialize," as
he says, the New South. The Southerners, black and white, had
heard plenty of Yankee opinions over the years. James does not
offer easy condemnation as if he were not implicated in the
America whose history this is. His revelation of what it means to

be a white man in the New South precludes any pretense to Olympian detachment. He offers instead of judgment an image and an instance of a relationship between the New South and himself, the "restless analyst," that might be of help in revising relations between the races. He plays the role of a therapist not a moralist.

And, of course, in order to be effective as a therapist, he has first to submit to analysis himself: he has to become conscious not only of his fears but of his attractions to the invalid figure before him so that his own "complexes" do not prevent him, as Freud says, from being "able to reconstruct the patient's unconscious."[54]

Mon Semblable, Mon Frère

Visiting the Confederate Museum, James may have been disappointed by the artifacts he found, but he could not have had better luck in his chance encounters with people there if he had arranged to have two representative "types" of the Old South on hand. The keeper of the museum was a quintessential Southern lady whose telling of the tales of the past made him feel that his "pilgrimage couldn't be a failure." She rehearsed "the old wrongs and the old wounds" until they had become "valuable, enriching, inspiring, romantic legend . . ." (385–6). The art of "thoroughly 'sectional' good manners . . . transported [him] as no enchanted carpet could have done" (385). This is the sense of the past longed for by the unredeemed Ralph Pendrell.[55]

This nostalgia-driven "enchanted carpet" took a sudden dive, however, when James struck up a conversation with a young Virginian doing homage to the relics of his ancestors in the Confederate Museum. (Ten years later James would meet in the National Gallery the young Canadian recruit whose profound ignorance of Western culture may have spurred him [James] to return to *The Sense of the Past*.) The filial piety of this "son of the new South" impressed James favorably at first.[56] He recalls that he

> complimented [the Virginian] on his exact knowledge of these old, unhappy, far-off things, and it was his candid response that was charmingly suggestive. "Oh, I should be ready to do them all over again myself!" (388)

This unselfconscious expression of the desire to repeat the past conflict brings James crashing back to earth. He had at first assumed that the museum's aesthetic blankness was "a pale page

into which he might read what he liked" (384). But face to face
with an unforeseen sign of the violence that sustained the "historic 'high' tone" he found so attractive in this gracious Son and
Daughter of the Confederacy, he found he was mistaken. The
"restless analyst" is forced to recognize that his desire to be
charmed by the past, to be seduced, almost blocked his recognition of the transference of the past conflict into the present
relationship. He realizes that he is not only the Yankee enemy
who might still be defeated in the next round of the struggle but
that he is also the object of the Virginian's fraternal affection:
they are white men together. Love and hate coexist.[57] James has
almost been seduced into an allegiance fighting for a cause that
is not his:[58]

> [The Virginian] was a fine contemporary young American,
> incapable, so the speak, of hurting a Northern fly – *as* North-
> ern; but whose consciousness would have been poor and
> unfurnished without this cool platonic passion. With what
> other pattern, personal views apart, *could* he have adorned
> its bare walls? So I wondered till it came to me that, though
> he wouldn't have hurt a Northern fly, there were things (ah,
> we had touched on some of these!) that, all fair, engaging,
> smiling, as he stood there, he would have done to a South-
> ern negro. (388–9)

James only knows what horrors are elided by his parenthetical
comment – "(ah, we had touched on some of these!)" – but this
trick of leaving the worst to his reader's imagination, which James
has used to such good purpose in *The Turn of the Screw,* is all the
more effective for the fact that these words and this image of the
Virginian engaged in doing unspeakable "things . . . to a Southern negro" are the final words of this section of the text.[59]

The charming Virginian has thus become in the reader's mind
capable of any horror *because* of the way James chooses to represent him. He represents him as a monster, "all fair, engaging,
smiling," because he sees through his rationalizations, just as he
had seen through the Southern "chivalry" of his own Basil Ransom in *The Bostonians.* Even while the misplaced Mississippian
feels in the yard of Harvard College "the soreness of an opportunity missed" and feels in the Memorial Hall "the sentiment of
beauty" inspired by the monument that "arched over friends as
well as enemies, the victims of defeat as well as the sons of
triumph," Ransom, nevertheless, torments Verena Tarrant: "In
playing with the subject this way, in enjoying her visible hesitation,

he was slightly conscious of a man's brutality – of being pushed by an impulse to test her good-nature, which seemed to have no limit."[60] The brotherhood's bond is forged at the expense of the relatively powerless other.

Although the Virginian took James's complicity *as* a white man for granted as the condition of his confidence, James is saved from this seductive appeal to racial brotherhood by the sudden intrusive return of the repressed image of the Negro to consciousness. A third term interrupts this dialogue between the North and the South. James recognizes that the abstract pattern of this "cool platonic passion" reigning in the Virginian's reconstructed but sparsely furnished consciousness still excludes the blacks from recognition as being equally human. The Virginian is intellectually isolated from the possibility of various and complex social relations between blacks and whites, perhaps more so (if Du Bois is right) than were his fathers before him. At this moment in his writing and by his writing, James represents the blacks as victims, not perpetrators, of violence and, by doing so, illustrates the ways in which two different interpretations of the same sign can exist simultaneously for him. This redefinition of the self in relation to the other is characteristic of James's narrative dynamics and an essential feature of the transference relationship necessary for successful psychoanalysis. The blacks do not mean only one thing to him, and this ambiguity and ambivalence disrupt the color line by inviting interpretation.

Having recognized that he is irrevocably implicated in the conflict he is analyzing because he cannot escape his own signifying body and yet believing that other outcomes of the conflict than those he reads in the living signs of Richmond are possible, James now resigns himself to act as a medium for the possible transformation of these relations. It is in this moment that he has understood something about the absolute value of race in Southern society. He has looked through Du Bois's veil; he has had, as Du Bois puts it, the "peculiar sensation, this double-consciousness, this sense of always looking at one's self through the eyes of others." Perhaps James could accept being identified as a white man when it meant that he might be the victim of the black teamster's violence; but he could not accept the consequences of the construction put upon his whiteness by the descendant of Confederate heroes.

Because James will not accept the identity as a white oppressor imputed to him by the Virginian, he finds himself in the position of being psychically a mulatto: he is white in the eyes of both black and white Southerners, but in his own eyes he must identify himself as *not* white because his race would place him in a position as oppressor that he refuses to occupy. His racial double consciousness comes into being because he will not accept the idea that his race determines his social and political position and beliefs absolutely. His resistance to this singular construction of his identity produces the ambiguity of his own racial identity that defies the monovalent Southern axiology. Resistance, ambiguity, and difference allow for new values to be formulated by the old things being in new relations to each other.

The monovalence of race in the South creates a dyadic opposition between black and white that is disrupted by the double consciousness of the subject who resists being defined as an object. "Double consciousness" in the sense that Du Bois and James are using this famous term would perhaps more accurately be described as a triadic relation. In this relation, the subject, by seeing himself or herself not only subjectively but also as the other sees him or her, triangulates the relation between self and other – and recognizes the possibility of the other being conscious of this same relation. By this triangulation, the existence of the subjectivities of both are acknowledged. At the same time, differences are recognized as the ground for a new relation rather than as the dead end of radical incommensurability. Black and white need not remain opposed values. Nor need the "mulatto" (psychic or otherwise) always be the same: it depends upon what third term comes into play to disrupt that opposition. The splitting or doubling of consciousness must be triangulated to disprovincialize the isolated mind of the South. Relations are multiplied; new meanings are possible.

James's response to the construction of race in the South is psychologically and morally very much like that of Du Bois. Repelled by the absolute division of people by their race, they both also saw that the double consciousness produced by resistance to this construction was itself of great use in overcoming the alienation between peoples that was created by segregation, that it was, in fact, invaluable to the disprovincializing of any consciousness that had isolated itself from the polyvalence of human relations.[61]

Being a psychic mulatto might well be, then, not a liability that would leave one isolated from a community, but rather the very means by which to establish fellowship with those (sometimes frighteningly) not like oneself. This belief in the value of difference is what makes James and Du Bois, one might almost say, soul brothers.

Retour

Bidding farewell to the young Virginian, James leaves the streets of Richmond and steps like a "strained pilgrim [into] a blessedly restful perch" (389) – the public library. Here was "the felt balm, really, of the disprovincializing breath" (391), the "especial restorative" (389) he had sought at first in the "romantic character" of the South. Although surrounded again by the pathetic memorabilia of the war, James nevertheless reflects hopefully:

> Disinherited of art one could indeed, in presence of such objects, but feel that the old South had been; and might not this thin tremor, on the part of several of those who had had so little care for it, represent some sense of what the more liberal day – so announced there on the spot – might mean for their meagre memories? (391–2)

This vision of the potentially redemptive power of a more liberal day is not, however, blithely idealistic or optimistic:

> They [the library and the university] are the *rich* presences, even in the "rich" places, among the sky-scrapers, the newspaper-offices, the highly-rented pews and the billionaires, and they assert with a blest imperturbable serenity, not only that everything would be poor without them, but that even with them much is as yet deplorably poor. (390)

There is no guarantee that establishing more and better relations with the Republic of Letters, with the traditions of thought and art found in the stacks and in the classrooms, will make the New South a place where only the best possible society will flourish.

Du Bois certainly had a similar hope in the power of culture to transform human relations. He signals the importance of this variety in the dual epigraphs to each chapter of *The Souls of Black Folk:* each is composed of a selection of lines of poetry from sources ranging from the Song of Solomon to Schiller to Byron to Mrs. Browning and a selection of melodies from the Sorrow Songs he recognized as the spiritual and artistic expressions of the African experience in America.[62] Never did he believe anyone deserved less than to participate fully in the culture of the world:

> I sit with Shakespeare and he winces not. Across the color line I move arm in arm with Balzac and Dumas, where smiling men and welcoming women glide in gilded halls.

From out the caves of evening that swing between the
strong-limbed earth and the tracery of the stars, I summon
Aristotle and Aurelius and what soul I will, and they come
all graciously with no scorn nor condescension. So, wed with
Truth, I dwell above the Veil. Is this the life you grudge us,
O knightly America? Is this the life you long to change into
the dull red hideousness of Georgia? Are you so afraid lest
peering from this high Pisgah, between Philistine and Ama-
lekite, we sight the Promised Land? (438)

James's belief in the need for cultural variety of a kind that was
impossible in the Old South and nearly so in the New is perhaps
best expressed by him in a letter to G. B. Shaw in which James
defends works of art for the very moral purposes Shaw thinks they
impede:

They are capable of saying more things to man about himself than any other "works" whatever are capable of doing –
and it's only by thus saying as much to him as possible, by
saying, as nearly as we can, all there is, and in as many ways
and on as many sides, and with a vividness of presentation
that "art," and art alone, is an adequate mistress of, that we
enable him to pick and choose and compare and know,
enable him to arrive at any sort of synthesis that isn't,
through all its superficialities and vacancies, a base and
illusive humbug.[63]

The duty that James has seen elsewhere is thus fulfilled by his
offering another work of art to the South, one that can be (and
obviously has been) interpreted in a variety of ways.

By his well-timed visit to the library, James represents an image
of the kind of relationship to the past that he thinks will be
helpful to his readers because they can borrow images from it.
And he puts the readers into a potentially creative relationship
with the South's ongoing conflicts when they read and interpret
his text. Reading the text is therapy in the sense that introducing
the possibility of multiple meanings coexisting defies the monovalent racism in which James has found himself to figure, to his
great discomfort. This complex narrative strategy is one James
had used to great effect, for example, in his 1896 tale "The Figure
in the Carpet," in which the reader becomes engaged in the same
quest for the ultimate pattern of an artist's work that the unhappy
hero of the story undertakes.

His chapter ends with a final lament for the effects on the

South "of having worshipped false gods," but not before he has praised the statue of Lee that ornaments a desolate intersection in Richmond. Wrought in "far-away uninterested Paris," it seems to him "as some precious pearl of ocean washed up on a rude bare strand" (393). A single great statue cannot, of course, suffice as the culture of the New South, but one of the reasons that this statue is effective is that it represents a different relationship of the New South to its past than James saw in the living signs, black and white. It is not a gross misrepresentation of the past that reenacts oppressive personal relations. Even the fact that the "high florid pedestal is of the latest French elegance" bespeaks a willingness to rely on "the beautiful openness to the world-relation" that James finds "disprovincializing." Also, it represents Lee, not Ivanhoe, as a hero to be remembered. The "medieval" nightmare may not be completely ended so long as imperial grand wizards were on the loose, but there are signs of an acceptance of history. The figure of Lee, unlike all the other equestrian representations of heroes on Richmond's Monument Boulevard, is facing South.

Furthermore, James's creative and critical response to this aesthetic artifact is an instance of the capacity of a work of art to generate further interpretations and thus create a variety of relations. Enough interpretations will bring the South out of the isolation imposed by its "cool platonic passion" by arousing its desire to engage in warmer and more significant relations.[64] James feels that his appreciation of the statue has the effect of bringing both of them into "sympathy – so that the vast association of the futile for a moment drops away from it" (394).[65]

James does not, however, end this chapter with the apotheosis of Robert E. Lee; he keeps all of the references that make that sign significant alive until the very end of the chapter so that the readers are left with the sense that there is much to be done, yet that things can be done. James does not let them off the hook, nor does he leave them without hope. In spite of his own discouragement at making anything interesting of "the senseless appearances about [him]," when he looked around one last time at the general aesthetic poverty of Richmond, he found *something* that he could praise for its "refinement of style," even if the desolate setting for the statue of Lee reiterates the lesson one last time of the devastating effects of isolation.

Finally, he offers his own work of art – his representations of acts of recovering the past and images for recovering from the past – in a *tone* that he believes his readers could bear to hear. He does not want to alienate them, to isolate them further, by chastising the present for all the sins of the past. He will not write off the New South, no matter how often the "questionable claims of the past" are muttered by a Confederate veteran lurking in the library like a bad conscience. The chapter on Richmond is his contribution to the literature of the South, his effort to make its "pale page" legible, not marginal.

THE RETURN OF THE ALIEN

ETHNIC IDENTITY AND JACOB A. RIIS

When Henry James returned to New York, the city of his birth, he found to his surprise that he did not return as a native but as an alien. He had expected to feel that he was coming home, and when he got home, he found that there was unexpected company. The ever increasing presence in his native city of a large population of immigrants presented James with yet another set of variables touching on the issue of the typical American sense of the past. Here was the reverse of the "international" situation: instead of a few rich Americans going to the Old World, the (generally) impoverished masses were coming to the New. He might have expected that the influx of a number of different people who had been living in "traditional" societies would prove an antidote to the American rage for the present. At the very least one might reason that if the denizens of Fifth Avenue were so fond of exotic signs of the past such as Renaissance chateaux and Gothic townhouses, they should welcome the equally exotic living signs of the past represented, for example, by their Bohemian or Neopolitan neighbors. But this was not the case. Furthermore, the leisure and business classes were no more content to let these signs of the past as embodied by the living remain intact than they were to leave their own mansions standing for more than a decade. James was very disturbed by this process of the destruction and loss of other cultural traditions in America, especially as he had such profound reservations, we have seen, about the direction that Anglo-American culture was taking.

During his visit and afterward while he was composing *The American Scene,* James began a process of redefining his conception of national identity in a way that bears careful consideration for what it suggests about how ethnic and racial identities are formed and transformed over time and under changing circumstances. He develops a description of how cultural transformation normally takes place and offers an analysis of how the business culture of America deforms that process. James's own sense of cultural dispossession becomes for him, not a cause for nostalgic bitterness or xenophobia as some have claimed, but a critical resource by means of which he creates a bond of solidarity with all those who have been dispossessed of their heritage, including the people whom we now call Native Americans. As he begins to trace the ways in which signs of various national pasts as represented by living people are distorted, if not obliterated, in America, he finds himself deeply implicated in the issues of national and native identity as an American and as a writer in the English language. Perhaps the title of Hardy's novel that he wanted to use for *The American Scene* would not have been the right one for his book after all.

James was shocked on a number of occasions he recalls in *The American Scene* by the consequences for human relations of business interests at work, particularly as they affected the most vulnerable immigrants. Recounting a visit to the Lower East Side, he writes that a "new style of poverty" has come into being in the New World. There is a higher standard of living than in the European old style of poverty, but the new poor pay in a different coin for the privilege of being exploited:

> You are as constantly reminded, no doubt, that these rises in enjoyed value shrink and dwindle under the icy breath of Trusts and the weight of the new remorseless monopolies that operate as no madnesses of ancient personal power thrilling us on the historic page ever operated; the living unit's property in himself becoming more and more merely such a property as may consist with a relation to the properties overwhelmingly greater and that allow the asking of no questions and the making, for co-existence with them, of no conditions. But that, in the fortunate phrase, is another story, and will be altogether, evidently, a new and different drama. There is such a thing, in the United States, it is hence to be inferred, as freedom to grow up to be blighted, and it may be the only freedom in store for the smaller fry of future generations.[1]

"The freedom to grow up to be blighted" is not one that would have been advertised at home or abroad. The degradation of the individual's value to "the living unit's property in himself" denotes the salient character trait of the "new style of poverty."

In a series of extended metaphors in which he rings his own changes on the cliché of the "melting pot," James explores his sense that the "conversion of the alien" that was taking place "under its own mystic laws" (123) was not usually in the best interest of the immigrants. Something about the way in which the aliens are changed by their new context strikes him as peculiar, even after taking into account the miracle of the scale (more than a million a year at this time) of what he calls the "visible act of ingurgitation on the part of our body politic and social, . . . constituting really an appeal to amazement beyond that of any sword-swallowing or fire-swallowing of the circus" (84). The alien seems to have lost his or her old national identity and character almost immediately upon landing:

> There are categories of foreigners, truly, meanwhile, of whom we are moved to say that only a mechanism working with scientific force could have performed this feat of making them colourless. The Italians, who, over the whole land, strike us, I am afraid, as, after the Negro and the Chinaman, the human value most easily produced, the Italians meet us, at every turn, only to make us ask what has become of that element of the agreeable address in *them* which has, from far back, so enhanced for the stranger the interest and pleasure of a visit to their beautiful country. They shed it utterly. . . . (128)

The loss of their typical manners has not come about naturally or culturally as James sees it but scientifically and mechanically. They have been ground not in "the very mill of the conventional,"[2] which converted Isabel Archer from an American innocent into a cosmopolitan heroine, but in the press of the dollar.

James does not pursue this line of argument in order to condemn business culture explicitly, but he turns his attention to the question of how this conversion compares with the ways in which he has always understood cultural transformations to work. Again and again he finds that there is a kind of disruption of the process of cultural development as he has known it to work in European cultures. Perhaps this symptom is the something "new . . . under the sun" that he speculates America will spawn (138).

The scientific force of this conversion is disconcerting because it seems uncanny rather than organic or mechanical. Trying to explain the odd effect of the "colourless" Italians, he introduces an extended metaphor in which a piece of fabric is neither color-fast in hot water nor able to tint "with its pink or its azure his fellow-soakers in the terrible tank." Where does the dye go? Or, more to the point for the novelist of manners:

> What *does* become of the various positive properties, on the part of certain of the installed tribes, the good manners, say, among them, as to which the process of shedding and the fact of eclipse come so promptly into play? It has taken long ages of history, in the other world, to produce them, and you ask yourself, with independent curiosity, if they may really be thus extinguished in an hour. And if they are not extinguished, into what pathless tracts of the native atmosphere do they virtually, do they provisionally, and so all undiscoverably, melt? Do they burrow underground, to await their day again? – or in what strange secret places are they held in deposit and in trust? The "American" identity that has profited by their sacrifice has meanwhile acquired (in the happiest cases) all apparent confidence and consistency; but may not the doubt remain of whether the extinction of qualities ingrained in generations is to be taken for quite complete? Isn't it conceivable that, for something like a final efflorescence, the business of slow comminglings and makings-over at last ended, they may rise again to the surface, affirming their vitality and value and playing their part? It would be for them, of course, in this event, to attest that they had been worth waiting so long for; but the speculation, at any rate, irresistibly forced upon us, is a sign of the interest, in the American world, of what I have called the "ethnic" outlook. The cauldron, for the great stew, has such circumference and such depth that we can only deal here with ultimate syntheses, ultimate combinations and possibilities. (129–30)

If in America these national characteristics are put still living in the grave, how have they otherwise come into being and survived in their native environments?

These questions take on a kind of urgency for James as he realizes that he himself is deeply implicated in the problem of losing the sense of national identity. He asks the question that is absolutely crucial for understanding American identity:

> Who and what is an alien, when it comes to that, in a country peopled from the first under the jealous eye of history? – peopled, that is, by migrations at once extremely recent, perfectly traceable and urgently required. They are still, it would appear, urgently required – if we look about

far enough for the urgency; though of that truth such a scene as New York may well make one doubt. Which is the American, by these scant measures? – which is *not* the alien, over a large part of the country at least, and where does one put a finger on the dividing line, or, for that matter, "spot" and identify any particular phase of the conversion, any one of its successive moments? (124)

James has come home to find himself dispossessed of the sense of himself as an American he had always assumed was inalienable. He makes his own marginal situation the occasion to ponder the whole question of national and ethnic identity.[3] Asking these questions is unexpectedly disconcerting.

To come face to face with the aliens on the scale that James saw them on his visit to Ellis Island is a revelation to the native. The effects of this vision are irrevocable:

I think indeed that the simplest account of the action of Ellis Island on the spirit of any sensitive citizen who may have happened to "look in" is that he comes back from his visit not at all the same person that he went. He has eaten of the tree of knowledge, and the taste will be for ever in his mouth. He had thought he knew before, thought he had the sense of the degree in which it is his American fate to share the sanctity of his American consciousness, the intimacy of his American patriotism, with the inconceivable aliens; but the truth had never come home to him with any such force. In the lurid light projected upon it by those courts of dismay it shakes him – or I like at least to imagine it shakes him – to the depths of his being; I like to think of him, I positively *have* to think of him, as going about ever afterwards with a new look, for those who can see it, in his face, the outward sign of the new chill in his heart. So is stamped, for detection, the questionably privileged person who has had an apparition, seen a ghost in his supposedly safe old house. Let not the unwary, therefore, visit Ellis Island. (85)

James experiences the presence of the alien as an invasion of his home (an image that he makes fictive use of in "The Jolly Corner," as we shall see) and an intrusion into the intimacy of what he calls his "supreme relation":

other impressions might come and go, but this affirmed claim of the alien, however immeasurably alien, to share in one's supreme relation was everywhere the fixed element, the reminder not to be dodged. One's supreme relation, as one had always put it, was one's relation to one's country – a conception made up so largely of one's countrymen and one's countrywomen. (85)

Yet even at his most astonished and unnerved, his inquiry begins to turn in another direction and to question his own presumed rights and the wisdom "of keeping the idea simple and strong and continuous, so that it shall be perfectly sound":

> To touch it overmuch, to pull it about, is to put it in peril of weakening; yet on this free assault upon it, this readjustment of it in *their* monstrous, presumptuous interest, the aliens, in New York, seemed perpetually to insist. The combination there of the quantity and their quality – that loud primary stage of alienism which New York most offers to sight – operates, for the native, as their note of settled possession, something they have nobody to thank for; so that *un*settled possession is what we, on our side, seem reduced to – the implication of which, in its turn, is that, to recover confidence and regain lost ground, we, not they, must make the surrender and accept the orientation. We must go, in other words, *more* than half-way to meet them; which is all the difference, for us between possession and dispossession. This sense of dispossession, to be brief about it, haunted me so, I was to feel, in the New York streets and in the packed trajectiles to which one clingingly appeals from the streets, just as one tumbles back into the streets in appalled reaction from *them,* that the art of beguiling or duping it became an art to be cultivated – though the fond alternative vision was never long to be obscured, the imagination, exasperated to envy, of the ideal, in the order in question; of the luxury of some such close and sweet and *whole* national consciousness as that of the Switzer and the Scot. (86)

What seems suddenly incongruous here is his example of "the Switzer and the Scot" as the ideal of "close and sweet and *whole* national consciousness." When he advocates "keeping the idea simple and strong and continuous," he cannot possibly mean that he wants Anglo-Saxon homogeneity if Switzerland – with its German, French, Italian, and Switzer constituencies – is his ideal of wholeness. If harmonious heterogeneity is, however, the ideal, then the native must consent to feeling dispossessed and haunted for a time while new features are introduced to the whole.

Here James has reinterpreted what national identity means: it is not a simple state in which one is born or to which one migrates; it is a complex relation one constructs between one's place of origin and the contexts of one's daily life, be they religious, political, or professional.[4] The question is then, how could such a hyphenated, complex cultural identity be made sense of in America? What kind of relations between natives and aliens must be created by a reinterpretation of their respective positions with regard to their various pasts in order for there to be an American future that includes them all and that does not efface their differences in the "terrible tank" that is now making them "colourless"?

Asking himself again whether it is possible that all of this foreignness so visible at Ellis Island can really be transformed by the "intendedly scientific 'feeding' of the mill" (84), he theorizes now in the context of his own destabilized sense of possession and identity that there must be something that does remain unassimilated, although what it is and how it retains its identity remains unanalyzable:

> You recognize in them, freely, those elements that are not elements of swift convertibility, and you lose yourself in the wonder of what becomes, as it were, of the obstinate, the unconverted residuum. The country at large, as you cross it in different senses, keeps up its character for you as the hugest thinkable organism for successful "assimilation"; but the assimilative force itself has the residuum still to count with. The operation of the immense machine, identical after all with the total of American life, trembles away into mysteries that are beyond our present notation and that reduce us in many a mood to renouncing analysis. (124)

Perhaps momentarily, but not for long, given that James himself has a considerable stake in the outcome of this dilemma of the invisible if "unconverted residuum." He will not renounce analysis for more than a passing moment but continues to work through the problem of his national identity by interpreting it in relation to the other national identities that are being constructed before his very eyes, especially on New York's Lower East Side. The past that he makes sense of here will be very close to home.

Worth a Thousand Words

A well-known figure, an expert on the conditions of life on the Lower East Side at the turn of the century wrote of the Chinese that "[h]e is by nature as clean as the cat, which he resembles in his traits of cruel cunning and savage fury when aroused."[5] Although the Chinese might be the least troublesome, according to the police of the "notoriously turbulent Sixth Ward," this is not a redeeming characteristic:

> The one thing they desire above all is to be let alone, a very natural wish perhaps, considering all the circumstances. If it were a laudable, or even an allowable ambition that prompts it, they might be humored with advantage, probably, to both sides. But the facts show too plainly that it is not, and that in their very exclusiveness and reserve they are a constant and terrible menace to society, wholly regardless of their influence upon the industrial problems which their presence confuses. The severest official scrutiny, the harshest repressive measures are justifiable in Chinatown, orderly as it appears on the surface . . . the poison that proceeds from Mott Street [opium and the prostitution of white girls] puts mind and body to sleep, to work out its deadly purpose in the corruption of the soul.
>
> This again may be set down as a harsh judgment. I may be accused of inciting persecution of an unoffending people. Far from it. Granted, that the Chinese are in no sense a desirable element of the population, that they serve no useful purpose here, whatever they may have done elsewhere in other days. . . .[6]

This same student of human nature writes of the Jew's "constitutional greed" and "natural talent . . . for commercial speculation":[7]

> Thrift is the watchword of Jewtown, as of its people the world over. It is at once its strength and its fatal weakness, its cardinal virtue and its foul disgrace. Become an overmastering passion with these people who come here in droves from Eastern Europe to escape persecution, from which freedom could be bought only with gold, it has enslaved them in bondage worse than that from which they fled. Money is their God. Life itself is of little value compared with even the leanest bank account. In no other spot does life wear so intensely bald and materialistic an aspect as in Ludlow Street.[8]

Yet the Negro is criticized for the opposite fault:

> He loves fine clothes and good living a good deal more than he does a bank account. . . . His home surroundings, except

when he is utterly depraved, reflect his blithesome temper.
. . . In the art of putting the best foot foremost, of disguising
his poverty by making a little go a long way, our negro has
no equal. . . . The amount of "style" displayed on fine Sun-
days on Sixth and Seventh Avenues by colored holiday-
makers would turn a pessimist black with wrath.[9]

Even in their most extreme formulations, these ethnic and racial
characterizations are occasionally disrupted by some appreciation
that the differences between cultures might have some value for
the culture as a whole. Irritating pessimists on a Sunday afternoon
seems like a culturally valuable activity, for example.

It is not, however, always easy to predict the relation of opinions to actions. The present writer, Jacob A. Riis, worked as a
"muckraking" journalist, lecturer, and photographer to improve
the living conditions of *all* immigrants on the Lower East Side
and elsewhere throughout his life. Reading Riis's texts – verbal
and visual – in dialogue with James's analysis of the cultural
situation of the Lower East Side helps us to see how these contemporaries understand the sense of the past as it is represented by
the different ethnic characteristics of the immigrants and how
each thinks about the process of creating a harmonious national
culture in America. In particular, reading these texts against each
other will show how James's conception of the role that ethnic
identity plays in the formation of a national identity depends
upon the perservation of ethnic differences, while Riis, like the
moguls and barons of industry and landlords against whom he
directed his attacks, wanted an ethnically homogeneous society,
albeit one that was more economically egalitatian than the moguls had in mind.

Riis's activism was directed toward very specific goals and was
sustained by the belief that improving the living conditions of
people then in tenements would eliminate the evils of crime,
alcoholism, infanticide, child abuse, and the like. When he first
began his work to bring these horrible living conditions to the
attention of people who had the power to change them, his
analysis of the causes of social depravity was somewhat confused,
however. His chapters in *How the Other Half Lives* (1890) on the
Chinaman and Jewtown are suspect not so much when he tries to
describe Chinese and Jewish differences in cultural habits as
when he condemns racial differences as the causes of moral
failure. The Italians are always liars; the Chinamen, perverts; the
Jews, greedy – and thus they will be until the end of time. Such

characterizations can be understood as confused not because they apply a model of biological determinism to cultural phenomena (in ways that are entirely consistent with turn-of-the-century scientific racism) but because these slurs were detrimental to his polemical purposes. By linking "racial" characteristics to particular human vices, Riis was distracting blame from those who were his real villains, the slumlords and corrupt politicians. He seems to have realized in some way that he was blaming the victim, and this ethnophobic aspect of his descriptions of slum life all but disappears in the 1902 *Battle with the Slum,* in which he focuses his outrage on the greed of the slumlords and corruption of the political machines, especially Tammany Hall.

Although one might be skeptical about the therapeutic powers of the small neighborhood park, one of Riis's long-term projects, Riis's photographs of slum life leave no doubt as to the ravages of the disease – moral and physical – that crowded, unsanitary, ugly living conditions bred. It was his photographs that made his case to his contemporaries with unmistakable force. It is for them that he is chiefly known today. In his preface to the 1974 volume of prints made by Alexander Alland Sr. from Riis's long-forgotten glass negatives, Ansel Adams writes: "For me these are magnificent achievements in the field of humanistic photography. . . . I know of no contemporary work of this general character which gives such an impression of competence, integrity and intensity." Adams writes of the "intense *living* quality of Riis's work" and his sense of identification with the subjects: "I am walking in their alleys, standing in their rooms and shed and workshops, looking in and out of their windows. And they in turn seem to be aware of me. . . . Do I hear the word 'empathy'?"[10] Although he was aware of Riis's writing and thought that everything should be judged together as a "consuming life work," Adams clearly could read the photographs without the text that would show Riis to be less empathetic with his subjects than Adams would like to believe.

In the lengthy biographical and critical essay that accompanies this printing of the photographs which made up the 1948 show of Riis's photographs, Alland devotes only one paragraph to this problem. His reticence and vehemence attest to his uneasiness with this aspect of Riis's work. He writes:

> Riis justifiably could be chided for his occasional exaggerated characterization of some groups in the polyglot population of New York. Some of his remarks have disturbed those

of us who have lent their voices in protest against the use of racial and ethnic stereotypes by public figures.

After telling about his own conversion to a "faith in racial brotherhood," as if to prove beyond the shadow of a doubt that his admiration for Riis does not implicate him in Riis's racism, Alland asserts: "In Jacob Riis's case, I am sure he wrote without malice. He had to develop a folksy style using the jargon of the lower depths where he worked."[11] Alland's apparently unconscious use of a phrase like "the lower depths" to characterize the slums when he has just finished speaking of "racial brotherhood" shows how difficult it is for one age to be consistently humanitarian or egalitarian or politically correct in the eyes of a later age.

The point is, however, that Alland is inclined to present Riis in the best possible light, and this interpretation of the materials contrasts vividly with the way in which James's critics have analyzed his remarks about immigrants and accused him of racism, elitism, and, at the very least, having "snobbish biases."[12] The images, dissociated from a context and from the text which they originally illustrated, lend themselves to the liberal humanitarianism favored by the "whig interpretation of history."[13] For a reader of images who is inclined to historicize and contextualize, of course, there would be ways to show how the conventions of imagery that are present in Riis's photographs represent his particular moral views of these subjects in ways that differ from other artists's visual representations of the poor immigrants.

Riis's own beliefs about the ideal human condition are more evident (to the reader of verbal texts) in the specific humanitarian goals to ameliorate the lives of the immigrants that he proposed. Improving the living conditions of the slums, even eliminating the slums altogether, is certainly a worthy goal, but Riis's ideal of what would replace them might give us pause. Sustaining his progressivist beliefs (he dedicated his 1902 volume to Theodore Roosevelt, a longtime friend and co-worker) is a kind of romantic belief in the therapeutic value of nature. He never fails to mention the joy that a bouquet of fresh flowers brings to the slum dweller old or young, and he speaks proudly of the tenement youngsters sent into the clean, healthy West who (for the most part) go on to become model citizens. Even the few boys who return, "lured by homesickness even for the slums," find that "the briefest stay generally cures the disease for good."[14] In a chapter called "The Genesis of the Gang" in *The Battle with the Slum,* he writes that "a boy who cannot kick a ball around has no

chance of growing up a decent citizen."[15] Not only must boys
have playgrounds on which to let off steam, grown men must
have their own homes on their own land:

> The simple fact is that the home-feeling that makes a man
> rear a home upon the soil as the chief ambition of his life
> was not there. . . . Man is not made to be born and to live all
> his life in a box, packed away with his fellows like so many
> herring in a barrel. He is here in this world for something
> that is not attained in that way; but is, if not attained, at least
> perceived when the daisies and the robins come in. . . . I say
> I believe it. I wish I could say I knew; but then you would ask
> for my proofs, and I haven't any. For all that, I still believe
> it.[16]

A few pages later, Riis again states his belief:

> I have dwelt upon the need of bracing up the home, or
> finding something to replace it as nearly like it as could be,
> where that had to be done, because the home is the key to
> good citizenship.[17]

Private property, home ownership in the suburbs, if not the country, and family values make what Riis believes to be a good citizen.
Although his analysis of the causes of urban misery shifts from
blaming ethnic and racial characteristics in *How the Other Half
Lives* to attacking Tammany Hall in *The Battle of the Slum,* his ideal
remains the same. There is one right kind of environment that
will produce the one right kind of American citizen. This conception of a homogeneous national identity thus serves the muckrak-
ers as well as the moguls, even if Riis's desire for conformity
seems more humanitarian and aesthetic than profit-oriented and
rational.

Riis's nostalgia for the virtues supposedly produced in a rural
culture is, interestingly, a significant "unconverted residuum," as
James calls it, of his own cultural heritage. There are two closely
related aspects to this particular "residuum." Riis's images of the
bucolic conditions that produce the ideal citizen hark back to his
own boyhood in rural Denmark. They easily harmonize, however,
with the American romantic idealization of nature because the
therapeutic value of nature is informed, in turn, by the virtues
(imagined or otherwise) of that traditional, rural way of life. A
close connection with nature is believed to be good for the soul
and for the citizen.

Riis's values do not appear to be foreign to the American

context, however, for yet another kind of reason. He envisions a harmonious society being created in and by the proper setting in America that is as ethnically homogeneous as was his rural Denmark. He can hold onto this desire for homogeneity not just because the ethnic characteristics of Danes would appear to blend in with those of the Anglo-Saxons more readily than do those of the Africans or Chinese but because the idea of homogeneity itself blends in. This yearning for a harmony of the whole is, of course, another aspect of the romanticism expressed in Riis's idealization of nature. Here is an instance of a sign of the past – Riis's romanticism – that is preserved in its new context; but the fact that it is preserved and not translated by coming into creative friction with some different belief makes its traditionalism more legible to us today.[18]

Perhaps it is also this romanticism infiltrating Riis's work that drove his contemporary Abraham Cahan, a man no less interested than Riis in representing the life of the immigrants, to dismiss Riis as "an amateur slumologist."[19] The Russian-born author of *The Rise of David Levinsky* and founder and longtime editor of *Forverts* (Jewish Daily Forward) may have felt that Riis had not, in fact, achieved that "empathy" with the immigrants from different ethnic backgrounds that Ansel Adams found so obvious and inspiring at a later date, that Riis's ideal of American citizenship would not have been able to accommodate in its bucolic realization the "unconverted residuum," for example, of Judaism. Abolishing the slums and moving everyone to the country would not turn the urban Jews into rural Christian Danes.[20] The poignant ending of Cahan's novel, in which David Levinsky feels himself divided between the orthodox world of his youth in anti-Semitic Russia and his lonely life as a New York millionaire, gives a haunting image of how this problem of articulating the living signs of the past into the present is not solved on economic terms alone. Melancholy as is the end of this novel, it keeps ethnic differences in play, and so there is still the possibility that different relations of these same values would lead to greater happiness for a Jew such as Levinsky – so long as those differences are not lost or erased or effaced or bleached out in the "terrible tank" of an oppressively homogeneous American culture.

The New Jerusalem

When James went on his tour of the Lower East Side, he was not looking for abuses of the housing codes, as Riis was, but for some evidence of the conditions in which he thought culture could grow. What was crucial was not the intact preservation of Old World culture – such as had blighted the economic prospects of the Bohemians who were so isolated from English-speaking Americans that they were virtually enslaved by their employers[21] – but a sense of the past that could be translated into the present. He found that the people best able to do so were the ones who had previous experience holding onto their identity while living on the margins of the mainstream, namely, the Jews.

It is not a little ironic that his assessment of the situation of the Jews in the New World has been read as proof of his anti-Semitism. As mentioned in the introduction to this book, Maxwell Geismar goes further than others when he writes that no one surpassed James in his desire to eliminate the Jews "unless it was the Germanic Hitler who used a more barbarous mythology, combined with all the skills of scientific industrial technology, to quell the same alien presence."[22] Peter Buitenhuis chides Geismar for his distortion of James's views, but he too finds that "[t]here is an aristocratic disdain in James's race-consciousness that makes these pages of *The American Scene* unpleasant reading."[23] Leon Edel seems to want to protect James from being held responsible for his remarks by claiming that James is repeating the clichés about Jews he learned from the English novel, especially Dickens.[24] Jonathan Freedman refers to "James's offhanded but nevertheless palpable anti-Semitism."[25] Yet read in the context of his wide-ranging speculations about the issue of ethnic and national identity, these comments on the Jews lend themselves to other interpretations.

What distinguishes the Jews from the other immigrant ethnic groups is that their traditional characteristics have not been effaced or repressed, although they have been transformed, in their new environment. Recalling his visit to the Lower East Side, which is surpassed only by "some shy corner of Asia" (131) for density of population, James speculates that his impression that "the scene hummed with the human presence beyond anything [he] had ever faced in quest even of refreshment" was, "moreover, no doubt . . . a direct consequence of the intensity of the Jewish aspect." What he means by this "intensity" is not analyzed but is illustrated by a series of metaphors:

> This [intensity of aspect], I think, makes the individual Jew
> more of a concentrated person, savingly possessed of every-

thing that is in him, than any other human, noted at random – or is it simply, rather, that the unsurpassed strength of the race permits of the chopping into myriads of fine fragments without loss of race quality? There are small strange animals, known to natural history, snakes or worms, I believe, who when cut into pieces, wriggle away contentedly and live in the snippet as completely as in the whole. So the denizens of the New York Ghetto, heaped as thick as the splinters on the table of a glass-blower, had each, like the fine glass particle, his or her individual share of the whole hard glitter of Israel. (132)

Not yet having explained the matter to his own satisfaction, he tries again:

This diffused intensity, as I have called it, causes any array of Jews to resemble (if I may be allowed another image) some long nocturnal street where every window in every house showed a maintained light. (132)

Of these three metaphors, only the first has received any critical attention, usually in conjunction with James's other zoologically inspired comparisons of his experience of being in the crowds of the Lower East Side to being

at the bottom of some vast sallow aquarium in which innumerable fish, of overdeveloped proboscis, were to bump together, for ever, amid heaped spoils of the sea. (131)

And his description of the fire escapes on the fronts of the typical tenement, which appear to transform it into

the spaciously organized cage for the nimbler class of animals in some great zoological garden. This general analogy is irresistible – it seems to offer, in each district, a little world of bars and perches for human squirrels and monkeys. The very name of architecture perishes, for the fire-escapes look like abashed afterthoughts, staircases and communications forgotten in the construction; but the inhabitants lead, like the squirrels and monkeys, all the merrier life. (134)

The cumulative effect of these zoological comparisons is to create an image of a place in which the inhabitants are not living as humans. They are crowded into structures that degrade them to the status of captive animals. The question here is whether it is

James's comparisons that degrade the inhabitants or whether it is degrading conditions against which he may be protesting – in his usual indirect way.

One of the reasons he might be indirect here, and thus especially liable to misinterpretation, is that the particular circumstances of his visit to the Lower East Side may have made him hesitate to speak more explicitly or negatively about the squalor of the tenements. His guide was the Yiddish playwright Jacob Gordin who, according to Leon Edel, took him to dinner with a Jewish family in a converted tenement and to the Yiddish theater.[26] James does not reveal the identity of his hosts in this episode of *The American Scene* anymore than he does when alluding to his visits with Edith Wharton, Owen Wister, or Henry Adams, visits that we know about from other sources, such as his correspondence. The distinction between public and private life was one he felt was little enough observed in America, and so he would probably be inclined to be particularly scrupulous about name-dropping when his hosts were famous and about invading the privacy of his less well known hosts by publicizing any details of their private lives. In other words, he would take pains not to become like his own 1882 creation, Henrietta Stackpole, who would like to write up her visit to Lord Warburton's castle for the American newspapers.

Protecting his hosts' privacy might, moreover, go beyond merely suppressing their names. Part of his obligation as a guest would be to avoid offending his hosts even after the fact by presenting them or their circumstances negatively. This may make James a poor journalist from one point of view, but the journalist's disregard for the distinction between public and private life was ever one of James's bêtes noires: witness Matthias Pardon in *The Bostonians* and the narrator of *The Aspern Papers,* the confrères of Miss Stackpole. Thus, the very similes, analogies, and the like. that strike the latter-day reader as offensive might have been intended to present the situation in its best rather than its worst light. James's image of the fire escapes as cages in which to make merry seems, on the one hand, indifferent to the suffering of the inhabitants, who would doubtless have preferred more indoor living space. But, on the other hand, his image may well have been inspired by the tone of the inhabitants's own effort to put the best face on a difficult situation. Also, there were worse places to live in New York at the turn of the century than in a zoo.

That the Lower East Side was densely populated and generally unsanitary at the turn of the century is not a matter for dispute.

Riis describes it as "swarming with unwholesome crowds" and says that "[c]orruption could not have chosen ground for its stand with better promise of success."[27] Riis includes an appendix with demographic statistics to his 1890 text and the contrast between the density of population to the square mile in Manhattan as a whole (73,299) and the density of population to the square mile in the Tenth Ward (334,080) and the Eleventh Ward (246,040) and the Thirteenth Ward (274,432) is striking enough. Two other statistics highlight the extremity of the situation. Although London's 1880 population was 3,816,483 and New York's was 1,206,299, the number of persons in a London dwelling was 7.9, and in New York there were 16.37 persons per dwelling. The death rate in London in 1881 was 21.3; in New York in 1880 it was 26.47. Although Riis did not have available at the time *How the Other Half Lives* went to press the 1889 figures for the number of persons in dwellings in London and New York, the difference in the death rates is indicative of a consistently dire situation in New York (1889 population estimated: 1,575,073), where it was 25.19, and a remarkable improvement in London (1889 population estimated: 4,351,738), where it fell to 17.4.[28] Riis's photographs of the infamous Mulberry Bend lined with carts and pedestrians, or of the illegal lodging house in which men would pay five cents for a spot on the floor already covered with sleeping bodies, or, finally, the stacks of coffins in the common grave in Potter's Field illustrate these conditions more vividly than the statistics can. Speaking of the Jewish tenements in particular, Riis says that the common practice of taking in lodgers made it "idle to speak of privacy in these 'homes.' "[29]

The fire escapes were ugly but were something to be grateful for, not only as important safety devices but as frequently used extensions of the families' inevitably crowded living space. Living thus in the open air in complete publicity may well have shocked James enough to have impelled him to try to depict this appalling situation in positive and playful terms rather than express his dismay. James's actual hosts were apparently relatively prosperous Jews – he mentions an internal fireproof staircase lined with white marble and describes the conditions as "so little sordid, so highly 'evolved' " – but he is nevertheless talking about a tenement with twenty-five families in it (135). One would not, however, need a personal invitation to see how most of the residents of the Lower East Side lived. The private life was all too public. To retail the squalor of the Lower East Side when it was so clearly the result of circumstances beyond the control of the inhabitants might have struck James as being in the worst possible taste and bad manners besides. These things were more important to him for his literary and moral purposes than reporting exactly what was there. Not everyone had to be a muckraker. James's effort to minimize grounds for prejudice against the Jews – to present them as thriving and "so little sordid" – can be read in a more complex context, not only of his style but of the social reality to which he was witness.

The issue of privacy versus publicity is one that concerns James on numerous occasions in *The American Scene,* but more to the point here is his struggle to find an adequate image of his sense of the difference of the Jews, the things that distinguish them from others, particularly from other immigrants, who habitually lost their distinguishing characteristics.

It took James three analogies to convey his sense of the way in which the Jews have maintained their identity before he is ready to move on to speculate as to the cause of this difference. What his zoological (snake or worm in bits) and his artistic (each "fine glass particle . . . [with its] individual share of the whole hard glitter of Israel") and his domestic (a light in every window of every house) metaphors have in common is the relationship of the part to the whole. In each metaphor the individual part is clearly defined as different from and yet part of a more complex whole: these are metaphors about synecdoche and metonymy. That separateness is not lost in an undifferentiated whole; neither is it isolated from the other parts with which it forms the whole. James has criticized American culture – manifested in forms as various as architecture and the Jim Crow laws – for being either eccentric or monotonous, what he called "individual loneliness" when speaking of the Fifth Avenue mansions and called "the great fatuity" of a modern slave-state when speaking of the South. The Jews had escaped falling prey to either of these typical American dangers, and they have done so by holding onto a sense of their past, by making continuity crucial to their ethnic identity:

> The advanced age of so many of the figures, the ubiquity of the children, carried out in fact this analogy [of the window lights]; they were all there for race, and not, as it were, for reason: that excess of lurid meaning, in some of the old men's and old women's faces in particular, would have been absurd, in the conditions, as a really directed attention – it could only be the gathered past of Israel mechanically push-ing through. The way, at the same time, this chapter of

history did, all that evening, seem to push, was a matter that made the "ethnic" apparition again sit like a skeleton at the feast. It was fairly as if I could see the spectre grin while the talk of the hour gave me, across the board, facts and figures, chapter and verse, for the extent of the Hebrew conquest of New York. With a reverence for intellect, one should doubtless have drunk in tribute to an intellectual people. . . . (132–3)

The "excess of lurid meaning" is what makes the Jews classic in Frank Kermode's sense of that word: there is a surplus of the signifier.[30] The Jews have been translated into many languages over the millennia without losing their own. They signify more than just the present or their individuality. Each also, but especially the old people, represents the "gathered past," that continuity of signs that makes them legible as Jews.

Nevertheless, this "fatal sense of history" has its discomforting aspect: no one invites a "skeleton [to] the feast." James is distinctly uneasy, but his discomfort can be understood in the context of his perplexity at the fate of ethnicity in the New World. He hesitates to yield to his "high elation," for he senses that any rejoicing at this survival of a traditional characteristic of the Jews, the "reverence for intellect," might not survive into the future:

The portent is one of too many – you always come back, as I have hinted, with your easier gasp, to *that:* it will be time enough to sigh or to shout when the relation of the particular appearance to all the other relations shall have cleared itself up. Phantasmagoric for me, accordingly, in a high degree, are the interesting hours I here glance at content to remain – setting in this respect, I recognize, an excellent example to all the rest of the New York phantasmagoria. (133)

Although James may have assumed the stance of a Jeremiah at times in *The American Scene*, he will not take on the role of an Isaiah. That the Jews have maintained their distinct cultural identity encourages him to believe that it is possible to do so in America, but whether they will continue to do so is far from certain.

Exactly how the Jews have maintained their living connection to this cultural past James does not attempt to explain beyond affirming his sense that it must be collective and inherited – "for race"[31] – rather than individual and voluntary – "for reason." The

Jews of New York seem the living signs of their history: "For what did it all really come to but that one had seen with one's eyes the New Jerusalem on earth?" (133). Compared with the "dark, foul, stifling Ghettos of other remembered cities," the "city of redemption" on Rutgers Street was an achieved thing of "splendour" (133), albeit that the splendour might have "this look of the trap too brilliantly, too candidly baited for the wary side of Israel itself" (135). Though it may sparkle primarily for others, "– yet its being moved to do so, at least, in that luxurious style, might be precisely the grand side of the city of redemption" (135). It achieves its "luxurious style" by creating a relation, in other words, with that which is different from it. Israel exists both in relation to its own past and in relation to the present others. This complexity of signs among which one's identity is constituted is the real richness of the New World.

It is this harmony of heterogeneity that, indeed, characterized the New Jerusalem (and the "close and sweet and *whole* national consciousness" of "the Switzer and the Scot"), about which Henry heard from his Swedenborgian father.[32] James's repeated use in these pages of this designation is anything but accidental, and his reluctance to prophesy about the future of ethnic groups in America might be inspired in part by his sense of the irony of it being the Jews – whom Henry Senior thought to be enslaved by the letter of the law – who had achieved the kind of style he (Henry Senior) had always believed to be the mark of the most highly evolved consciousness, the consciousness that had a lively sense of the similarities and differences between itself and the other.

James does not attempt to explain in more general terms the reasons exactly how the Jews have succeeded in maintaining their ethnic identity when other groups have failed (although Judaism's tradition of making distinctions among things in its laws and customs might have appealed to James, who protested so frequently about the American habit of "effacement of the difference" [167]). It could also be that the whig interpretation of history that sustained the perpetual revolution of white Anglo-Saxon Protestant capitalism would be quite foreign to the people of Moses guided by the economics of a very different tradition and working within a very different conception of history. This surrender of analysis when facing the real thing that reverberates with enough associations is his characteristic response in *The American Scene*. The real thing always has a sense of the past.

A much earlier text by James gives a clue, however, to James's possible reluctance to speak too knowingly about the character of the Jews. In an 1876 review of *Daniel Deronda* – an amusing dialogue among three readers of the serialized novel – one of the many subjects on which they disagree is the relationship of the author to the "noble subject," as Theodora puts it, of the Jewish revival in which Deronda becomes involved even before he knows he is a Jew. Constantius, who represents the voice of moderation in this debate, says that he thinks the Jewish revival is not possible and that the Jews probably "take themselves much less seriously" than George Eliot has. She "takes them as a person outside of Judaism – aesthetically. I don't believe," he continues, "that is the way they take themselves." Pulcheria, who is consistently small-minded in this discussion, makes a nasty comment about the Jews being dirty, and Theodora responds that "George Eliot must have known some delightful Jews." The ever moderate Constantius responds:

> Very likely; but I shouldn't wonder if the most delightful of them had smiled a trifle, here and there over her book. . . . I don't quite know what [Deronda's mission] means, I don't understand more than half of Mordecai's rhapsodies, and I don't perceive exactly what practical steps could be taken. Deronda could go about and talk with clever Jews – not an unpleasant life.[33]

Interpreting a culture so different from one's own is a difficult and delicate task, and Deronda's discovery that the ancient ways and truths of Mordecai and Miriam are not those of the other but his own illustrates the drama of expanding empathetic consciousness, however right or wrong Eliot may have been in the detail.

James's hesitation to explore the causes of the difference between the Jews and other ethnic groups is nevertheless an uncharacteristic retreat from the challenge to make sense of that which seems foreign and strange. If he could reach an understanding of the Southern blacks, as I suggest he did (by a very complex strategy), then why should the Jews have presented a greater challenge, given that he had known in his continental life many more Jews than he ever had people of African descent? Had he pursued his analysis of their success, he might have seen that "the luxury of some such close and sweet and *whole* national consciousness as that of the Switzer and the Scot," which he had praised as a concept of national identity, described the situation of the Jews (87).

For millennia, the Jews had been faced with the problem of living as aliens, and, far from being an impediment at all times, this alienation had worked to their and to the gentile's positive advantage. Or so suggests Veblen in his essay "The Intellectual Pre-eminence of Jews," in which he explains in cultural and historical terms the fact that Jews had contributed a disproportionate amount to European civilization. It was the occasional, gifted Jew's dispossession from both the traditions of his people and from gentile society that encouraged in him the "skeptical frame of mind" that is "[t]he first requisite for constructive work in modern science, and indeed for any work of inquiry that shall bring enduring results."[34] Deflating the claims of racist biologism and inverting the usual, negative meaning of exile, Veblen explains his theory of this unique cultural development:

> It appears to be only when the gifted Jew escapes from the cultural environment created and fed by the particular genius of his own people, only when he falls into the alien lines of gentile inquiry and becomes a naturalised, though hyphenate, citizen in the gentile republic of learning, that he comes into his own as a creative leader in the world's intellectual enterprise. It is by a loss of allegiance, or at the best by a divided allegiance to the people of his origin, that he finds himself in the vanguard of modern inquiry.[35]

Veblen does not say that there are not gifted Jews who might contribute to the continuation of their traditional knowledge, but his point is that what has been taken to be a deficit – alienation – is, for the life of Western culture, a benefit. Thus the success of the Jews cannot be understood on the mystical grounds of race, but it can be made sense of as the result of a reinterpretation of the signs of one's own past. The preeminence of the Jews, as Veblen analyzes it, would not, importantly, lead to either anti- or philo-Semitism because it is not based on the same grounds as are the age-old stereotypes of the Jew.[36]

The hyphen that joins the country of origin to the place of residence is the sign of the possible semiosis of new and valuable signs – for any people. A recent theory of the possible meaning of the Jewish diaspora as a model for other complex identities is offered by Daniel and Jonathan Boyarin:

> Diasporic cultural identity teaches us that cultures are not preserved by being protected from "mixing" but probably can only continue to exist as a product of such mixing.

Cultures, as well as identities, are constantly being remade. While this is true of all cultures, diasporic Jewish culture lays it bare because of the impossibility of seeing Jewish culture as a self-enclosed, bounded phenomenon. . . . In other words, diasporic identity is disaggregated identity. Jewishness disrupts the very categories of identity because it is not national, not genealogical, not religious, but all of these in dialectical tensions with one another.[37]

The multiple possibilities for reinterpretation of these signs of identity, which exist to a greater or lesser degree depending on the relation of the signs, allow for the accent that is necessary, as James wrote in an essay about the charm of Italy, for the creation of "type." Type is not a thing in itself, but "the supreme right accent or final exquisite turn to the immense magnificent phrase" that makes "style."[38] And style is highly desirable to a complex civilization.

Writing a Different Subject

James had written years before about his own hyphenated position that, he felt, worked to his benefit as an artist in search of a style. In 1888 he wrote to William about his sense of the "continuous or more or less convertible" English and American worlds. This passage follows a remark about his sister Alice's passionate interest in Home Rule for Ireland and perhaps is a response to this claim for separate, exclusive interests. Although he speaks of the differences between the England and America as "melting together . . . or at any rate as simply different chapters of the same general subject," he does not desire a loss of their differences so much as a fluency of translation from one to the other:

I have not the least hesitation in saying that I aspire to write in such a way that it would be impossible to an outsider to say whether I am, at a given moment, an American writing about England or an Englishman writing about America (dealing as I do with both countries), and so far from being ashamed of such an ambiguity I should be exceedingly proud of it, for it would be highly civilized.[39]

The cosmopolite can speak, not as a native, but with an accent that does not compromise understanding. The accent lends interest to how the thing is said. The ambiguity, the different interpretations, the variety of accents, mark a work as classic. This complexity is one of the signs of civilization always making a different sense of itself. And it is hard work.

Henry had written earlier in this same letter to William of the exhausting labor of writing to Louis Stevenson, whom he adored. Mrs. Stevenson had written from "some undecipherable cannibal-island in the Pacific" and their situation is almost beyond the comprehension of the cosmopolitan, polyglot James. But he does not surrender to the perceived difficulty of deciphering the situation: "They are such far-away, fantastic, bewildering people – that there is a certain fatigue in the achievement of putting one's self in relation with them."[40] Nevertheless, the affectionate letters to these aliens continued until Stevenson's too early death. The relation was worth the effort.

The semiotic work of making a different sense of himself as an American than he had anticipated is not completed in the writing of *The American Scene,* but the grounds of the semiosis are traced in several places in the text where James interprets his relations to the aliens. The tones of these scenes vary considerably, representing the different kinds of relations between the "restless analyst" and his subject. Some are more productive of anxiety than others.

He could hardly argue with the established residence of the immigrants in his hometown. Having accepted his own alienation from what he had thought of as the ground of his "supreme relation," he is prepared to greet the aliens on equal terms:[41]

> The great fact about his companions was that, foreign as they might be, newly inducted as they might be, they were *at home,* really more at home, at the end of their few weeks or months or their year or two, than they had ever in their lives been before; and that *he* was at home too, quite with the same intensity: and yet that it was this very equality of condition that, from side to side, made the whole medium so strange. (125)

Members of this first generation are at home, but they are not recognizable as relatives. There can be "no claim to brotherhood with aliens in the first grossness of their alienism."

But with the second and third generations, the children who have become Americans by means of the common schools and the newspaper, they are "the stuff of whom brothers and sisters are made" (120). When the natives and the aliens have shared a common past for several generations, a past that cannot help but be complex and composed of various elements of ethnic experience, then brotherhood is possible, says James, now risking some prophecy as to the admirable goal, if not to the inscrutable process.

This extension of relations will not, however, be without serious consequences for the earlycomers. For the process that brings about such a brotherhood will, James fears, entail the loss of the most precious part of his own heritage: his native language.

As he wandered about New York and as he crossed the continent, James was increasingly aware that the language he had taken for granted – as he had taken for granted his birthright in the New World – was changing profoundly. And it was not just the alien who was threatening the English language. The "native" Americans may have been perceived as an even greater source of corruption. He made this problem the topic of his commencement address, "The Question of Our Speech," to the graduating class at Bryn Mawr in 1905, and he made it the topic of a four-part series of articles on "The Speech of American Women" in *Harper's Bazar* beginning in November 1906, printed after his return to England.[42] Part of what he means by "speech" is quite literally the way the language is spoken: its pronunciation, its articulation. He found American speech sloppy to the point of incomprehensibility, but his "plea for the mild effort of differentiation," was met with indifference, if not scorn.[43] Between the threat to the language posed by the alien – whose cafés are "torture-rooms of the living idiom" of the language, not unlike the rooms in the "Tower of London, haunted by the shade of Guy Fawkes" – and the "slobbering Boston misses" he chides in the pages of *Harper's Bazar*, he fears for the life of the language he has known:

> The accent of the very ultimate future, in the States, may be destined to become the most beautiful on the globe and the very music of humanity (here the "ethnic" synthesis shrouds itself thicker than ever); but whatever we shall know it for, certainly we shall not know it for English – in any sense for which there is an existing literary measure. (139)

The past of literature in English would not be an adequate standard for the language as it was, inevitably, going to be transformed. That future seems indecipherable, or at least unpronounceable, to him now:

> it is as if the syllables were too numerous to make a legible word. The *il*legible word accordingly, the great inscrutable

> answer to questions, hangs in the vast American sky, to
> his imagination as something fantastic and *abracadabrant,*
> belonging to no known language. (121–2)

The future may be "illegible" to him, and his fear is that he will
also be illegible to the future. Whatever "literary measure" comes
into being, it may well be one that threatens to make his version
of American English extinct.

It is perhaps his sense of the impending extinction of his
literary identity in his native land that inspires Henry James's
astonishing conclusion to *The American Scene* in which he, the
paleface sine qua non, identified himself with the "beautiful red
man" who has been fatally "dispossessed" of his land.

In his closing exhortation, James takes on the persona of the
"native American," a designation to which he has surrendered his
rights as a descendant of William James of Albany, and, identifying now with the dispossessed, he directs his anger against the
white men whose national origins he had assumed he, Henry
James, shared. He turns on his brothers in order to do something
to redress the imbalance of power that had so nearly obliterated
the signs of the past, both natural and cultural, all across the
land:

> If I were one of the painted savages you have dispossessed,
> or even some tough reactionary trying to emulate him, what
> you are making would doubtless impress me more than what
> you are leaving unmade; for in that case it wouldn't be to
> *you* I should be looking in any degree for beauty or for
> charm. Beauty and charm would be for me in the solitude
> you have ravaged, and I should owe you my grudge for every
> disfigurement and every violence, for every wound with
> which you have caused the face of the land to bleed. (463)

Having dispossessed the natives of their land, having rendered it
hideous wherever possible, the white man lives on in his "vast
general unconsciousness and indifference," while the "restless
analyst" is haunted with the sense of "the unretrieved and the
irretrievable" (464). James's horror at "all the irresponsibility
behind" the Pullman, which symbolizes this process of destruction to him, may have deterred him from tracing the path of its
"criminal continuity" any further, beyond the Mississippi or into a
second volume.

This passage is part of the last chapter that was missing when
the American version of his book was originally published in

1907. T. S. Eliot may have believed that "one needs the enemy" in order for a culture to develop creatively.[44] Perhaps the editors at *Harper's* felt that with friends like James, enemies would be redundant.

James's haunting sense of imminent extinction, of dispossession, of disfigurement, and despair returned, however, to be confronted on the more familiar domestic territory of "The Jolly Corner." In this story, whose germ James lifted directly from the then abandoned *Sense of the Past,* the absentee returns home to find his splendid house haunted by the spirit of what he might have become had be stayed in America and become a businessman. This ghost, whom the hero finally turns on and chases, is both the perpetrator of horrors and himself a horror with a trauma particularly threatening to a writer: he is missing two fingers. Spencer Brydon triumphs over this alien self only when he recognizes it as himself and accepts the possibility of guilt without, for that, accepting the responsibility for the possible violence. He might have done these awful things; but he did not. He does not reach this understanding of himself and the alien powers alone, however, but with the help of a third figure, a woman who helps him to interpret his experience, and thus the story stands virtually alone (with the unfinished *Sense of the Past*) in the Jamesian canon for its remarkable, traditional happy ending.

The role of this woman is crucial in understanding the mediation of the native (Brydon) and the alien (the ghost). She is what makes the reinterpretation of the familiar past identity and the foreign present one possible. She is the hyphen that joins the signs of the past and those of the future. She is, in Peirce's terms, the interpretant, the Third. She is, in psychoanalytic terms, the transferential figure (like Nan) who loves agapically and makes the future not only possible but desirable.

James's traumatic return home seems to have given him the terms in which to reformulate his sense of himself as a writer in and by his great retrospective labors: the New York Edition and his autobiographies. In these volumes he labored to ensure his place in the Anglo-American literary world, a place from which he must have believed that he might be less easily dispossessed than he had been from his place of birth. Only another great trauma, the outbreak of the Great War, would again stimulate the return of the memory of his dispossession and inspire him to examine in *The Sense of the Past* the dangers of losing a living connection with the past, a loss he had seen illustrated in and by

America with such ill effect for the development of the culture. The shock of being legally defined in wartime by the British government as an "alien"[45] in his own Lamb House in Rye would move him, finally, to hyphenate himself not only in the history of literature as an Anglo-American writer but also in the eyes of the law as an Amer-British subject.

PART THREE

PATRIMONY AND MATRIMONY:
THE IVORY TOWER

HETEROSOCIAL ACTS

THE AMBIGUITY OF GENDER IN THE NEW WORLD

In *The Ivory Tower* James begins to dramatize the social and cultural life he had analyzed in *The American Scene*. He had surmised in that text that the way that Americans made sense of the past (or not) created both strange cultural artifacts and very peculiar social relations, particularly between men and women: "This failure of the sexes to keep step socially is to be noted, in the United States, at every turn, and is perhaps more suggestive of interesting 'drama,' as I have already hinted, than anything else in the country." He attributes the lack of social coordination to "that foredoomed *grope* of wealth" trying to find out "what civilization really *is*."[1] Groping, as might be expected, leads to some very awkward movements. Failing "to keep step socially," men and women are more likely to tread on each other's toes than to move gracefully together. James is struck by "the appearance of a queer deep split or chasm between the two stages of personal polish, the two levels of the conversible state, at which the sexes have arrived" (65). Such a lack of coordination, such a gap in the conversation thwarts James's attempt to dramatize this moment in the history of manners and indicates a crisis in matrimony as an institution for transmitting the past.

As he begins to write the story of men and women in the most recent version of the New World he had witnessed, James finds that the drama he had thought would be so "suggestive" stalls. This fragment of a novel has not so much a "misplaced middle" as a series of first acts that do not lead to the second act in which the conflict of differences would begin to be interesting. It resists becoming dramatic because the differences and conflicts – the differences between the genders – on which drama depends are not well defined. He cannot get the right cast of characters: he sees all about him that "nothing [is] so characteristic as this apparant privation, for the man, of his right kind of woman, and this apparent privation, for the woman, of her right kind of man" (65). The values of gender do not consort meaningfully in the New World.

As James had seen in so many contexts, this lack of meaning is the typical consequence of the American habit of effacing differences. In *The Ivory Tower* he begins to show how the loss of the kind of articulated distinctions that could transform "groping" into some more graceful form of movement affects one of the major institutions by which a society constructs itself and transfers the sense of the past into a desire for the future, namely, matrimony. In a society that "abhorr[ed] ... discrimination" (305), it would be hard to imagine how the drama and ritual of heterosexual mating could be played out.[2] In the Newport of *The Ivory Tower* the game of matrimony is stalemated because the gender of the players is uncertain.

The blurring of distinctions that is endemic to this novel differs from James's interest in the proliferation of gender roles that is played out in so many of his writings, novels and stories in which men and women find themselves at odds with the status quo but are at least able to define themselves in relation to it.[3] Olive Chancellor may have been "unmarried by every implication of her being," but she was not, for all that, at a loss to define herself by opposition to the norms of Boston society. The difference and the resistance did not make her happy; but they made it possible for her to know that her own desires were thwarted. Ned Rosier in *The Portrait of a Lady* may have failed to meet Osmond's criteria for a suitable suitor for his daughter; but there was no doubt in Pansy's mind that he was the right man for her. In "The Death of the Lion," the use by two writers of pseudonyms of the opposite gender leads the bewildered narrator to wonder at first "if there were three sexes" but not to doubt that, in the end, he would be able to tell them apart.[4] The play of gender is complex and various in these works, but it differs from the situation in *The Ivory Tower* where the lack of gender differences leaves the characters at a loss to know how to act.

This confusion exists in spite of the fact that the donnée of this novel is one in which it would seem that nothing could be easier than the happy ending exemplified in the history of the novel by marriage. The kinds of obstacles that have thwarted so many of James's star-crossed lovers are not there. Graham Fielder, a European-bred American, suddenly and unexpectedly inherits a fortune of millions of dollars from his uncle. Why should he not make the marriage of his fondest dreams? Yet he refuses to consider marriage at all:

"Well" – Gray was here at least all prompt and clear – "I keep down, in that matter, so much as I can any *a priori* or mere theoretic want. I see my possibly marrying as an effect, I mean – I somehow don't see it at all as a cause. A cause, that is" – he easily worked it out – "of my getting other things right. It may be, in conditions, the greatest rightness of all; but I want to be sure of the conditions."[5]

This conception of matrimony makes it into a thing to be possessed – like a fortune that buys the trophy bride – rather than a living, meaningful relation by which one defines and redefines oneself as a gendered social being. Graham is imposing the monological values of the institution of patrimony onto the institution of matrimony, this being another instance of the kind of homogenization of values and particularly the domination of business values to which James objects so strenuously throughout *The American Scene*.

Gray's difficulty in imagining that a relationship with a member of the opposite sex would help him on his quest to figure out his life is thus not only a personal problem but a social one. All the relations between men and women that are depicted in this novel exhibit aspects of this alienation between the male public world of money-making and business and the female social world of consumption and display, with the result that no marriage between the values of these worlds seems meaningful – or even possible. The world of men and the world of women seem absolutely at odds with one another.

James does not, however, despair – even if he does abandon this novel to return to the world of *The Sense of the Past* in which he knew how to conduct the play of gender values so that a happy ending is imaginable, so that a future is desirable. In *the Ivory Tower*, in his commencement address to the 1905 graduating class of Byrn Mawr College, and in several essays about American women that he wrote shortly after his visit, he analyzes what he sees as a crisis in relations between men and women. His explicit purpose in the essays is to suggest ways in which those relations might be reconfigured so that men and women would see that they might benefit by reestablishing relations with each other that did not segregate them by gender but allowed them to speak to each other meaningfully by way of those differences. One possibility that he seems to consider at this historical juncture is that it would be worthwhile trying to differentiate heterosexuality – with its reproductive imperative that serves the continuity of society at large – and heterosociality, which also serves society but in a cultural rather than a biological sense. Heterosociality is one of the necessary conditions for an interesting culture because it is the ground for varied and beneficial relations between men and women. Without such a possibility of sociality, one would wonder not only what "civilization really *is*" but what it is for.[6] James found that in America men and women, off in their own separate spheres, were barely on speaking terms, and he wants to show them how critical to their own social well-being it is that they make sense of themselves by talking to each other. *The Ivory Tower* is, by contrast, filled with the kind of awkward silences that are the horror of any host or teacher.

The loss of differences between the genders in *The Ivory Tower* is figured in that novel as confusion and embarrassment at various moments of social interaction. It also, importantly, figured as an impediment to the kind of transference (in the psychoanalytic sense) that James thought invaluable to the individual's social development. In *The Ivory Tower* this kind of heterosocial relationship fails. Whereas Rosanna was able to play the transferential role for Gray at a crucial juncture in his life when they were much younger, this relationship that worked in Europe fizzles in Newport (40–1). The ground of Rosanna's power to play this role earlier is clearly delineated: "She had been involved in something, produced by something, intimately pressing upon her and yet as different as possible from herself; and here was the concentrated difference . . ." (87). Having been formed by some kind of encounter with something other than herself, she has been able to embody that meaning to and for Gray in such a way as to provoke his own transformation – whatever it might be.[7] Now in Newport, she fails him. Amid other disappointments he senses

> a return of a queer force in his view of Rosanna as above all somehow wanting, off and withdrawn verily to the pitch of her having played him some trick, merely let him in where she was to have seen him through, failed in fine of a sociability implied in all her preliminaries. (266)

Her "concentrated difference" has become a blank. Significantly, the other instance of a productive transference in the novel – between Cissy Foy and Mr. Northover – has also taken place in Europe (66). Different as these heterosocial relationships are insofar as they involve very different configurations of the genders and ages of the participants, they have both benefited all of the players at critical moments in their lives. These benefits are only possible in the world that James represents when there are differences in play. The gender differences create the possibility of such play.

In these last two novels James suggests why heterosociality should be cultivated, even as heterosexual matrimony must also undergo reconstruction in a cultural context in which, among other things, the transformations in the laws and nature of patrimony were changing the economic basis of relations between men and women. James's understanding of the economic grounds and consequences of this social disorder echoes Charlotte Perkins Gilman's analysis in *Women and Economics,* and his analysis of the pitfalls of compulsory heterosexuality prefigures in important ways the complaints of Adrienne Rich against the institution of matrimony.[8] Yet it is no small irony in *The Ivory Tower* that James shows how, at this moment in the historical transformations of the relations between patrimony and matrimony, the two women who have independent fortunes are no more able to create the kinds of social relations they desire than are the men of business or the character who is always James's best last hope – the American Girl – here represented by Cissy Foy.[9] Economic equality alone will not reform social relations in a desirable way. The millionairess Rosanna Gaw, who has arranged that Gray inherit his millions from his uncle, suddenly realizes when she has done her good deed that there is no one in Newport to whom she wants to introduce him once he has arrived. She is appalled by her society:

> What Rosanna most noted withal, and not for the first time either, every observation she had hitherto made seeming now but intensified, what she most noted was the huge general familiarity, the pitch of intimacy unmodulated, as if exactly the same time, from person to person, bound the whole company together and nobody had anything to say to anyone that wasn't equally in question for all. . . . She would have liked to be intimate – with someone or other, not indeed with every member of a crowd. . . . (46)

This lack of social discrimination, this veritable promiscuity, precludes the possibility of meaningful differences; it confuses the value of gender; it thwarts the promise of matrimony that a happy ending can be desired in perfect good faith, the promise that a human relationship can really matter, that it can make a difference.

Clueless in Newport

The loss of gender differences in *The Ivory Tower* affects men and women both in their separate spheres and when they attempt to socialize together. In recent decades the work of social and feminist historians has made familiar the division between the "spheres" of men and women that characterized nineteenth-century society. Although descriptions of these "spheres" often make them seem like natural or essential or, in any case, unchanging social divisions, they are not in James's view, stable, hypertrophied, hierarchical arrangements of differences. Social relations are always characterized in his work by the possibility of changing their meanings as they are reconfigured in different contexts. But in American society the lack of contact between the genders and their consequent lack of marking makes each sphere potentially meaningless.

The loss of marking in Newport is played out in the ambiguous representation of Gray's gender.[10] Sometimes he is feminized; sometimes his gender is indeterminate. His rich uncle, Mr. Betterman, announces to Gray on his first visit, "You're like the princess in the fairy-tale" (119), and speaks of him in terms that suggest the perfection of the virginal: "I've got you – without a flaw" (109). Horton claims to see Gray "up in the blue, behind your parapet, just gracefully lean over and call down to where I mount guard at your door in the dust and comparative darkness" (216). This Rapunzal lacks, however, the personal property that could contribute to her liberation.

Most comically (and most tragically, as Miss Gostrey's creator might add) indicative of the ambiguity of gender in *The Ivory Tower* is the question of Gray's moustache. When Horton cannot recall whether his friend had, when they had met previously, such facial ornamentation, Cissy Foy appeals to Gray's neighbor Davey Bradham, who has just returned from a call on the heir apparent, to answer this question, "as if the fate of empires depended on it" (179). But it happens that Davey has no recollection of apparent facial hair and so the "sense of a moustache" being in doubt seems to leave "the sense of difference in things, and of their relations and suitabilities" also very indeterminate (175–6).

This feminization of Gray is, however, not merely a reversal of the attribution of the conventional signs of gender. James plays with this simple kind of reconstruction for comic effect, as when he has Gray notice that Mr. Betterman's male physician is "addressed rather as he had heard doctors address nurses than nurses doctors" (84) by the attendant Miss Mumby. But the problem is not that gender roles are reversed or that opportunities for women have expanded over the decades. The problem is that these social transformations have alienated men and women from each other and made them illegible to each other.

The ambiguity of gender is staged most fully in *The Ivory Tower* not in opposite-sex but in same-sex relations and especially in the relations between Graham and the man he picks to be his financial adviser, Horton Vint. Like Gray, Horton is also characterized on occasion as ambiguously gendered, as when James describes his laugh: "no sound of that sort equally manful had less of mere male stridency" (164). In any reading of their relationship, it is clear that the masculinity of both Gray and Horton is very much in question insofar as it is recognizable as a set of shared socially recognizable conventions. At a few points early in the development of the story it seems possible to read their homosocial relation as a viable alternative to the discontents of heterosexuality. Homosocial bonds thrive in structures that effectively use a variety of strategies to exclude women.[11] At first blush, this seems to be the meaning of Horton's indifference to the good opinion of him held by women to which Gray refers when explaining his decision to make Horton his financial advisor. The "confidence" of women, he says,

> is concerned only with the effect of their own operations or with those to which they are subject; it has no light either for a man's other friends or for his enemies: it proves nothing about him but in that particular and wholly detached relation. (237)

This indifference to the opinion of women could work to support the homosocial bond – but only in a social context in which that exclusion confirmed gender differences rather than exposed the collapse of difference.

But at first the homosocial bond offered by his relation with Horton as a refuge from the complications of marriage had had its own seductions for Gray. The scene of their first confidential conversation is highly erotically charged:

Wonderful thus the little space of his feeling the great wave
set in motion by that quiet worthy break upon him out of
Gray's face, Gray's voice, Gray's contact of hands laid all
appealingly and affirmingly on his shoulders, and then as it
retreated, washing him warmly down, expose to him, off in
the intenser light and the uncovered prospect, something
like his entire personal future. Something extraordinarily
like, yet, could he but keep steady to recognize it through a
deepening consciousness, at the same time, of how he was
more than matching the growth of his friend's need of him
by growing there at once, and to rankness, under the
friend's nose, all the values to which this need supplied a
soil. (197)

The thrill of this sensuous, earthy communication is soon compromised.

James shows how that same-sex bond cannot be sustained when
the differences between it and heterosexuality are as attenuated
as they are in the world of *The Ivory Tower*. He runs the gamut of
different relations between the two men, as if desperately seeking
some way in which they might be configured to benefit each
other. In the first stage of their relation their economic inequality
reproduces the typical situation of the man with money and the
dependent woman without it, and the result is the play of eroti-
cism in the foregoing scene. But in order for there to be a sequel
of the kind Gray wants to this scene, the values cannot be so
unequally distributed. He wants more give-and-take; he wants a
kind of reciprocity that is only possible when the trump card of
economic power is not always his. He attempts to create a new
game when he reverses the economic roles by surrendering control of his fortune to Horton. This strategy does not, however,
work, and his dissatisfaction is tellingly characterized by his
sense of the loss of difference that had been so exciting to him
in their first encounter. When he finds that Horton will not
disagree with him, Gray is "mystified as he had several times been,
and somehow didn't like too much being, by having to note
that to differ at all from Vinty on occasions apparently offered
was to provoke in him at once a positive excess of agreement"
(254). The resistances that gave their first scene of union such a
pleasurable tension have been obliterated. Difference collapses
into sameness, and thus even the promise of homosociality is
thwarted.

In a world where men cannot relate to men nor women to

women (a point, alas, I have no space to illustrate), how can men and women learn to "keep step socially" well enough so that they might sometimes marry?

They must begin, James suggests, by learning again to talk to each other. From that new beginning, other steps, other conversations, other relations might in time develop. A new heterosexuality, a new matrimony would certainly emerge from a heterosociality that valued good talk between men and women. This is how Rosanna had worked her good for Gray in earlier, European days:

> It was a joy to me to feel it clear up – with the good I had already done him, at a touch, by making him speak. I saw how this relieved him even when he practically spoke of his question as too frightful for his young intelligence, his young conscience – literally his young nerves. (40)

By conversing with a sympathetic person – "he understood that I was somehow inspired for him" – his confusion is transformed into an understanding of the possibility of new, meaningful relationships, which themselves are transformations of relationships of the past. In *The Ivory Tower* James does intend that Gray should again find someone who will help him by talking to him. Cissy "is the being, up and down the place, with whom he is going to be able most to *communicate*" (304), regardless of whether this means that by the logic of romance that rules *The Sense of the Past* they will marry. It seems unlikely, however, that the "talking cure" could be effective, that such transferences could take place, in the absence of the kind of speech that James takes to be a high sign of civilization.[12]

So how shall the heterosocial conversation come about?

Articulating Matters

In *The Question of Our Speech* James proposes by means of a complex analogy between speech and marriage a theory about the relation between language and heterosociality and an explanation of why differential values are essential to their social functions. Speech is "the very hinge of the relation of man to man" – but only if women are also speaking and being spoken to.[13]

In this address (which has many more dimensions than can be explored here) James explains the grounds on which he ascribes a supreme value to speech as the means by which civilization is transmitted and circulated:

> This imparting of a coherent culture is a matter of communication and response – each of which branches of an understanding involves the possession of a common language, with its modes of employment, its usage, its authority, its beauty, in working form; a medium of expression, in short, organized and developed. (6)

More than just a liberal arts education in the "clear humanities" depends absolutely on the possibility of mutual understanding through the medium of speech (5):

> We may not be said to be able to study – and *a fortiori* do any of the things we study *for* – unless we are able to speak. All life therefore comes back to the question of our speech, the medium through which we communicate with each other; for all life comes back to the question of our relations with each other. These relations are made possible, are registered, are verily constituted, by our speech, and are successful (to repeat my word) in proportion as our speech is worthy of its great human and social function; is developed, delicate, flexible, rich – an adequate accomplished fact. The more it suggests and expresses the more we live by it – the more it promotes and enhances life. (10)

The cultivation of speech is a sign of the maturity of culture. It is "the touchstone of manners, is the note, the representative note – representative of its having (in our poor, imperfect human degree) achieved civilization" (12). Respect for "a settled character, a certain ripeness, finality and felicity" (35) of speech shows respect for humanity at its best – by which James means at its most social.

By the terms of this scheme, America has singularly failed to achieve "civilization." Launching into his jeremiad, he prophesies that "the doom of the slovenly" (25) is imminent. American abhorrence of discriminations is expressed in speech by the lack of "any approach to an emission of the consonant," making it "a mere helpless slobber of disconnected vowel noises" (25). James offers "a closer account of the evil against which [he] warn[s] you" (23): continuing in this manner will reduce human speech (and with it human civilization) to the rudimentary "grunting, the squealing, the barking or the roaring of animals" (16).

After explaining the historical reasons why he thinks that American English has been subjected to unique demands because of the influx of immigrants who have had to use it as a serviceable instrument for survival first and foremost, he insists that a distinction be made between the practical value of the language when it is used in this simple way and its possible social functions as they would be fulfilled in more elaborately developed forms. James calls upon his audience in his peroration to be "models and missionaries, perhaps a little even martyrs, of the good cause" (52).

The women of this leisure/graduating class of 1905 at Bryn Mawr are not compelled by the same economic pressures as are the recent immigrants for whom English is their second language. By speaking the language they have inherited well, these new graduates and their ilk are making possible "developed, delicate, flexible, rich" personal relations (10).

Of course, cultivating speech does require a certain effort on the part of these young women and is bound to feel awkward at first. However, with practice, with discipline, with a "*care* for tone," they might achieve "the ease that comes from the facing, the conquest of a difficulty," rather than "the ease that comes from the vague dodging of it." Here the voice of the experienced craftsman is heard: "In the one case you gain facility, in the other case you get mere looseness" (32). Only with skill is art possible. He asks them only to take as much care in their personal relations as they do in their personal appearance. In the new world of the Gilded Age this absence of the kind of "*care* for tone" (13) is, he says, all the more surprising in American society, given the general tendency to perfect the public presentation of the person. At similar carelessness shown in "any other of our personal functions," "we should blush" (23–4). No woman worth her Worth would be caught dead showing such looseness in the matter of corsets. In that realm of self-representation she makes distinctions and is quite willing to suffer discomfort to achieve her desired end – and her desired middle.

Just as no fashion endures forever, however, so no standard of speech is permanent or universal (any more than there is one correct literary language). James does recognize that the language will be transformed in unpredictable ways by, for example, the "ethnic synthesis." It must, of course, be able "to respond, from its core, to the constant appeal of time, perpetually demanding new tricks, new experiments, new amusements of it: so to respond without losing its characteristic balance." That "balance" is maintained so long as the conservative interest, which should always predominate, remains, equally, the constant quality; remains an embodied, constituted, inexpugnable thing. The conservative interest is as indispensable for the institution of speech as for the institution of matrimony. (46–7)

This analogy insists upon the sociality of both of these institutions. Either is only meaningful as "a common language" (6) when shared by a group of speakers:

Abate a jot of the quantity, and, much more, of the quality of the consecration required, and we practically find ourselves emulating the beasts, who prosper as well without a vocabulary as without a marriage-service. It is easier to overlook any question of speech than to trouble about it, but then it is also easier to snort or neigh, to growl or to "meaow," than to articulate or intonate. (47)

James may well, of course, have underestimated the complexity and sociability of the languages of animals, but his point is that speech and marriage are both semiotic systems that are only meaningful by the articulation of differences that are conventionally recognized by the parties concerned.

This understanding of the values of language has become common knowledge since the dissemination of Saussure's linguistic theory.[14] In speech, the differential values are phonemes, words, and the like. In marriage, the differential values are heterosexual conventions. They provide the common language that makes the institution meaningful, understandable – and as flexible as a language is in the way they allow for an infinite number of new formulations.

It is important to note that James's defense of the "conservative interest" does not prescribe an essential or permanent nature for the institution's differential relations. In such a theory of the change of value systems, there can be no absolutes, no "male" and "female" for all time. What he does think is necessary in order for there to be heterosocial relations is that there be continuity in enough of the values so that they can be understood well enough by all concerned parties. There is no inherent reason why every aspect of the institution could not change so much over a long enough time as to be unrecognizable to the present view: a ship afloat can be completely rebuilt – but only a bit at a time. A word can shift its meaning so greatly that it can no longer be used for its earlier purposes. Just so the values of gender and the institution of marriage might change so much over time as to be unrecognizable to us now. Too much change too rapidly, however, would leave the players in the game of heterosexual unions as bewildered about which maneuvers move them toward their goal pragmatically as is the postmodern parent listening to teenagers speak their private language for their own social purposes. Such is the state of collapse in the meaning of gender relations in *The Ivory Tower.*

It is very important to recognize at this point in the analysis of James's argument that he is not defending the status quo or urging a return to some imaginary perfect past – or for that matter prophesying the ideal future of relations between the sexes in any specific terms. The closest that James ever comes to experimenting in utopian visions is in the romance of *The Sense of the Past,* in which we have seen that he planned to resolve the discordances of past and present by putting his hero in a situation in which gender roles were paralyzing to him and showing how, through the transformative heterosocial love of Nan, he might arrive at a revision of his present that makes it a desirable heterosexual future.

As early as his 1868 review of a collection of essays titled "Modern Women, and What Is Said of Them," James insists that the attempt to blame the "increased freedom" of women for social problems is as "supremely absurd" as to "endeavor, with a long lash and a good deal of bad language, to drive women back into the ancient fold." Their "increased freedom [is] a part of the growth of society" (334), and, in fact, since it is men who "give the *ton* – [who] pitch the key," they are more responsible for these problems in heterosexual relations than are women:

> It is impossible to discuss and condemn the follies of "modern women" apart from those of modern men. They are all part and parcel of the follies of modern civilization, which is working itself out through innumerable blunders. . . . We are all of us extravagant, superficial, and luxurious together. It is a "sign of the times." Women share in the fault not as women, but as simple human beings.[15]

To acknowledge the inevitability of "blunders" is not to surrender the right to criticize any particular forms social life might take.

In the essays in "The Speech of American Women" and "The Manners of American Women"[16] that James wrote after his return to England his most iterated point is that the isolation of the American woman from the American man has, in spite of her

apparent increase of freedom, impoverished rather than enriched her social relations: as "[t]he product of an order in which
no presence was really so taken for granted as her own, her
view of relations was thereby inordinately simplified" (33). This
gender segregation is yet another manifestation of what he calls
"a civilization addicted to nothing if not to waste" (77). What is
wasted here are the benefits to sociality that are embodied in
conventions of speech and manners that are inherited and that
must, of course, be transformed if they are to remain meaningful
as society changes. But Americans do not seem to understand the
value of cultivating these conventions:

> It has never been without profit to the individual American,
> I think, to have taken in the truth, as societies other than
> his own put it before him, that in a difficult and complicated
> world it is well to have had as many things as possible dis-
> criminated and well thought out and tried and tested for us,
> well to remember that the art of meeting life finely is, what
> the art of the dramatist has been described as being, the art
> of preparations. (68)

This "art of meeting life" is laid waste by what James refers to as
"our too habitual, too national belief in the sweet sanctity of free
impulse." James writes of the "unlighted chaos of our manners,"
of a world in which criticism might as well belong to "the economy of another planet" (41).

He sees heterosociality as providing what he variously calls
"educative forces" (72), "criticism" (33), and, more problemati-
cally, "the male privilege of correction" (78). In this last formulation he seems to confirm the kind of hierarchical relation that is
often characterized as patriarchal. Although he specifies that it is
in "societies other than ours" that gender relations have been
arranged so that the male has the wider exposure to public life
that educates the domestic sphere by adding new values to it, he
does not say that it must always be so. What is more important in
this conception of the relative functions of the different genders
is that he insists (as he did in the 1868 review) that it is "as a
social creature" that woman

> gets her lead and her cue and her best sanction for her
> maintenance of her [speech]; since she is never at all thor-
> oughly a well-bred person unless he has begun by having a
> sense for it and by showing her the way: when – oh then
> beautifully and wonderfully and in a manner all her own! –

she often improves on it and carries it, in the detail of application, much further than he. (78)

For certain readers of James this little-known passage from an obscure essay will confirm what they have long believed about Henry James and his father before him: namely, that they subscribed to the most conventionally sexist beliefs of their respective ages.[17] But the qualification that it is "as a social creature" that woman relates thus to the male "social creature" makes an absolutely crucial difference in the meaning of James's description of their relation.

If the male has the "privilege of correction," it is not the last word in the conversation. Nor the most beautiful and wonderful. The female art of conversation, as I might call it, improves upon the correction that has improved upon the homogeneous simplicity of impulse. It is only then that the kind of sociality that brings different kinds of speech, that brings different kinds of people together in a shared, meaningful experience is possible. Heterosociality is created for the benefit of all by the reciprocity of conversation rather than unilateral instruction.

To appreciate how and why this analysis of the necessary conditions for heterosociality is conducted in the terms of gender and follows these three stages of natural impulse, correction, and the art of sociality, it will be useful to return to James's own patrimony, his father's psychospiritual story of the individual as a social being. And it is in the context of the story of the genesis of the individual as social that it becomes clear why the differences that must be in play in order for heterosociality to come about do not correspond to the assignment of these male and female conversational roles to particular men and women. There is no reason why a woman might not by her criticism exercise the "male privilege of correction"; and no reason why a man might not cultivate the "female art of conversation." There just must be both. The differential values necessary to conversation depend upon gender differences being in play. Conversation in the Jamesian sense is only possible when heterosexual conventions lead to the pleasures and variety of heterosociality. For without conversation, there is no social life at all for anyone.

8

ODD COUPLES

HENRY JAMES SENIOR AND JACQUES LACAN

The differential and creative roles that gender plays in the development of the individual as a social and artful being are theorized in Henry James Senior's psychospiritual version of Genesis. James Senior was very much a man of his times in his enthusiasm for a new vision of society, and he was very much his own man in the idiosyncratic interpretation he gave to some of the ideas of the New Age. The touchstone of his originality is the theocentrism of his ideas, but this emphasis only becomes eccentric in time. Long after socialism had relinquished its religious foundation, he persisted in basing his social vision on Christianity. His later writings on marriage suffered at the hands of his contemporaries because he continued to believe in Fourier's feminist principles *and* to insist on a religious basis for his understanding of sexual difference. Had he done one or the other, chosen either Fourier or Swedenborg as his guide, he might have found himself better understood and with a few more intellectual cohorts. As it was, he found himself an easy mark for attacks from radicals and conservatives alike – but he never gave up trying to make his point clear.[1]

James Senior's effort is always to understand the spiritual meaning of actual worldly experience. He attempts to portray the "spiritual world" – which, Henry Junior writes in his autobiography, "we were in the habit of hearing as freely alluded to as we heard the prospect of dinner or the call of the postman"[2] – as a realm that could be described just as well as the physical and social worlds could. This double perspective does mean that it is not always clear – even to such a sympathetic reader as C. S. Peirce[3] – what kind of point James is trying to make at a given moment. Is he offering a theory of the spiritual meaning of heterosexuality in his reading of Genesis? Or is he offering a critique of marriage as it was actually practiced in the 1840s? There tends to be a good deal of slippage between his genres (see Chapter 2), at times leading the reader unfamiliar with the theological foundation of the critique to confuse theoretical claims about gender differences with prescriptive definitions of gender roles.[4] This is especially the case with James's remarks about women.

At the heart of James's critique of the institution of marriage as he saw it practiced was his condemnation of the economic dependency of women. Fourier calls such marriage practices "conjugal slavery," which James explains as meaning that the claim to "absolute property" in any human being is abhorrent, "that is, a property unvivified by the other's unforced, spontaneous gift."[5] In the current state of affairs, marriage was often "concubinage" concerned only with "personal" interests of the parties instead of the "social" and "race interest" of true marriage.[6] James agreed with Fourier that monogamous marriage enforced only by the letter of the law was, as Fourier said, "Yes, prostitution, more or less prettied up . . ." and that women suffer most from this state of things.[7] Fourier had a complex remedy for this unhappy state of affairs that far surpasses any of our attempts to move beyond the binarism of sex;[8] James Senior restricted himself to the critique of monogamy in the terms of his religious beliefs.

His condemnation of the economic dependence of women must be seen in the context of his underlying belief that it is as a *social* institution that marriage is holy.[9] James saw that the woman is habitually "dependent" upon man "for her outward subsistence and honor" in the "isolated family," but (unlike many of his liberal contemporaries, such as John Stuart Mill) he is less concerned with remedying the economic or legal inequities of the individual's situation than clarifying the spiritual meaning of marriage as a "crude earthly type or symbol of a profounder marriage which, in invisible depths of being, is taking place between the public and private life of man, or the sphere of his natural instinct and that of his spiritual culture. . . ."[10] Marriage as legally constituted and characteristically practiced is the opposite of what it should be, "the crown only of the most perfect culture known to humanity."[11] The true sanctity of marriage is realized by its transformative, relational possibilities: "It is the sole nursery of the social sentiment in the human bosom . . . [it] symbolizes to the imagination of the race . . . the essential unity of mankind."[12] Moreover, marriage is the very model of the harmonization of differences existing in nature: "The only original inequality known to the human race is that of the sexes, and marriage in annulling this forever sanctifies weakness to the regard of the strong, or makes true manhood to consist no longer in force but in gentleness."[13]

Thus woman's economic dependence is to be abhorred because marriages based on "conjugal slavery" retard the coming of "a perfect society or fellowship of man with man in all the earth."[14] James's whole conception of marriage depends on the freedom and spontaneity of both parties. And the woman has a special role in making marriage realize its highest social purpose:

> [M]arriage is the apotheosis of woman.... For woman means not human nature, but human culture . . . woman in my opinion symbolizes humanity no longer in its merely created or physical or moral aspect . . . but in its regenerate, or social and aesthetic aspect, in which it feels itself divorced from any legal vassalage even to God, and becomes, on the contrary, freely and frankly at one with him.[15]

The vivifying, spontaneous love of the woman is the essential element in the scheme of redemption:

> an absolute or final phase of human nature rather than a contingent or complementary one; . . . she is . . . something very much more than either male or female – something, in fact, divinely different from either . . . In short, the sole dignity of marriage, practically viewed, lies in its abasing the male sway in our nature, and exalting the feminine influence in its place.[16]

It is at points like these that it is least clear whether James is referring to actual wives or to some female principle. James often refers to this final stage of individual spiritual evolution as "the female Adam," and describes this being as one who is "something very much more than either male or female – something, in fact, divinely different from either." Evidently, if the goal of this scheme of development is a kind of androgyny in which there will still be differentiated genders, there cannot be a necessary alignment between actual men and women and the male and female principles. Each individual man and woman seems to have male and female principles psychospiritually speaking – but the spiritual evolution that James is describing depends upon heterosexual relations being in play socially, not spiritually or solipsistically. The values of gender are, as we shall see, more complicated and various in James Senior's scheme than appears at first blush.

A belief in the transformative role of gender differences is the crucial concept that connects James's critique of the actual institution of marriage and his psychospiritual theory of the individual. These complex relations between beings of differentiated genders are necessary for the development of what I have called in the last chapter heterosociality and what James Senior calls "fellowship" or the "divine-natural-humanity." Without gender differences having played their crucial roles along the way, there can be no "female Adam" – and thus no hope of fellowship for society as a whole. Heterosexuality is necessary to heterosociality.

The Genesis of Gender

The crux of James Senior's originality is the interpretation he offers of the genesis of gender in his reading of the biblical text: "in the image of God created he him; male and female created he them." Although the contradiction between this description in Genesis 1:27 and the account offered in 2:21–4 – God taking the rib from the side of the man and fashioning it into woman – has provoked many conflicting interpretations of the spiritual, human, and political status of woman over the millennia, James's account is not troubled by the inconsistency because he is not trying to use scripture to justify misogyny. On the contrary. When in "The Woman Thou gavest with me" he protests against those opponents of the women's movement "who obstinately regard woman as the mere sexual counterpart and diminutive of man," he dissociates himself unequivocally from two major ideologies of female inferiority and subordination.[17] On the one hand, there were the age-old arguments postulating woman's inferiority that claimed there was only one sex, which existed in its perfect (male) and its imperfect (female) forms. These arguments derived their authority from the classical belief that woman's sex was the physical inversion of man's and various biblical doctrines, including the story of Eve's derivative origin from the rib of Adam and of her tempting of him to disobey God's law. The new-age arguments, on the other hand, conceived of the two sexes as different and incommensurate and used those differences to enforce woman's dependence and subjugation. Sexual difference cannot be used, as James sees it, to justify oppression because the reason the two sexes exist is to redeem each other together. There is no possibility for domination and submission, for superiority and inferiority, in the fellowship between divine-natural-humans.

What James is proposing in his reading of Genesis is that Eve is the means by which Adam becomes human, and thus she is the agent for eventual redemption, not of original sin. James regards the whole concept of original sin as unspeakably puerile. But he is not quite of the traditional "fortunate fall" party either, because Christ plays a wholly illustrative and in no way exceptional role in his theology, being simply the first instance of the divine-natural-humanity that all persons will incarnate eventually. Indeed, one of the reasons that his interpretation of Genesis might have been rejected by his contemporaries is that he virtually negates the salvific power of Christ and gives a crucial role in humanization and in socialization to a female figure. But his is not a simple stereotype of the morally redeeming characteristics of the angel of the Victorian household. There are both positive and negative aspects to Eve. And the negative can become the positive and vice versa, depending upon what moment in this progressive process one is describing.

James means the creation of "Adam" in the etymologically correct sense of the generic human being, which exists in two sexes. The Hebrew word for "man" insists upon this generic quality in its association with the word for "soil, ground": *'ādām* and *'ªdāmā* might be translated more accurately and poetically, one scholar suggests, as "earthling" and "earth."[18] James calls the two aspects of "the Adam" the *homo* and the *vir*, but the masculinity of both of those Latin terms is destabilized by his characterization of them and their shifting gender relations. It is in James's description of the relations between the *homo* and the *vir* that his theory of the transformation of the individual consciousness into the social consciousness is revealed.

The *homo* is easier to describe than is the *vir*, for his characteristics are those shared with mineral, vegetable, and animal life: "On my physical side – my fixed, organic, passive, maternal side – by which I am related to nature or outlying existence, I am my own object."[19] Other characteristics found in the *homo* are "the race principle, the principle of universality, or community" (141). He is, in a word, natural, and he lives a life of unmitigated brutality until the *vir* arouses him to consciousness and conscience. The *vir* is that which is distinctly human: "On my moral or personal side – my contingent, free, active, or paternal side by which I am related to man or my kind, I am my own subject" (137). Other characteristics of the *vir* are "the family principle, the principle of individuality or difference" (141). The *vir* is social.

The oppositions between the body and the spirit, necessity and freedom, maternal and paternal are familiar enough. But what is odd here in the alignment of these binary oppositions is that if Adam is the *homo*, then Eve is the *vir*, and this means that Eve is the paternal principle. Not only that. She is also identified, because she is the *vir*, with the "intelligent sonship" of "contingent relations" between creator and creature that are essential to the eventual redemption of all of humanity (136). She creates this freedom or contingency by incarnating "the principle of individuality or difference" that brings conscience into being and thus "bring[s] forth a human, which is a moral or individual form, everyway commensurate with the universality of mineral, vegetable, and animal existence" (147).

James pithily writes in the table of contents: "Adam impotent and imbecile until vivified by Eve." But how is he "vivified"? The climax of his story defies the conventions of linear narrative. Too much is happening at once:

> But now what is the method of this great achievement? How can we rationally conceive of the *vir* being spiritually begotten by the divine power out of the *homo?* In other words, what conceivable ratio is there between the wholly unconscious life of mineral, vegetable, and animal, and the wholly conscious life of man? Between the blind instinctual groping of Adam, and the clear intelligent will of Eve? (141)

The originality of his scheme of redemption becomes more apparent as this question is restated in a variety of ways, as he asks how there can be a connection

> Between the utterly unselfish nature of the *homo*, and the utterly selfish nature of the *vir?* Between the innocence which characterizes all our distinctively *humane* tendencies and affections, and the guilt which stains all our distinctively *virtuous* ones? (141-2)

The paradox implicit in his interpretation of the so-called fall of man begins to emerge. How can virtue be stained with guilt? One moment James is ascribing to Eve the task of raising the Adam from his purely creaturely bondage to nature, and the next he is identifying her selfishness with guilt and virtue. Clearly her role is ambiguous.

But much is at stake in understanding it: "It is a question about the genesis of consciousness, or as to the precise *nexus* that obtains between physical and moral existence" (142). This is the real concern of the story of Eden:

> We read accordingly in the symbolic *Genesis,* that while all the lower things take name from man (or derive their quality from their various relation to the human form), man himself (Adam or the *homo*) remains void of self-consciousness, void of moral or personal quality, remains in short wholly unvivified by the *vir,* until creation itself gives place to redemption, or nature becomes complicated with history, in that remarkable divine intervention described as the formation of Eve or the woman out of the man's rib: by which event is symbolized of course an inward or spiritual divine fermentation in man which issues at last in his moral consciousness, or his becoming subjective as well as objective to himself. (148)

Adam's fermented and vivified moral consciousness, a.k.a. Eve, a.k.a. "selfhood," (a.k.a. the "proprium," in Swedenborg's terms), is not the medium by which he knows good and evil in absolute terms, but the means by which he is able to differentiate everything and anything at all. Her value is not as a list of commandments, but as the principle by which discriminations can be made.

This capacity to discriminate is indispensable to the process of becoming human, and it is always ambiguous. Vivification is ambiguous. Its effect is positive insofar as it creates conscience; and it is negative in that it leaves man under the illusion that he is alienated, not only from God, but from his fellows. The one effect is not possible, however, without the other.

James's description of the creation of conscience, "the true logical *differentia,* or point of individuation, between man and animal" is the most psychologically subtle part of his theology:

> The *vir* is begotten of the *homo* (or nature becomes spiritually vivified) exclusively through the instrumentality of *conscience,* which is a living though tacit divine word in every created bosom, leading it to aspire only after infinite knowledge. Conscience does not give this counsel to the *homo* in direct or explicit, but only in indirect or implicit terms. Its precept is negative, not positive, saying "thou shalt *not* eat of the tree of the knowledge of good and evil (i.e. finite

knowledge), for in the day thou eatest thereof thou shalt surely die." (150)

In other words, this prohibition splits consciousness: the *vir* is begotten; the Adam can now make distinctions between things; and it is this negating ability that makes him human, this thanks to the "irresistible influence" of Eve, "God's own best gift to him" (153).

The negative consequences of this gift must not be overlooked, however, for the ability to make discriminations also limits human beings. It "makes the seeming life but most lethal death" by isolating human beings from each other, by letting them believe (temporarily) that they are self-sufficient and alienated from man and God through a "a stupendous though most merciful illusion" (155). The very "differential element" (154) that makes the now vivified creature human and is necessary to make (Adam)Eve become the divine-natural-human "female Adam," does, in the meantime, not only alienate (Adam)Eve from God and all the other (Adam)Eves, but makes (him)her a "prig." And, as James Junior recalls in his autobiography,

> Our father's prime horror was of *them* – he cared only for virtue that was more or less ashamed of itself. . . . Thus we had the amusement, since I can really call it nothing less, of hearing morality, or moralism as it was more invidiously worded, made hay of in the very interest of character and conduct; these things suffering much, it seemed, by their association with the conscience – that is the *conscious* conscience – the very home of the literal, the haunt of so many pedantries.[20]

Nevertheless, his alienation and isolation are exactly what will eventually allow for "our social and aesthetic regeneration."

The vivified, split conscience gives the creature the freedom which (he)she will later discover to be the grounds of (his)her fellowship with God. In the meantime, it causes all sorts of complications that alienate (Adam)Eve from God, just "as the image necessarily stands in subjective antagonism to its original" (46):

> And this conscious or contingent separation of creature from creator is all that is meant by the creator giving him natural selfhood, or *quasi* life in himself. A creative – which of necessity is an infinite – love can have no shadow of respect to itself in creating, but only to the creature, or what is not itself. Hence its supreme aspiration must be to lift its

creature at any risk out of dumb creatureship into intelligent sonship, i.e. out of fatal into free conditions of life, out of necessary into contingent relations with itself, by endowing him with self-consciousness (which means sensible *alienation from, or otherness than,* itself), that so his subsequent frank and spontaneous reaction towards infinite goodness and truth may be eternally secured and promoted. (136)

Prefacing his further remarks on this aspect of the development of conscience and consciousness with a plea – "Let me insist then upon being perfectly understood" (136) – that signals his desperate sense of the difficulty of explaining how the *vir* is begotten, not created, of the *homo,* James forges on trying to describe how the *vir* "stamps me consciously free, i.e. makes me to my own perception praiseworthy or blameworthy as I do well or ill." This ground of conscience prepares the future for the divine-natural-humanity by allowing the possibility of "a spiritual fellowship or equality between [God and humans]"(137).

Just as the begetting of the *vir* was difficult to describe because it both suggests and denies what the state of relations between actual men and women is and should be (in other words, the allegorical is conflated with the literal and historical), so does this next transition from the human to the divine-natural-human fellowship (the "female Adam") defy a description that does not seem prescriptive of a behavior that reinforces many aspects of the oppressive status quo of domestic relations between men and women. Yet the difference is that in James's revision of heterosexual relations, each person is there freely, spontaneously. No true marriage can tolerate coercion. To illustrate how this transition is to take place James uses the example of the obligation the father/husband owes to his family and other dependents as head of the family not to use his "domestic rule" for his own benefit but only for theirs, a position and power he will gladly renounce "whenever they are ready to discern the spiritual scope of the law, and accept all the obligations it imposes."[21] The father cannot claim authority over them without provoking "their well-grounded disgust and aversion" and thus losing any claim even to their "forbearance." If he is "habitually false, tyrannical, or simply self-seeking," he deserves "to be treated only as a madman" and would be in a just society. But if his "domestic rule" is challenged when he is not being odious, then his responsibility is to offer another interpretation of his position to the rebel:

He, to be sure, is the provisional head of the family, but they are the family itself; and he can only vindicate his headship, therefore, by persistently ruling the family primarily in the interest of justice and only derivatively thence in his own.[22]

It is thus by a series of acts of spontaneous resistance, not by perpetual obedience to the law, that the creature becomes first human and then the divine-natural-human. Only by exercising his/her freedom in these revolts against the constraints first of nature and then of moralism is the spontaneous creativity of the divine-natural-human realized and fellowship attained at last. The "female Adam" comes into being as an inclusive heterosocial relation, a relation that is possible only because there have been and continue to be gender differences in play in the lives of each individual man and woman.

Oedipus and Eve

For the modern reader it is impossible not to consider these issues of gender difference in psychoanalytic terms. It is, moreover, particularly useful to do so because this comparison clarifies the common assumption in James Senior's and Freud's versions of gender difference, an assumption that was not shared by their contemporaries, namely, that sexual identity is not biologically determined but rather that it is created simultaneously with consciousness. James Senior's enigmatic and ambiguous conception of Eve shares with the theory of the castration complex a refutation of the naturalistic and metaphysical dogmas concerning the meaning of sex.

Freud refuted the biologically deterministic beliefs of his contemporaries with his theory of the Oedipus complex as the explanation of the creation of gender identity. Men and women are not born but made. Freud's interest is in how that difference comes into being, and here he is on common ground with James Senior. He, too, would be ready to ask: "How is moral life generated of mere physical existence?" although not ready to follow with James Senior's (theo)logical restatement of that question: "How does the dull opaque earth of our nature become translucent with heavenly radiance?"(148). Freud came to reject any theory that assumed that gender identity was natural, and (according to Juliet Mitchell, on whose clear interpretation of this complex history I rely) his later writings on the castration complex can be understood as corrections of the biologistic assumptions that still haunt the earliest formulations of the theory of the Oedipus complex, specifically, the assumption that heterosexuality was the natural resolution of this complex.[23]

Equally as important as the rejection of a biological explanation for gender identity is the way Freud explains in his later writings on the castration complex how the subject comes into being through a process much like that James Senior calls "vivification." In "The Splitting of the Ego in the Process of Defense" (the unfinished paper he was working on at the time of his death)[24] Freud argues that the subject only comes into being as divided and as gendered. This paper, Mitchell writes, "describes the formation of the ego in a moment of danger (of threatened loss) which results in a primary split from which it never recovers" (25). The split is caused by "the ineffable presence of a symbolic threat (the 'event') to which one is inevitably subjected as the price for being human" (17). Lacan's description of the subject as "a being that can only conceptualise itself when it is mirrored back to itself from the position of another's desire" emphasizes the division that creates the self as well as the role of the Other by means of which the self becomes a subject, an "I" (5). This coming into being is, however, anything but pacific. "Once more," writes Mitchell, "Lacan underlines and reformulates Freud's position. The castration complex is *the* instance of the humanisation of the child in its sexual difference" (19).

In Henry James Senior's theology, the creation (or rather begetting) of the subject takes place by means of alienation and consciousness of that "subjective antagonism" between individuals and God. In spite of this painful alienation, which is enacted as self-denial and felt as frustration, the reward is the humanization of the natural man in the sense that (he)she now participates in the exchange of "differential element[s]" (154), as James Senior says, or, as Lacan would say, language, or the symbolic. As with the story of "vivification," it is difficult to explain in linear narrative terms what is going on when at this moment of transformation. Samuel Weber characterizes the problem lucidly:

> this form of repression [of the castration complex] is supposed to differentiate the psychic apparatus and yet, as it is also a purely intrapsychic instance, it must presuppose this differentiation. Yet as soon as one ceases to consider primal repression as an intrasubjective product and begins to see it as an effect of the signifier in the structuring of the subject, the paradox becomes intelligible. It can be understood as

an allegory of the difference that *renders* discursive logic and its linearity possible while simultaneously restricting and displacing them. It is in this sense that Lacan can claim that language is the condition of the unconscious, for the unconsious "is" only (before) the bar that strikes and subjects the subject to the signifier.[25]

The humanization that is made possible by the prohibitions that engender the castration complex – this entry by the split gendered subject into the realm of the symbolic – necessarily brings with it the dissatisfaction indicated by this alienated doubleness. Freud wrote: "We must reckon with the possibility that something in the nature of the sexual instinct itself is unfavourable to the realization of complete satisfaction."[26] To be a (gendered) subject is to be lacking. The subject, as Lacan described it, is the "being created in the fissure of a radical split" (5), a gap that can never be breached. This gap has been created by the prohibition of the protosubject's desire. What James has called the "paternal" principle that Eve exercises, Lacan calls "the Name of the Father." Their prohibitive function is a mixed blessing: it makes the subject human and defines humanity as such as being dissatisfied.

The remedy, such as it is, to dissatisfaction is misrepresentation. Lacan explains in "The Signification of the Phallus" why creating a relation between the sexes depends not on the satisfaction of desire but on the involuntary and unavoidable misrepresentation of desire:

> Thus desire is neither the appetite for satisfaction, nor the demand for love, but the difference that results from the subtraction of the first from the second, the phenomenon of their splitting [*Spaltung*].
>
> One can see how the sexual relation occupies this closed field of desire, in which it will play out its fate. This is because it is the field made for the production of the enigma that this relation arouses in the subject by doubly "signifying" it to him: the return of the demand that it gives rise to, as a demand on the subject of the need – an ambiguity made present on to the Other in question in the proof of love demanded. The gap in this enigma betrays what determines it, namely, to put it in the simplest possible way, that for both partners in the relation, both the subject and the Object, it is not enough to be subjects of need, or objects of love, but that they must stand for the cause of desire.

> This truth lies at the heart of all the distortions that have appeared in the field of psychoanalysis on the subject of sexual life.[27]

The "doubly 'signifying' " role of sexual difference works by its ambiguous and (mis)representative function: it "must stand for the cause of desire" – but it cannot be it. Thus misrepresentation or distortion is necessary to the development of the subject in relation to all objects of desire. James would have learned this from Swedenborg's celestial testimony, if from no more earthly source.[28]

The doubling of discourse is what makes the speaking, gendered subject possible. The subject only becomes possible because differences of gender are already in play – and remain in play. And so also with differences of language:

> This negative place, this "dislocation," comes to be occupied by various instances: first by the mother as that utterly Other in the sense of the demand for love; then by the father as the forbidding, castrating instance which also introduces the law; and finally the phallus "itself," as the selfless, self-effacing mark that bars the place and splits the subject. While the phallus thus marks the *decisive* moment of bifurcation in the trajectory of the subject, it at the same time remarks the structural condition of the latter's subjection – to language as medium of articulation and of difference.[29]

Lacan's famous formulation that the man has the phallus and the woman is the phallus has caused much puzzlement. Perhaps there is then no great risk in suggesting, in the hope of clarifying both that statement and James Senior's conception of "the female Adam" that each phallocentric description of the subject includes rather than effaces the history of gender differences that have made the subject possible and makes *gender* rather than *maleness* the necessary differential value.[30]

Neither Freud nor Lacan would have shared James Senior's optimistic vision of the divine-natural-humanity or "the female Adam" insofar as it foresees the harmonization of human desires. Jacqueline Rose characterizes the pessimism of psychoanalysis nicely when she writes: "The subject has to recognise that there is desire, of lack in the place of the Other, that there is no ultimate certainty or truth, and that the status of the phallus is a fraud (that is, for Lacan, the meaning of castration)."[31] But the value that Freud and Lacan both place on language as the subjecting, differentiating medium through which human relations are made more or less satisfactory suggests that an adequately complex use of language might make fellowship possible, if never perfect. Divine-natural-humanity is (obviously) not a simple but a complex social relation. The phallus may well be a fraud; but "the female Adam" is one who perhaps makes interesting use of her complex subjectivity for the sake of fellowship such as it can be in this world. The female art of conversation that makes use of the doubled, split, differentiated trope of irony for the sake of heterosocial relations might be not a fraud, but as real a thing as is possible.

IRONY MAKES LOVE

MRS. HENRY JAMES AND WASHINGTON, A.C./D.C.

One need not waste time arguing that James Junior did not exactly share his father's vision of "the female Adam" and the divine-natural-humanity or Fourier's "calculus of passionate attraction,"[1] as concocted in *Le nouveau monde amoureux*.[2] But the assumptions that sustained this theology did become a part of the son's characteristic way of interpreting social relations generally and gender relations specifically. He took for granted the basic premises of his father's Christian socialism: that meaning was not made individually, but socially; that meaning was made by difference, not essence; that the transformation of the individual took place by relations with other people who were different from oneself; and, thus, that the other people were necessary (even if they were irritating) to the process of increasing one's own sociality. James wonderfully summed up these lessons when he recalled the frequent paternal injunction, "that we need never fear not to be good enough if we were only social enough: a splendid meaning indeed being attached to the latter term."[3]

Although James claimed in his later autobiography that his father's ideas stood about like "so many scattered glasses of the liquor of faith," which one could taste or not as one pleased – and that he generally abstained – it is clear that he was fluent in the fundamental beliefs of his parent.[4] For example, Henry James "Junior" read his father's review of John Stuart Mill's *The Subjection of Women* and Horace Bushnell's *Woman's Suffrage: The Reform against Nature* and wrote to his father in the paternal idiom, speaking of "the fate of collective humanity" and the "organization of the actual social body."[5] For my present purposes it is especially important that the point he sees fit to make about the *Atlantic* review concerns gender differences and that he recognizes that his father's version of difference was not the conventional one. James writes that he "decidedly liked" his father's article – "I mean for the matter" – and then specifies the grounds of his pleasure: "I am very glad to see someone not Dr. Bushnell and all that genus insist upon the distinction of the sexes."[6] Dr. Bushnell's version of the distinction of the sexes was, properly speaking, sexist, for it proclaimed that the power of man over woman was justified on natural and divine grounds.

An odd couple of examples in which I will trace the connections between the beliefs of the Henry Jameses Senior and Junior concerning the value of gender, heterosexual and heterosocial relations will conclude my analysis and will also indicate the way in which the transformation of the past into the present for the sake of the future is worked out in the most social of human relations. First, James's narration of a scene from the story of his own Oedipal drama brings into focus his conception of how irony makes love in the conversation of that most ephemeral member of this famous family, Mrs. Henry James. Second, James's astonishing personification of the nation's capitol in *The American Scene* is the most utopian narrative in all his oeuvre, being almost phalansterian in its vision of the possibilities for civilization once the relations between men and women have been revived by means of an artful conversation in which the woman's use of irony in conversation creates the ever unfulfilled (but necessary) promise of heterosocial happiness.

The (Out)Law of the Mother

It is fitting that it should be in James's own recollection of a scene of his Oedipal drama that the mark of his father's hand is most visible just at the moment that it is being overwritten by the son's construction of his identity as a writer who was *not* his father. In spite of his claim in the autobiography that his father's religious instruction within the family was "issued in all the vividest social terms" (337) and not in didactic, coercive ones, James Senior's writing is relatively abstract. In order to become a speaking/ gendered/writing subject, young Henry must find a style of his own. He is able to do so because his mother's art of conversation makes irony the occasion for love.

The story of how young Henry becomes the subject of his own writing makes sense in the context of his representation of his parents's marriage in this autobiographical volume. He was well aware of the terms in which his father conceived his own marriage. In the last letter James Senior wrote to Henry, his idiosyncratic meaning of "social" is nicely illustrated. He recalls how much his recently deceased wife doted on their second son, the "angel" of the family, and confesses (no doubt not for the first time) what his marriage meant to him:

> She was not to me a "liberal education," intellectually speaking, as some one has said of his wife, but she really did arouse my heart, early in our married life, from its selfish torpor, and so enabled me to become a man. And this she did altogether unconsciously, without the most cursory thought of doing so, but solely by the presentation of her womanly sweetness and purity, which she herself had no recognition of.[7]

By arousing his "heart ... from its selfish torpor," Mrs. James played in her husband's case the role he believed proper to the oppositely sexed partner in the course of spiritual development: she was Eve, the *vir*, who made him human. She vivified him by her spontaneous love. Henry seems to see the redemptive, salvific potential of this marriage in terms very similar to those offered by his father when he writes that: "It showed us more intimately still what, in this world of cleft components, one human being can yet be for another ..." (343).

Of course, Henry saw this relationship from a different perspective insofar as it relates to him as the child of this happy union. The scene (narrated in a very brief, page-long passage) he recalls as the one in which his relations with his parents were supremely significant for him was his father's reading aloud to his mother from his " 'papers' that were to show her how he had this time at last done it." This scene was not unique but repeated frequently: it would be narrated in the imperfect tense. Though Henry was there under some coercion – "as I yielded first and last to many an occasion for being [present]" – his mother was, to his sense of things, there in all her freedom:

> No touch of the beautiful or the sacred in the disinterested life can have been absent from such scenes – I find every such ideally there; and my memory rejoices above all in their presentation of our mother at her very perfectest of soundless and yet absolutely all-saving service and trust.
> (342)

Attempting to sketch a portrait of this particular lady presents the artist with a peculiar challenge, however. He finds that it is difficult to represent her because she does not seem to exist except in relation to the other characters in this scene. She does not have a character of her own.

On the one hand, the "complete availability and . . . smoothness of [her] surrender" makes for childhood bliss:

> We simply lived by her, in proportion as we lived spontaneously, with an equanimity of confidence, an independence of something that I should now find myself think of as decent compunction if I didn't try to call it instead morbid delicacy, which left us free for detachments of thought and flights of mind, experiments, so to speak, on the assumption of our genius and our intrinsic interest, that I look back upon as to a luxury of the unworried that is scarce of this world. (342)

She allows the children perfect freedom. She creates "the harmony that was for nine-tenths of it our sense of her gathered life in us, and of her having no other."

And yet, on the other hand, she is not without some kind of (omni)presence: "what account of us all can pretend to have gone the least bit deep without coming to our mother at every penetration?" How could she both have been so undefined and yet so defining to the family as a whole? This ambiguity troubles Henry:

> The only thing that I might well have questioned on these occasions was the possibility on the part of a selflessness so consistently and unabatedly active of its having anything ever left acutely to offer; to abide so unbrokenly in such inaptness for the personal claim might have seemed to render difficult such a special show of it as any particular pointedness of hospitality would propose to represent. . . . She lived in ourselves so exclusively, with such a want of use for anything in her consciousness that was not about us and for us, that I think we almost contested her being separate enough to be proud of us – it was too like our being proud of ourselves. (343)

First stating the problem again abstractly – she was "our possibility of *any* relation" – James then addresses this paradox metaphorically: she was "the very canvas itself on which we were floridly embroidered. . . ." The relation of the "florid" figure to the blank ground leaves unspecified the agent of this work. She makes the differentiating mark possible, but how does she do this, when she herself is without any "particular pointedness"?

Mrs. James's ambiguous role can be understood in the terms offered by her husband's scheme of psychospiritual salvation but only as they are dramatized in the writing of her son. She seems to represent two different incommensurable relations to her children only if the whole story is not told. Told, and told again. Imperfectly, yet with the same happy ending each time.

Looking back again at the image of "our mother listen[ing], at her work, to the full music of the 'papers,' " James begins to offer his critique of his father as a writer that shows how important both parents are, how important their differences are, to his development as a subject and a writer. His father's intrusion into the pre-Oedipal bliss of his undifferentiated union with his mother is experienced as a prohibition of the pleasure that is most desired by the son: "The fun was of course that I wanted in this line of diversion something of the coarser strain" than that offered by the father's performance for the mother:

> *There* was the dim dissociation, there my comparative poverty, or call it even frivolity, of instinct: I gaped imaginatively, as it were, to such a different set of relations. I couldn't have framed stories that would have succeeded in involving the least of the relations that seemed most present to *him;* while those most present to myself, that is more complementary to whatever it was I thought of as humanly most interesting, attaching, inviting, were the ones his schemes of importances seemed virtually to do without. Didn't I discern in this from the first a kind of implied snub to the significance of mine? – so that, in the blest absence of "pressure" which I have just sought here passingly to celebrate, I could brood to my heart's content on the so conceivable alternative of a field of exposure crammed with those objective appearances that my faculty seemed alone fitted to grasp. (339)

The father's "implied snub" to that which the son desires makes the son defiant. Prohibition begets negation.

The process of the son's differentiation as a writing subject begins as a critique of the paternal style, which is deemed to be limited:

> Was not the reason [I most of all seemed to wish that we might have been either much less religious or much more so] at bottom that I so suffered, I might almost have put it, under the impression of his style, which affected me as somehow too philosophic for life, and at the some time too

living, as I made out, for thought? – since I must weirdly have opined that by so much as you were individual, which meant personal, which meant monotonous, which meant limitedly allusive and verbally repetitive, by so much you were not literary or, so to speak, *largely* figurative. My father had terms, evidently strong, but in which I presumed to feel, with a shade of irritation, a certain narrowness of exclusion as to images otherwise – and oh, since it was a question of the pen, so multitudinously! – entertainable. (344)

By extrapolating from the patrimonial semiotic web of otherwise eccentric associated meanings – "individual" means "personal" means "monotonous" means "not literary," thus not an overwhelming figure – the son indulges in an iconoclastic appropriation of the father's instrument of signification par excellence: the pen. He revises the standards by which style is judged even while he abides by its supreme importance as a value. His rebellion, which is still an identification with the father's literary propensities, is a submission to the letter of the law of the father – but with a revisionary difference:

> Variety, variety – *that* sweet ideal, *that* straight contradiction of any dialectic, hummed for me all the while as a direct, if perverse and most unedified, effect of the parental concentration, with some of its consequent, though heedless, dissociations. I heard it, felt it, saw it, both shamefully enjoyed and shamefully denied it as form, though as form only; . . .
> (344)

This veritable revel of revolt against the exclusionary isolation of the father's "dialectic" is "perverse" because it is heterogeneous: it is made possible by the heterosexual difference of the mother from the father. This sentence continues:

> and I owed thus supremely to my mother that I could, in whatever obscure levity, muddle out some sense of my own preoccupation under the singular softness of the connection that she kept for me, by the outward graces, with that other and truly much intenser which I was so little framed to share. (344)

The paternal letter is, no matter what its intention, always already inadequate for the son's needs, which can only be satisfied not *by* his mother but by the way in which *she represents for him the "other."*
Her difference indicates for the son the incompleteness of the

father and prefigures the possibility of his own independence. She does this by breaking her silence without surrendering her "all-saving service and trust." She does it by the most delicate irony:

> The happiest household pleasantry invested our legend of our mother's fond habit of address, "Your father's *ideas,* you know – !" which was always the signal for our embracing her with the last responsive finality (and, for the full pleasure of it, in his presence). Nothing indeed so much as his presence encourages the licence. . . . (333)

This is irony at the father's expense, which he can well afford because he is immediately recompensed by the family as a whole. The mother dissents from the letter of the paternal law and thereby begets familial harmony. For the son in question, her irony mediates his rebellious yet submissive relation to his father: she represents the possibility of being otherwise without forsaking the pleasures of human relations.

By representing irony as the means by which the differently gendered person creates a sense of possible transformation for the subject, James renders a recognizably human version of the story of divine-natural-humanity. He shows how the same person – his mother – can play two different roles for him when the configuration of relationships changes. The mother, by her doubleness, seems to embody as well as speak irony. When the intrusion of the father (here the Eve, *vir*) disrupts their bliss, she is no longer undifferentiated but can act as a transformative sign for her son in the course of his own development. (She can be the natural Adam at one moment, and the "female Adam" at another – as need be.) It is her difference *and* her ability to make the kind of difference that is characteristic of irony as a trope that are crucial to the happy ending of this story, however many times it is repeated.[8] She is and acts as an alternative to the letters of the father, speaking in her own style, and thus she represents the possibility of another point of view that does not exclude the first one but changes its meaning. She uses irony to make love.

This is obviously a very different reading of the possibilities for resolution of the Oedipus complex than those offered by Freud or Lacan. In the preceding chapter I suggested that for both of them language (or more generally the symbolic) offered the best hope for some satisfaction in the inevitably frustrating condition of being a split, gendered, human subject. Both Jameses imagine that this entry into the symbolic, into the realm of culture, might work out better than that. One important difference in these conceptions of the formation of the gendered subject is that what was *not* important was that he defined himself in relation to the phallus, which is the crucial step in the formation of the subject for Freud and Lacan. Mitchell explains that for them "the father stands in the position of the third term that *must* break the asocial dyadic unit of mother and child."[9] It is a symbolic function and thus actual fathers, like actual threats of castration, are not in question. It is the symbolic, imagined threat that differentiates the sexes by forbidding to the child the position of being the phallus desired by the mother. The phallus as Lacan theorizes it is the "mark around which subjectivity and sexuality are constructed [which] reveals, precisely, that they are constructed, in a division which is both arbitrary and alienating."[10]

But the third term in James's story does not only break a unity (the Adam split by Eve); it both is and creates a new one (the "female Adam"). There is a double movement in this genesis of gender by which James writes himself into being in relation to sexually differentiated beings.[11] His self-definition is not phallocentric but heterosocial.

It may be that these differing conceptions of the resolution of the Oedipus complex are possible because Lacan is relying on a Saussurian dyadic notion of the sign and James on something more like a triadic Peircean notion. John K. Sheriff finds "Peirce's theory superior to structuralist theory because Peirce emphasizes that humans are freed, rather than enslaved, by language." Elsewhere he formulates this difference in terms that are more closely related to the Lacanian description of the symbolic: "Symbols, according to Peirce, enable us to see. A Symbol for Peirce, like Thirdness in general, is a medium; a symbol for Derrida, like language in general, is a substitute." And this difference has very important social consequences:

> According to Peirce's theory of signs, we at least have some justification for the sense of certainty we have about our existential experience. Unlike the dyadic sign in which the world is lost in the crack, gap, abyss of nothingness, or whatever, the triadic sign gives us faith that we do indeed come to the world through signs, and the objects of experience do have meaning for us that is understandable to others whether or not they agree with the correctness of our views.[12]

One consequence of this kind of understanding of the value of difference is that, instead of having his object of desire always already being lost in the realm of the symbolic, as Lacan's is,

James is engaged in a network of differences that keeps him connected with other human beings.

Although Lacan was explicitly relying on the Saussurian notion of the sign in his reformulations of psychoanalytic theory and particularly in his important revision of the castration complex, it seems to me on the basis of my analysis of several important moments of personal transformation in James's work – particularly *The Sense of the Past* and this autobiographical anecdote – that something more like a Peircean, triadic notion of the sign might underlie the relationship of transference as it is practiced and theorized in psychoanalysis.

As I have suggested in several ways, at several points in the course of this book, the heterosociality of transference allows it to be transformative. Henry James Senior's belief in divine-natural-humanity may have given his son a dynamic story about the psychosocial development of individuals, but Henry abstracted from that story an understanding of the value of heterosocial relations in a way that freed him to imagine a variety of creative relations between men and women where his father had privileged marriage. Marriage for Henry was only one of several possible social institutions in which salvific heterosocial relations could flourish. He was both more phalansterian and more modern than his father.

But there must be gender differences in order for any institutions that govern social relations to thrive. His anxious and distressed analysis of the collapse of sexual distinctions in the America of 1904 is based upon his understanding of the beneficial role that this difference plays in the creation of identity, whether on the greater social or the intimate family scene. On only one occasion during his visit did he have occasion for any hope that American society would recognize the value of having the two differently defined sexes in ongoing social relations with each other. The nation's capital was unique in this sense.

Washington, A.C./D.C.

The only place in America in which James sees the beginnings of an alternative to the social segregation of the sexes is in Washington, D.C. There seems to be a different social standard that is in play there. He speaks of the way in which the behavior of the diplomatic corps introduces a currency of "smiles and inflections ... Washington being the one place in America, I think, where those qualities are the values and vehicles, the medium of ex-

change," and he indicates the grounds on which this difference
is possible when he speaks of the beauty and nobility of Mount
Vernon as being unthinkable detached from the person of
George Washington, "[s]ince it is not the possessive case, but the
straight, serene nominative, that we are dealing with. The whole
thing *is* Washington – not his invention and his property, but
his presence and his person. . . ."[13] The nominative is not the
customary case in America; the possessive is rather its distinguishing mark:

> It might fairly have been, I used to think, that the charming
> place – charming in the particular connection I speak of –
> had on its conscience to make one forget for an hour the
> colossal greed of New York. (342)

Washington might offer an alternative to the hyperpossessive case
of New York by creating its own alternative, nominative identity.

The possibility that Washington is organized by an alternative
axiology is also indicated by James's designation of it as "The City
of Conversation." Given his critiques in "The Question of Our
Speech" and "The Speech of American Women" of the impoverished condition of American speech and the high value he attributes to developed systems of articulation, such a nomination is
already a compliment. And the grounds on which this use of
"smiles and inflections" as the "medium of exchange" is possible
are almost foreseeable in the light of his estimate of the reasons
for the decline of speech and manners: "The value here was at
once that the place could offer to view a society, the only one in
the country, in which Men existed, and that rich little fact became
the key to everything." The reason why "Men" existed in Washington society was simple, yet awesome in its consequences: "Nobody
was in 'business' – that was the sum and substance of it; and for
the one large human assemblage on the continent of which this
was true the difference was huge" (345). This difference means
that the conversations in this city are not like those elsewhere in
America but more like those in Europe – not because of differences in topics of conversation but because both genders participate in them.

And because of this heterosociality, it is possible that Washington will develop an identity fitting for a national capital. The
means by which it develops this identity are not unlike those
by which the young Henry James did (as represented in the
autobiographical passage analyzed previously), and James takes a
great interest in, even identifies with, this adventure:

What *was,* at all events, better fun, of the finer sort, than
having one's self a stake in the outcome? – what helped the
time (so much of it as there was!) more to pass than just to
join in the so fresh experiment of constitutive, creative talk.
(344)

Conversation is thus the medium of self-creation in the capital, as
the development of his own style of writing was the young James's
medium. And the city, likewise, must go through a variety of
relations with others in order to make itself the sexually differentiated subject capable of the discriminations that are necessary
for "constitutive, creative talk."

Although James does not by any means belabor the allegorical
aspect of this description of how the City of Conversation is
creating it(her)self, the by-now-familiar outlines of this process of
self-definition can be discerned. This effort to create a subject
capable of making the distinctions that are necessary to its own
identity and to its negotiations with the world is one with which
James himself identifies as an American and as an artist. It is,
indeed, much like the struggle he himself had defining himself
in relation to his parents.

As with James Senior's version of the begetting of the subject
(the conscience, the paternal principle, Eve, or the *vir*), some
unexpected gender assignments make for a few slippery passages
between the allegorical and the literal descriptions of the value of
sexual difference. James is concerned both with the actual men
and women of Washington and with Washington herself. His
choice of this gender for the city named for the Father of Our
Country is, moreover, highly significant as an indication of his
revision of the emphasis on the male that haunts the phallocentric terminology of the castration complex. Washington (A.C.)/
D.C. is his "female Adam," the gender of the progenitor having
been transformed by heterosocial relations.

The story of Washington becoming a subject, a nominative,
begins, of course, with the undifferentiated state from which the
subject is to emerge, call it the natural Adam in James Senior's
terms or the "asocial dyad of mother and child" in Lacan's. The
territory of undifferentiation from which Washington is emerging
is the world of business, a world that, as James has claimed frequently throughout *The American Scene,* eschews, abhors, and
scorns difference:

What could strike one more than that it was the only way
in which, over the land, a difference *could* be made, and

than how, in our vast commercial democracy, almost any difference – by which I mean almost any exception – promptly acquires prodigious relief. (345)

Thus, oddly enough, the male world of "business" defines the "asocial" state of undifferentiated relations – usually associated with the mother – that must be disrupted for the subject to come into being.

But so does the "social" sphere of women present a landscape unblemished by variety. With the businessman's abdication of the social field to the woman, the territory appears to James as featureless: "It lies there waiting, pleading from all its pores, to be occupied – the lonely waste, the boundless gaping void of 'society' " (345). In James's terms it is the absence of sexual difference that makes the social wasteland sterile, not the presence, as it were, of a "feminine" absence or void. No such "traditional" assignments of gender are feasible in this scenario as it develops. This is the barren situation of the American "woman produced by a woman-made society" who "in her manner of embodying and representing her sex has fairly made of her a new human convenience" serving, unwittingly, the businessman by taking care of all the nonbusiness in a way that James thinks unprofitable to herself in the long-run, as soon as the "first flush of . . . triumph" at having the field to herself has passed (347, 351).[14]

The crisis, or as James calls it in a running head, "The Rupture of the Compact," occurs when this order of things is challenged. The protosubject's longing to continue in this undifferentiated state is frustrated. The woman, for whom the undisputed domination of society is as dear as it has been rare, will not surrender her dominion willingly, and will, understandably, resort to all sorts of subterfuge and deception to maintain her position of power. Her "masterstroke," James says, has been "to represent the situation as perfectly normal." In this she has been aided by "her so 'sleeping' partner, the strange creature, by her side." James's metaphor evokes both Genesis and the mysteries of the market that trades in intangible property interests. It is as if Eve awoke to find Eden hers alone to do with it what she would, or as if she were engaged in some sleazy business deal and fraudulently represented herself as the only person involved. This odd couple, in any case, "disposed together in the American picture, . . . testif[ies], extraordinarily, to the *successful* rupture of a universal law . . ." (346). That "universal law" is simply that society is heterosexual, that gender differences are marked.

The force that threatens to disrupt these sexually undifferentiated states of male business and female "society" is thus a representative of that "universal law." It is, as another running title informs us, "The Presence of Men" in society that precipitates the crisis. Having "discovered that he *can* exist in other connection than that of the Market, and that all he has therefore to settle is the question of whether he may," the "Man" has "socially found himself" and the scene is transformed: "Man is solidly, vividly present, and the presence of Woman has consequently, for the proposed intensity, to reckon with it." But how has he done this?

> It would be awkward and gross to say that Man has dealt any
> conscious blow at the monopoly of his companion, or that
> her prestige, as mistress of the situation, has suffered in any
> manner a noted abatement. (349)

If he has not consciously insisted upon his own importance as an element in the equation of society, perhaps he has unconsciously done so by means of becoming involved in relations other than those of the "Market." There is another kind of man in Washington.

The "universal law" is represented in Washington by the European "diplomatic body," which, however, James finds "more characteristically 'abysmal' [there] than elsewhere, more impenetrably bland and inscrutably blank" (344). The "Father" may be somewhat broken down, but he is still a force to reckon with because he knows who he is, while the emerging subject (Washington) does not yet. His blankness in the face of this upstart's "positive quest of an identity of some sort, much rather – an identity other than merely functional and technical" – is understandable: it is not his "concern to help the place intellectually to find itself." Not only does he not have "a stake in the game," but to have one "was the last thing a foreign representative would wish to confess to, this being directly opposed to all his enjoined duties." It is rather his "mission to leave all such vaguely and, so far as may be, grotesquely groping: so apt are societies, in finding themselves, to find other things too." The "spirit of the old-time Legations" is expressed by their "detachment from the whole mild convulsion of effort" and aloofness, "alarm" and "amusement." Such is the paternal role and attitude toward the aspiring subject in whose attainment of an identity and its attendant critical perspective he has no interest. It is, in fact, contrary to his interest to have a subject in competition with himself.

Nevertheless, he unwittingly plays two roles that are important

in the development of Washington's identity: he is both a forbidding antagonist against whom Washington must define herself in
their struggle for the same desired end of having an identity; and
he is the representative "European" man who is distinguished
from the usual American man by his participation in a society
composed of both men and women. He makes "The Return of
the Male" (another running title!) possible in principle, not because he *is* male but because he represents a sexually differentiated and related subjectivity. He is, in James Senior's theology,
the aspect of the *vir* or the Eve that is the law that makes conscience possible by alienating the subject from himself or herself.
In Lacanian terms, he is the Name of the Father.

But what needs to be emphasized here is that the "Europe"
that he represents is not the imposition of male authority and
privilege. He represents the creation of identity by means of
gender difference, which can be and has been historically realized in a variety of ways. This is the meaning that James gives to
"Europe" in his closing remarks on the subject of Washington's
emerging identity. He suggests that the "social picture" of Washington is "harmonious" because the women are "happily, sooth-
ingly, proportionately, and no more than proportionately, participant and ministrant." Yet this is not because they have simply
reconstructed or submitted to the imposition of some replica of
the Old World gender hierarchies. Having been the dominant
"participant[s]" in their own territory, they will not be merely
"ministrant[s]" in their reunited state:

> They could not, one reasoned, have been, in general, so
> perfectly agreeable unless they had been pleased, and they
> could not have been pleased without the prospect of gain-
> ing, by the readjusted relation, more on the whole, than
> they were to lose; without the prospect even again perhaps
> of truly and insidiously gaining more than the other benefi-
> ciary. That *would* be, I think, the feminine conception of a
> readministered justice. Washington, at such a rate, in any
> case, might become to them as good as "Europe," and a
> Europe of their own would obviously be better than a Eu-
> rope of other people's. There are, after all, other women on
> the other continents. (351–2)

Presumably these "other women" make of "the readjusted relation" their own "Europes" as well, such as suit their social needs.

For Washington to have a "Europe" of her own, she must learn
how to make the most of having different genders in relation to

each other. Obviously, the allegorical and the literal dimensions of James's analysis are enmeshed here because he refers to "Washington" as "she," and yet what makes her different from other American cities is that her identity is constituted by the sexual difference that means "male" and "female." In other words, the purpose of forming a social identity is so that men and women will learn to get along in ways that contribute to their common welfare, or, in James Senior's terms, fellowship. Again, Washington is gendered heterogeneously: A.C./D.C, the "female Adam."

And it is at this point that things begin to get really interesting. For now consciousness begins to create interest; it comes into its own by making what it has inherited into something new. James recalls the law of his father *and* his mother:

> As I reconsider both my own and my brother's early start . . . it is quite for me as if the authors of our being and guardians of our youth had virtually said to us but one thing, directed our course but by one word, though constantly repeated: Convert, convert, convert![15]

Or, as he might convert the parental injunction to fit the present case: Converse, converse, converse!

The beneficial effect on the character of Washington of the participation in this conversation by men and women (for "[t]he victim of the effacement, the outcast at the door, has all the while we have been talking of him, *talked himself* back" onto the social scene [351]) will be shown by the increasing refinement of the good conversation and good manners that are now possible. Men and women and Washington, most of all, will benefit by the criticism of the other sex from which they had been shielded in their separate spheres. If the American woman may be "the least criticized object, in proportion to her importance, that ever adorned" a social scene (348), the American uncriticized man is just as appalling. Writing of the drummers he encountered everywhere on his train journeys, he sees them as "victims and martyrs" because "they hadn't *asked,* when one reflected, to be almost the only figures in the social landscape," anymore than had the women in their wasteland. What is lacking is "other *kinds* of persons, other types, presences, classes." Or, as James poses the point in his most theoretical terms:

> Wondrous always to note is this sterility of aspect and this blight of vulgarity, humanly speaking, where a single type has had the game, as one may say, all in its hands. Character

is developed to visible fineness only by friction on a large scale, only by its having to reckon with a complexity of forces – a process which results, at the worst, in a certain amount of social training.

No kind of person – that was the admonition – is a very good kind, and still less a very pleasing kind, when its education has not been made to some extent by contact with other kinds, by a sense of the existence of other kinds, and, to that degree, by a certain relation with them. . . . They [the drummers] would fall into their place at a touch, were the social proposition, as I have called it, completed; they would then help, quite subordinately assist, the long sentence to be read – relieved of their ridiculous charge of supplying all its clauses. (427–9)

These men have suffered from their lack of contact with women: "What women did they live with," James asks after observing their manners and their speech, "what women, living with them, could yet leave them as they were?" (426); just so has the woman – "a new human convenience" (347) – suffered by her isolation from men.

Thus the sequel to the "male privilege of correction" to which James refers in his *Harper's Bazar* essay is realized in the heterosociality of Washington:

The tone was, so to speak, of *conscious* self-consciousness, and the highest genius for conversation doubtless dwelt in the fact that the *ironic* spirit was ready always to give its very self away, fifty times over, for the love, for any quickening of the theme. (344; my emphasis)

Here James theorizes what he had witnessed at home, the salvific irony of Mrs. James, the trope that simultaneously divides and unifies for the sake of generating meaning and more meaning. Here also is delight in social intercourse as the re-creation of human freedom: the pleasure in giving of the self that makes of society a fellowship and of life an art.

The split in the consciousness of the subject that is so catastrophic in the psychoanalytic theory of the castration complex can be formulated as irony that is highly productive of meaning. Freud would agree with this proposition so far – sublimation is an alternative to suffering – but James seems to allow for a happiness that goes beyond sublimation and becomes love, the transformation of "*conscious* self-consciousness" into the sense that "quicken[s]" life. Washington must be gendered as a heterosocial woman because of the role that she is to play in the development of the nation. This attribution of transformative powers to the woman is a residue of his father's conception of the "female Adam" – "something very much more than either male or female – something, in fact, divinely different from either" – in the redemptive scheme of divine-natural-humanity.[16] Washington cannot play her role without being both male and female, without being both George of Mount Vernon and (the District of) Columbia, but it is by her ironic interpretation of past social relations that new and better ones become possible. In his allegory of asymmetrical sexual difference, it is the heterosocial woman who is characterized as making a difference for social relations. I think, for example, of Maggie at the end of *The Golden Bowl*, having gotten at least some of what she wanted and needed by interpreting and thus recreating her marriage. I recall Ralph Pendrel's enigmatic statement in *The Sense of the Past*, when he declares that Aurora is one of "The women. *The* women" who make a difference he cannot explain but which he comes to understand, happily, through his otherworldly journey.[17] I think of the one moment in *The Ivory Tower* when social relations are transformed from the awkward to the harmonious by the irony of Cissy Foy, who turns a faux pas into the possibility for greater heterosociability. But can the ironic "grace" of one girl make a difference in a social setting like that of Newport or will irony show its other side: Rosanna Gaw wonders whether "a young creature you weren't quite sure of [could] use a weapon of such an edge only for good?"[18]

The relationship between men and women is neither hierarchical nor symmetrical in James's schema. Each gender exercises a corrective effect on the other in the course of their ongoing social relations and thereby contributes to the "friction on a large scale" and the "complexity of forces" that alone can develop "character . . . to visible fineness."

But what is the character that Washington, the representative of all that might be possible for American society, refines? Standing on the verge of this better world, as the natural-human, (Adam)Eve, has stood on the verge of union with the divine, what is the next step that carries her/him/them forward? What in the world do they talk about once the conversants are again on speaking terms? Why, the only possible subject of perennial interest: "Washington talks about herself, and about almost nothing else . . ." (342–3).

James explains immediately that this is one of the characteristics of capitals. Washington is just

> falling superficially indeed, on that ground, but into line with the other capitals. London, Paris, Berlin, Rome, goodness knows, talk about themselves: that is each member of this sisterhood talks, sufficiently or inordinately, of the great number of divided and differing selves that form together her controlling identity. (343)

Talking about oneself is anything but monotonous if identity is conceived as being composed of a "great number of divided and differing selves." Such is the case with the capital James knows best:

> London, for instance, talks of everything in the world without thereby for a moment, as it were, ceasing to be egotistical. It has taken everything in the world to make London up, so that she is in consequence simply doomed never to get away from herself. (343)

Although Washington is not yet doomed by her empire to be *that* interesting, her self-centered conversation represents

> one of the most natural and happiest, cases of collective self-consciousness that one knows . . . in ardent pursuit of some workable conception of its social self, and trying, meanwhile intelligently to talk itself, and even this very embarrassment, into a *subject* for conversation. (343)

She creates, in other words, by her ironic and complex conversation, both herself and the closest thing to social fellowship likely in this life. This is not the happy ending of the marriage allowed by the conventions of the romance in *The Sense of the Past;* it promises, however, a more real possibility for infinite conversation between men and women. As an alternative to the matrimonial stalemate of *The Ivory Tower,* this representation of heterosociality seems not only tolerable but desirable. Men and women are once again on speaking terms. Among other things, they might now begin to make sense of the past for the sake of the future. And with that happy thought, I end.

EPILOGUE

ON THE THIRD HAND

Or I would end, if there were not, as James well knew, always something more to be said. In this instance, what must be said now is both retrospective and prospective insofar as my conclusion ought to look toward some future if I have learned my lesson from James. That is to say, if I have learned not how to copy but how to interpret his method of making sense of the past to serve my own purposes.

Reading this fourth and last phase of James's career has shown the importance and complexity of connections between his writing and his cultural and political worlds. In the case of *The American Scene,* these connections have always been conspicuous in a way that they are not in *The Sense of the Past* and *The Ivory Tower.* This book has endeavored to show that the "geometry of his own" constructed by the artist reaches into realms of social life that James has generally been regarded as having ignored.

The weblike nature of James's constructions of meaning initially provided me with a model for exploring the historical relations of his texts to their times. Herbert Butterfield's description of a historical methodology that would eschew the "whig" interpretation of history suggested that metonymy might provide a methodological trope that would trace contiguities and differences, and thereby represent the past in terms that hinted at its own complexity rather than delineating its possible similarities to the present. To this end, I have read James's texts in dialogue with those of his contemporaries in order to show how terms and concepts such as "waste," "race," and "ethnicity" could be differentially interpreted at the turn of the century. Tracing these contemporary contiguities and differences of meaning displaces any sense of the past as being monolithic and clarifies James's position on a spectrum of political and social values that has been inadequately described by the binary opposition of "liberal–conservative."

However, this dialogue between contemporary texts might easily fall victim to another illusion of historicist writing, namely, that one could capture an image of the past as it *really* was, the very illusion that James critiques by placing the hero *The Sense of the Past* under its sway. In order to escape from this illusion, the hero must be saved by a very special kind of love. Recognizing this kind of love as a model for an interpretive possibility makes a critical (and unrecognized) feature of James's "geometry" come into focus. His web of signifying relations is not a rhizome; it is a construction of triads. The introduction of a third term into the dialogue is what makes new meanings possible, what makes a future possible that never repeats the past as it really was.

The third term assumes many guises in the situations I have analyzed in the course of this book. As many forms as it assumes, however, there are conventions that can be traced in the way it works to make meaning. I admit gladly that these conventions are only discernable to me in retrospect, having emerged from the process of looking for answers to particular questions about James and culture rather than from an a priori conviction. The third term – which is never a golden mean between opposites – always performs two semiotic functions simultaneously: by its introduction, it disrupts the relation between the first and second terms (a relation that can thwart the growth of semiosis and degenerate into dualistic opposition) by providing a ground for the recognition of their difference; also and at the same time, it creates a new meaning by introducing a link to a different set of possible relations than had been in play in the previous relation of the first two terms. The process is creative and endless and unpredicatable. Thus, it always suggests the possiblity of yet another (future) meaning.

James makes use of this triadic semiotic practice again and again to disrupt the various social impasses he witnesses: for example, the dyadic paralysis of nostalgia that polarizes relations between the past and present; or the black–white biologistic binarism that perpetrates racism; or the male–female social segregation that sustains sexism. The form of third term – acting like Peirce's interpretant – cannot be predetermined because it must assume a particular guise to relate to the circumstances at hand, the already given first and second terms. Thus, for Ralph Pendrel in *The Sense of the Past*, it is the transferential, agapic love of Nan that transforms his nostalgic fixation on the past into a desirable relation to the future; in *The American Scene* the dyad of taste and waste is transformed by the third term taking the form of excess out of which future use might be made; between blacks and whites a double consciousness that creates the triangulating possibility of seeing oneself as one is seen by the other may be disprovincializing; between men and women it is ironic, heterosocial conversation that vivifies relations, opening the possibility of using symbolic forms to create fellowship and art.

This interpretive practice is thus discernible as a kind of convention, one that forgoes being prescriptive as a kind of law. Because the model of this convention is found in Henry James Senior's psychospiritual theology, I believe that it would be possible to trace this semiotic practice throughout James's work. I have, however, focused on the specific forms it takes in the "fourth phase" in which he writes his last romance because *The American Scene* helps to make the cultural stakes of this practice clear. The flexibility and variety of the forms of the third term keep it from appearing as a repeated "figure in the carpet," but these attributes also indicate that in any situation, in any circumstance fraught by conflict, it is possible to find a third term to generate a new meaning in relation to the first and second terms. Without the third term, conflicts become polarized and paralyzed. When a suitable third term is brought into play by the interpreter, the sign of its success is the increased sociality of the parties concerned. In this Peircean sense James's interpretation is always pragmatistic, always directed toward the increase of meaning and social relations.

The creative, social role of the third term is what gave James the faith – no matter how dire the straits, how void the social scene, how gaping the conversation – that it was always possible to make new meanings, to find consciousness interesting, to create art, to make culture work for greater sociality. Tracing the conventions of his semiotic practice has cultural value for us (we who are James's future) when we make our own sense of James (who is our past).

In my own practice in this book I have experimented with this convention of the third term by explicitly introducing the concerns of my contemporaries into the dialogue of James with his contemporaries. My series of third terms is composed of theoretical issues articulated by Bataille (waste), Lacan (gender), Appiah (race), and others. My interpretations of James's texts thus are generated triadically in a way that avoids the presentism of the "whig" interpretation of history. My metonymic procedure does not claim an absolute and causal connection between the past and present as does the metphoric or analogic practice of the "whigs" or the New Historicists. My metonymic associations allow rather for the possibility of their own displacement – and for the growth of semiosis – because of a certain amount of arbitrariness in the selection of this third term: some other triad of contiguous associations could very well be as fruitful, although it would not necessarily serve the same use. Each chapter has its own framework or story because there is a variety of social uses and institutions I wish to interpret in these late texts by James, and thus I have chosen to vary the critical and cultural and theoretical contexts in which the reading takes place. By leaving some gaps between my critical frameworks, moreover, I also allow for the reader to continue the process of interpretation in which James is always interested for the sake of developing more rich and various social relations. By setting his texts in relation to those of his contemporaries and to a shifting series of third terms, I hope to have made a contribution to the conversation of interpretation that he believed is critical to creating a society in which it is meaningful to live and to love.

APPENDIX

EXCERPTS FROM THE *1900* AND *1915*
MANUSCRIPTS OF
THE SENSE OF THE PAST

―――――

The typescripts for both versions of *The Sense of the Past* are held by the Houghton Library at Harvard University (bMS Am 1237.8 boxes 1 and 2 and bMS Eng 1213 [73]), and are quoted by permission of the Houghton Library, Harvard University, and Bay James, Literary Executor of the James Estate.

The first passage in the selections given is from the 1915 New York Edition; the numbers preceding the passage refer to the pages of the New York Edition. The second passage, enclosed in brackets, is from the 1900 typescript. In each case James elaborates and subtly shifts the conception of the past and the hero's relation to it. What he wants to make clear is that, in spite of the comparison of Ralph's sensibility to that of the artist, there are important differences, and that Ralph's relation to the past is bound to get him into trouble because he wants the thing itself rather than the traces of its survival in the present.

Aurora to Ralph

33. At the intensity required, as you said, by any proper respect for itself, you proposed if possible yourself to arrive – art, research, curiosity, passion, the historic passion, as you called it, helping you.

[At the intensity you proposed, if possible yourself to arrive – art, research, curiosity, passion – yourself to arrive.]

Aurora Quoting Ralph's Book

34. "There are particular places where things have happened, places enclosed and ordered and subject to the continuity of life

216

mostly, that seem to put us into communication, and the spell is sometimes made to work by the imposition of hands, if it be patient enough, on an old object or an old surface." It's very wonderful, you know, your having arrived at that, your having guessed it, in *this place, which denies the old at every turn and contains so few of such objects and surfaces . . . I hope your old house will contain plenty of them.*

["There are particular spots where things have happened, that seem to put us into communication, and the spell is sometimes made to work by the imposition of hands, if it be patient enough, on an old object." . . . I hope your old house will contain plenty of such.]

* * * * * *

34. Her quotation of this twaddle, as it struck him, from his small uninformed Essay . . .,

[Her quotation of this twaddle, as it struck him, from his small Essay,]

The Cousin's Gift of the House

42. It was a mere town tenement, and none of the newest, but it was the best repayment of his debt he could make. He had nowhere seen the love of old things, of the scrutable, palpable past, nowhere felt an ear for stilled voices, as precious as they are faint, as seizable, truly, as they are fine, affirm a more remarkable power than in the pages that had moved him to gratitude.

[It was a mere town tenement, and none of the newest, but it was the best he could do. He had nowhere seen the love of old things, and the sense of what they might have still to say so vividly embodied as in the pages in question.]

* * * * * *

43. There were old things galore in Mansfield Square; the past he considered, held its state there for those with the wit to make it out; and, should his young kinsman accept his bequest, he would

find himself master of a scene in which a chapter of history –
obscure, though not so remote as might perhaps have been
wished – would perhaps by his intervention step more into the
light. The generations at least had passed through it, clinging
indeed as long as they might, and couldn't have failed to leave
something of their mark, which it would doubtless interest Mr.
Ralph to puzzle out. It was the testator's wish that he should do
so at his ease. The letter in fine was, as Ralph said, a deucedly
beautiful gentlemanly one, and the turn of the wheel of fortune.
The material advantage might be uncertain; but it was blessedly
not for the economic question, it was for the historic, the aesthetic, fairly in fact for the cryptic, that he cared. A big London
house sounded in truth on the face of the matter less like an aid
to research than like an exposure to rates and taxes, a legacy of
the order vulgarly known as thumping. But verily too even London, for our rare young man, was within the pale of romance,
His "other" passion in short had soon begun freshly to glow.

[There were old things in Mansfield Square; and, should his
young kinsman accept his bequest, he would find himself master
of a house in which a chapter of history – obscure, though not so
remote as might have been wished – would perhaps show a little
clearer. The generations at least had passed through it, and left
something of their mark. It was, as Ralph said, a deucedly beautiful gentlemanly letter, and the turn of the wheel of fortune was
simply prodigious. The material advantage might be equivocal;
but it was not for the economic question, it was for the historic,
the aesthetic, that he cared. A London house sounded in truth
on the face of the matter less like a contribution to it than like a
legacy of the order vulgarly known as thumping. But in truth too
even London, for poor Pendrel, was within the pale of romance,
His "other" passion in short glowed again.]

The House

46. Should he begin to make his way into the secrets, as they
hovered and hung there, wearing a sort of sensible consistency,
who could say where he might come out, into what dark deeps of
knowledge he might be drawn, or how he should "like," given
what must perhaps at the best stick to him of insuperable modern
prejudice, that face of some of his discoveries?

[Should he begin to read into the secrets, who knew where he might come out, or into the shadow of what strange knowledge he might find himself drawn?]

Ralph's Relation to the Past

48. On the day he disembarked in England he felt himself as never before ranged in that interest, counted on that side of the line. It was to this he had been brought by his desire to remount the stream of time, really to bathe in its upper and more natural waters, to risk even, as he might say, drinking of them. No man, he well believed, could ever so much have wanted to look behind and still behind – to scale the high wall into which the successive years, each a squared block, pile themselves in our rear and look over as nearly as possible with the eye of sense into, unless it should rather be called out of, the vast prison yard. He was by the turn of his spirit oddly indifferent to the actual and the possible; his interest was all in the spent and the displaced, in what had been determined and composed round-about him, what had been presented as a subject and a picture, by ceasing – so far as things ever cease – to bustle or even to be. It was when life was framed in death that the picture was really hung up. If his idea in fine was to recover the lost moment, to feel the stopped pulse, it was to do so as experience, in order to be again consciously the creature that had been, to breathe as he had breathed and feel the pressure that he had felt. The truth most involved for him, so intent, in the insistent ardour of the artist, was that art was capable of an energy to this end never yet to all appearance fully required of it. With an address less awkward, a wooing less shy, an embrace less weak, it would draw the foregone much closer to its breast. What he wanted himself was the very smell of that simpler mixture of things that had so long served; he wanted the very tick of the old stopped clocks. He wanted the hour of the day at which this and that had happened, and the temperature and the weather and the sound, and yet more the stillness from the street, and the exact look-out, with the corresponding look-in, through the window and the slant on the walls of the light of afternoons that had been. He wanted the unimaginable accidents, the little notes of truth for which the common lens of history, however the scowling muse might bury her nose, was not sufficiently fine. He wanted evidence of a sort for which there had never been documents enough, or for which documents mainly, however

multiplied, would never *be* enough. That was indeed in any case the artist's method – to try for an ell in order to get an inch. The difficulty, as at best it is, becomes under such conditions, so dire that to face it with any prospect one had to propose the impossible. Recovering the lost was at all events on this scale much like entering the enemy's lines to get back one's dead for burial; and to that extent was he not, by his deepening penetration, contemporaneous and present? "Present" was a word used by him in a sense of his own and meaning as regards most things about him markedly absent. It was for the old ghosts to take him for one of themselves.

[On the day he disembarked in England he felt himself as never before counted on that side. It was to this that his desire to reascend the stream of time, really to bathe in its upper waters. No man, he believed, had so much wanted to look back – to scale the high wall into what the years, each a squared block, pile themselves behind us and see as nearly as possible with the eye of sense what is on the other side. He was by the nature of his mind, [of?] a comparative indifference to the actual and the possible; his interest was for what had been determined round him, presented as a subject by ceasing – so far as things ever cease – to be. It was when life was framed in death that it really made the picture. His fancy in fine was to live again the lost moment, to be again in consciousness the creature that *had* been, to feel and breathe and touch and taste the foregone. What the ardour of the artist all insistent and reconstructed had most to say to him was that art was capable of an energy to this end never yet fully required of it. It could draw the foregone much closer to its breast. Its wooing had been too shy, its embrace too weak. It had lacked – for to this the matter came – the supreme passion. He wanted the very smell of the simpler mixture of things; he wanted the very tick of the old stopped clocks. He wanted the hour of the day at which things had happened, and the temperature and the weather and the sound from the street, and look of the window and the slant on the walls. He wanted the unimaginable accidents, the little notes of truth for which the common lens of history, however she might bury her nose, was not sufficiently fine. He wanted things of a sort for which there had never been documents enough, or for which documents only, however many, would never *be* enough. That was indeed in any case the artist's condition – to try for an ell in order to get an inch. The difficulty, in this light, is so dire that to face it with any prospect one had to want the impossible. Recovering the lost was at all events on this scale much like entering the enemy's lines to get back one's dead for burial; and to that extent was he not, by his deepening penetration, contemporaneous and present? "Present" was a word he used in a sense of his own. It meant as regards most things about him absent. The old ghosts might mistake him for one of themselves.]

The London Light

65. However else this air might have been described it was signally not the light of freshness and suggested as little as possible the element in which the first children of nature might have begun to take notice. Ages, generations, inventions, corruptions had produced it, and it seemed, wherever it rested, to have filtered through the bed of history. It made the objects about show for the time as in something "turned on" – something highly success-ful that he might have seen at the theatre. What was one to call the confounding impression but that of some stamp, some de-posit again laid bare, of a conscious past, recognizing no less that it recognized?

[Whatever else it had, this last element, it had the property of not being the light of freshness. It suggested as little as possible the air in which the first children of nature might have made their observations. Ages, generations, inventions, corruptions had pro-duced it, and it seemed, wherever it rested, to have filtered through the bed of history. It made the objects about him show for the time as in something "turned on." What was one to call it, at any rate, but the look of the conscious past?]

NOTES

================

Prologue

1. The inevitable question of any mutual influence between these writers is probably simple in the case of James and Veblen: although James may have heard of *The Theory of the Leisure Class* from his friend and editor William Dean Howells, I have found no evidence that he knew it or any of Veblen's other, more technical works or that Veblen read any of Henry James's work.

   In the case of James and C. S. Peirce the connection is more complicated. Peirce frequented the James family house in Cambridge and was a friend and colleague of William at Harvard. The enduring and heretofore unrecognized influence of Henry James Senior on Peirce's semiotics will be addressed in the first chapter of Part Two, "Civilization and Its Contents."

   There is a direct connection between Veblen and Peirce: while Peirce was a temporary lecturer at Johns Hopkins, Veblen, before failing to win a scholarship that would have allowed him to pursue his study of philosophy there, attended Peirce's 1881–2 lectures on "Elementary Logic." See Joseph Dorfman, *Thorstein Veblen and His America* (1934; New York: Viking,1945) 41.

   Du Bois, William James's student at Harvard, and Henry just missed meeting in Paris, but Henry read *The Souls of Black Folk* with admiration.

   I know of no contact between James and Riis or his work.

2. Stanford: Stanford UP, 1990; New York: Oxford UP, 1991. Other important works in this emerging tradition that have been recently published are Nancy Bentley's *The Ethnography of Manners: Hawthorne, James, Wharton,* Cambridge Studies in American Literature and Culture, vol. 90 (Cambridge: Cambridge UP, 1995) and Sara Blair's *Henry James and the Writing of Race and Nation,* Cambridge Studies in American Literature and Culture, vol. 99 (Cambridge: Cambridge UP, 1996), the latter published too late for me to take account of it in this work.

3. I should mention that I do not address these questions in the context of the autobiographical volumes and the New York Edition revisions, in part, because I found myself with more than enough to say about the three texts on which I focus and on which there is relatively little criticism and, in part, because there are several relatively recent works, especially William R. Goetz, *Henry James and "the Darkest Abyss of Romance"* (Baton Rouge: Louisiana State UP, 1986), Philip Horne, *Henry James and Revision: The New York Edition* (Oxford: Clarendon, 1990), and David McWhirter, ed., *Henry James's New York Edition: The Construction of Authorship* (Stanford: Stanford UP, 1995), that do focus intensively on these other productions.

Introduction

1. Henry Adams, *Mont Saint-Michel and Chartres,* ed. Ernest Samuels and Jayne N. Samuels (1904; New York: Library of America, 1983), 695.
2. Walt Whitman, "A Backward Glance O'er Travel'd Roads," in *Walt Whitman: Poetry and Prose,* ed. Justin Kaplan (New York: Library of America, 1982), 671.
3. Hamlin Garland, *Crumbling Idols* (Chicago: Stone and Kimball, 1894), 189.
4. Ralph Waldo Emerson, "The American Scholar," in *Essays and Lectures,* ed. Joel Porte (New York: Library of America, 1983), 70; Karl Marx, *The Eighteenth Brumaire of Louis Napoleon,* in *Selected Writings,* ed. David McLellan (Oxford: Oxford UP, 1977), 300.
5. See Anthony Grafton's "Renaissance Readers and Ancient Texts," in *Defenders of the Text: The Traditions of Scholarship in an Age of Science, 1450–1800* (Cambridge: Harvard UP, 1991), 23–46, for an excellent demonstration of how classical texts are read differently by two conflicting schools of humanists in order to see how foreign these scholars' ways of posing the problem of the relation of past and present are to the American assumption that one can break utterly with the past.
6. The romance as a genre lends itself, of course, to various kinds of play with temporal dislocation, be it into the future or the past. The classic study of the American romance tradition is Richard Chase, *The American Novel and Its Tradition* (Garden City, N.Y.: Doubleday, 1957). Two recent studies of the importance of the romance in American historical consciousness are by Emily Miller Budick: *Fiction and Historical Consciousness: The American Romance Tradition* (New Haven: Yale UP, 1989) and *Engendering Romance: Women Writers and the Hawthorne Tradition, 1850–1990* (New Haven: Yale UP, 1994). George Dekker's *The American Historical Romance* (Cambridge: Cambridge UP, 1987) is particularly valuable for the focus on Scott's contribution.

7. Henry James, *The American Scene*, introd. and notes by Leon Edel (1907; Bloomington: Indiana UP, 1968), 112–13.

8. Sigmund Freud, *Civilization and Its Discontents*, trans. James Strachey (1930; New York: Norton, 1961), 19, 17, 18.

9. David Lowenthal, *The Past Is a Foreign Country* (Cambridge: Cambridge UP, 1985); Anthony Kemp, *The Estrangement of the Past: A Study in the Origins of Modern Historical Consciousness* (New York: Oxford UP, 1991).

10. Paul de Man, "Literary History and Literary Modernity," in *Blindness and Insight: Essays in the Rhetoric of Contemporary Criticism, Theory and History of Literature* 7 (Minneapolis: U of Minnesota P, 1983), 142–65.

11. Warner Berthoff, "American Literature: Traditions and Talents," in *Fictions and Events: Essays in Criticism and Literary History* (New York: Dutton, 1971), 174.

12. Jean Seznec, *The Survival of the Pagan Gods*, trans. Barbara F. Sessions (1940; Princeton: Bollingen, 1953), 322.

13. Erwin Panofsky, "Renaissance and Renascences," *Kenyon Review* 6:2 (Spring 1944): 201–36.

14. Kemp's tracing of the association of innovation with heresy in the eyes of the church fathers *and* in the eyes of Luther is particularly valuable because it shows how unrevolutionary Luther intended to be, how much his ambition was to return to the pure, original state of Christianity, and how that desire for the origin becomes, in spite of itself, disruptive of any possibility of continuity.

15. John Carlos Rowe, *Henry Adams and Henry James: The Emergence of Modern Consciousness* (Ithaca: Cornell UP, 1976). See particularly the conclusion of the chapter on *The Education*. I am also referring, of course, to Frederick Jackson Turner's scheme of the progress of American civilization as famously articulated in "The Significance of the Frontier in American History," in *The Early Writings of Frederick Jackson Turner*, ed. Edward E. Everett (Madison: U of Wisconsin P, 1938), 183–229.

16. Herbert Butterfield, *The Whig Interpretation of History* (1931; London: G. Bell & Sons, 1951). All further references to this text are noted parenthetically.

17. In the introductory chapter, "The Idea of Conservatism," of *The Conservative Mind: From Burke to Eliot*, 7th rev. ed (Chicago: Regnery Books, 1986), Russell Kirk lists the "Belief in a transcendent order, or body of natural law, which rules society as well as conscience" as the first of what he calls the "six canons of conservative thought" (8). James would be disqualified on these grounds alone from any orthodox conservatism, important as his father's religious ideas were for him, a point I will make in a variety of ways in the course of this book.

18. James, *The American Scene*, 113.

19. Hayden White, *Metahistory: The Historical Imagination in Nineteenth-Century Europe* (Baltimore: Johns Hopkins UP, 1973).

20. In identifying the processes of selection and those of metaphor (and contrasting them with the processes of combination and metonymy), I am relying on the classic analysis of Roman Jakobson in "Two Aspects of Language and Two Types of Aphasic Disturbances: Metaphor and Metonymy," in *Fundamentals of Language* by Roman Jakobson and Morris Halle (Gravenhage: Mouton, 1956), 55–82. I realize that synecdoche is usually considered a subcategory of metonymy, but I would argue that it is then the form of metonymy that is located schematically at the point at which the axis of metaphor and the axis of metonymy intersect because synecdoche isolates the feature from its whole context in the way that metaphor does and metonymy does not. See my essay, "The Sin of Synecdoche: Hawthorne's Allegory against Symbolism in 'Rappaccini's Daughter,' " *Texas Studies in Literature and Language* 29:3 (Fall 1987): 278–301.

21. In her review of Stephen Greenblatt's *Learning to Curse: Essays in Early Modern Culture,* Anne Barton writes that he "amasses evidences which bear in upon and often seem to control works that are cited, for the most part, in ways that prevent them from speaking to the reader in anything like their full complexity." His selective, synecdochal method is, in her judgment, troubling: "Greenblatt's fondness for dealing with literary texts selectively, detaching a single passage and making it speak for the whole, is another somewhat disquieting characteristic." *New York Review of Books* 33:6, 28 March 1991, 53.

See also Carolyn Porter, "Are We Being Historical Yet?" *South Atlantic Quarterly* 87:4 (Fall 1988): 743–86, esp. 761–2 where Porter analyzes the way that Greenblatt uses analogy so that functional resemblance becomes structural equivalence.

22. Brook Thomas, *The New Historicism: and Other Old-Fashioned Topics* (Princeton: Princeton UP, 1991), 12–13. See the chapter on Walter Benn Michaels's *The Gold Standard and the Logic of Naturalism: American Literature at the Turn of the Century* for a particularly clear analysis of Michaels's use of the "modernist technique of montage," which "might satisfy aesthetic tastes trained to expect unity (*ars* originally meant 'fitting together'), but only by neglecting the messiness of history" (132–3).

23. J. G. A. Pocock, *The Ancient Constitution and the Feudal Law: A Study of English Historical Thought in the Seventeenth Century, a Reissue with a Retrospect* (1957; Cambridge: Cambridge UP, 1987), ix.

24. See Mark Seltzer, *Henry James and the Art of Power* (Ithaca: Cornell UP, 1984), for this kind of paradigmatic use of Foucauldian theory, esp. 154, 174.

25. Lee Patterson, *Negotiating the Past: The Historical Understanding of Medieval Literature* (Madison: U of Wisconsin P, 1987), 64–72.

26. Henry James, "The Figure in the Carpet," in *Eight Tales from the*

Major Phase, ed. Morton Dauwen Zabel (New York: Norton, 1958), 149.

27. Henry James, preface to *Roderick Hudson,* in *Literary Criticism: French Writers, Other European Writers, Prefaces to the New York Edition,* ed. Leon Edel (1907; New York: Library of America, 1984), 1041.

28. Clifford Geertz says that "the essential task of theory building here is not to codify abstract regularities but to make thick description possible, not to generalize across cases but to generalize within them." See "Thick Description: Toward an Interpretive Theory of Culture," in *The Interpretation of Cultures* (New York: Basic Books, 1973), 3–30.

29. See J. Laplance and J.-B. Pontalis, " 'Over-Determination' and 'Over-Interpretation,' " in *The Language of Psycho-Analysis,* trans. Donald Nicholson-Smith, introd. Daniel Lagache (1967; New York: Norton, 1973), 292–4.

30. Eric Sundquist, *To Wake the Nations: Race in the Making of American Literature* (Cambridge: Harvard UP, 1993), 21.

31. Stephen Toulmin, "The Marginal Relevance of Theory to the Humanities," *Common Knowledge* 2:1 (Spring 1993): 83.

32. Several of the reviews contemporary to the publication of *The American Scene* that exhibit in varying degrees the critical position toward James's politics are Frederic Tabor Cooper, "The American Scene," *North American Review* 185 (17 May 1907): 218; review of *The American Scene, Manchester Guardian,* 12 February 1907, 5; review of *The American Scene, Standard,* 30 January 1907, 9; Michael Monahan, "Side Talks by the Editor," review of *The American Scene* by Henry James, *Papyrus: A Magazine of Individuality,* 9 October 1907, 27–30; review of *The American Scene, Times Literary Supplement,* 8 February 1907, 44.

More recent instances are found in Van Wyck Brooks, *The Pilgrimage of Henry James* (New York: Dutton, 1925), 39, 170; John Crowe Ransom, "American Aesthete," review of *The American Scene* by Henry James, *Nation,* 7 December 1946, 652; Edmund Wilson, "Henry James and Auden in America," *New Yorker,* 28 September 1946, 94–5; Jean-Christophe Agnew, "The Consuming Vision of Henry James," in *The Culture of Consumption: Critical Essays in American History, 1880–1980,* ed. Richard Wightman Fox and T. J. Lears (New York: Pantheon, 1983), 78; Louis Auchincloss, "Henry James's Literary Use of His American Tour (1904)," *South Atlantic Quarterly* 74 (April 1955): 139–51; D. W. Sterner, "Henry James and the Idea of Culture in 'The American Scene,' " *Modern Age* 18 (1974): 283–90; David Furth, *The Visionary Betrayed: Aesthetic Discontinuity in Henry James's* The American Scene (Cambridge: Harvard UP, 1979); Harold Beaver, "In the Land of Acquisition," review of *The Future in America: A Search after Realities* by H. G. Wells and *The American Scene* by Henry James, *Times Literary Supplement,* 18–24 September 1987, 1020–1; Laurence B. Holland, "Representation and Renewal in

Henry James's *The American Scene,"* in *The Expense of Vision: Essays on the Craft of Henry James* (1964; Baltimore, Johns Hopkins UP, 1982), 423, 428–9; Susan L. Mizruchi, *The Power of Historical Knowledge: Narrating the Past in Hawthorne, James, and Dreiser* (Princeton: Princeton UP, 1988).

For another interpretation of the meaning of the hostility toward James, see Wright Morris, "Use of the Past," in *The Territory Ahead* (New York: Harcourt Brace and Company, 1958), 98–9.

33. Lionel Trilling, "The Princess Casamassima," in *The Liberal Imagination: Essays on Literature and Society* (New York: Doubleday, 1957), 55–88. Even Trilling does not give James's knowledge of socialism the credit it deserves when he fails to distinguish between the kinds of Utopian, Fourierist socialism James knew intimately in his youth and the later economically based forms of socialism that are preached by the characters in *The Princess Casamassima*.

34. One of the most intolerant reviews Anderson's *The American Henry James* (New Brunswick, N.J.: Rutgers, 1957) received was from Leon Edel in *American Literature* 29:4 (1958): 493–4, who dominated certain parts of James studies for several decades. Edel is particularly hostile to Anderson's claim that James uses the religious symbolism of his father's Swedenborgianism "allegorically." Allegory was, indeed, in bad repute in 1958, but Edel may rely too much on James's own disavowals of knowledge of his father's theology. See Chapters 8 and 9.

35. H. G. Dwight, "Henry James – 'In His Own Country,' " *Putnam's Monthly* (May 1907, July 1907), reprinted in *Henry James: The Critical Heritage*, ed. Roger Gard (London: Routledge & Kegan Paul, and New York: Barnes and Noble, 1968), 444–6.

In her comprehensive survey, "Henry James's *The American Scene:* Its Genesis and Its Reception," *Henry James Review* 1 (1979): 195, Rosalie Hewitt notes the repetitiveness of the criticism of the book and the "almost complete reversal" in critics' evaluation of James treatment of the South.

36. Irving Howe, introduction to *The American Scene* by Henry James (New York: Horizon Press, 1967), vii.

37. Paul B. Armstrong, *The Phenomenology of Henry James* (Chapel Hill: U of North Carolina P, 1983), 189; see also 235 nn. 13–14.

38. F. O. Matthiessen, *Henry James: The Major Phase* (New York: Oxford UP, 1944), 110.

39. Alan Trachtenberg, "The American Scene: Versions of the City," *Massachusetts Review* 8 (1967): 281–95; Alfred Habegger, *Henry James and the "Woman Business"* (Cambridge: Cambridge UP, 1989), 230–8.

40. Hayden White, "The Context in the Text: Method and Ideology in Intellectual History," in *The Content of the Form: Narrative Discourse and Historical Representation* (Baltimore: Johns Hopkins UP, 1987), 190.

41. Maxwell Geismar, *Henry James and the Jacobites* (1962; New York: Hill and Wang, 1965), 350; Mark Seltzer, *Henry James and the Art of Power* (Ithaca: Cornell UP, 1984), 146.

42. William James, "To Henry James," 4 May 1907, in *Selected Letters of William James*, ed. and introd. Elizabeth Hardwick (Boston: Godine, 1980), 234–5. For some contemporary reactions in the popular press see *Life* 47, 22 February 1906, 240; *Life* 47, 12 April 1906, 466.

43. Dwight, "Henry James – 'In His Own Country,' " 444–6.

44. Except of course in the wonderful collage by Donald Barthelme titled *Henry James, Chief* in which HJ appears in a headdress and warpaint. A black-and-white reproduction of this collage appears in John Carlos Rowe's *The Theoretical Dimensions of Henry James* (Madison: U of Wisconsin P, 1984), 13.

45. Ezra Pound, "Henry James," in *The Literary Essays of Ezra Pound*, ed. T. S. Eliot (1918; New York: New Directions, 1935), 295–6.

46. Rowe, *The Theoretical Dimensions of Henry James*, 169, 98. In his earlier work, *Henry Adams and Henry James: The Emergence of a Modern Consciousness* (Ithaca: Cornell UP, 1976), Rowe had spoken of the tendency "of James's characters [to] divest themselves of a dead past through the vital act of making their own history" (146), putting James more in the camp of Hamlin Garland who would dispose of the "crumbling idols" of the past.

47. This scapegoating of an author for political reasons is not unprecedented, as Jeffrey M. Perl observes in *Skepticism and Modern Enmity: Before and after Eliot* (Baltimore: Johns Hopkins UP, 1989). See Part Three, Chapters 6 and 7. Perl argues that the postmodern culture has, to its loss, polarized the conflict between itself and the moderns, using Eliot as its scapegoat, lest it seem to ally itself with any anti-democratic, antipopulist, anti-Semitic forces. In order to protract this conflict, to keep the ambivalence unnoticed, the postmodern artists and critical establishment have ignored the postwar developments in the art and critical practice of Eliot and Pound as well as Picasso and Stravinsky, for example.

48. Giles B. Gunn, *F. O. Matthiessen: The Critical Achievement* (Seattle: U of Washington P, 1975). See the chapter "From James to Dreiser" for a detailed account of Matthiessen's various political affiliations during this period of his life.

49. William E. Cain, "Criticism and Politics: F. O. Matthiessen and the Making of Henry James," *New England Quarterly* 60:2 (June 1987), 163–88, esp. 166, 172. Cain's study of the political dimensions of Matthiessen's attitude toward James is evenhanded and informative, but his attempt in the later part of the essay to redeem the passages in *The American Scene* that Matthiessen has condemned as racist suffers from a lack of historical contextualization that leaves James's remarks subject to the vagaries of the critic's interpretation.

50. F. O. Matthiessen, *The James Family: Including Selections from the Writ-*

ings of Henry James, Senior, William, Henry, and Alice James (1947; New York: Vintage, 1980), 646.

51. Ibid.
52. Reginald Horseman, *Race and Manifest Destiny: The Origins of American Racial Anglo-Saxonism* (Cambridge: Harvard UP, 1981), 63–4, 72, 76, 177, 180–2.
53. Quoted in ibid., 72.
54. It is worth noting as well that James explicitly (relatively speaking) repudiated the doctrine of racial supremacy later ascribed to him in early reviews of two volumes of Francis Parkman's *France and England in North America*, namely, the 1867 and 1874 reviews of Parkman's *The Jesuits in North America in the Seventeenth Century* and *The Old Régime in Canada*, respectively, in which he is quite ironic about the progressivist view of history represented therein. See Henry James, "Francis Parkman," in *Literary Criticism: Essays on Literature, American Writers, English Writers*, ed. Leon Edel (New York: Library of America, 1984), 568–79.

Chapter 1. Sense of the Present

1. Laurence Lafore, *The Long Fuse: An Interpretation of the Origins of World War I*, 2nd ed. (New York: Lippincott, 1971), 260.
2. Ibid., 189.
3. Henry James, "To Edith Wharton," 19 August 1914, *Henry James Letters*, ed. Leon Edel, 4 vols. (Cambridge: Belknap Press of Harvard UP, 1974–84), 4:715–16.
4. Henry James, *Within the Rim and Other Essays: 1914—1915* (London: Collins, 1918).
5. Theodora Bosanquet, *Original Diaries: 1898–1960*, bMS Eng 1213.1 and bMS Eng 1213.2, ms. and ts., Houghton Library, Harvard University, 8 August [1914]. Quoted by permission of the Houghton Library, Harvard University.
6. Vernon Louis Parrington, *The Beginnings of Critical Realism in America, 1860–1920* (1930; New York: Harcourt, 1958), 240.
7. Henry James, *The Middle Years* (1917), in *Autobiography*, ed. Frederick W. Dupee (1956; Princeton: Princeton UP, 1983), 569–70. All further references to this text will be noted parenthetically.
8. Martha Banta, in "Beyond Post-Modernism: The Sense of History in *The Princess Casamassima*," *Henry James Review* 3 (1982): 106, makes a similar point in her discussion of James's view of "the rich accessibility of history-as-experience," namely, that "What saved James from a fate similar to Hyacinth's [the hero of the novel] was the faith he gave to the creation of texts." Also from a fate similar to Adams's, we might add.
9. James, "To Henry Adams," 21 March 1914, *Letters*, 4:705–6. In *Henry Adams and Henry James: The Emergence of a Modern Consciousness* (Ithaca: Cornell UP, 1976), 130, John Carlos Rowe remarks about

this exchange of letters: "Adams despairs at last of that very process James finds so novel and enlivening. The endless necessity of interpretation confirms Adams's degradationist view of man and culture. James would come to see the failure of the modern age as its inability to sustain the free play of human signification. The unity Adams vainly longs for is the true 'beast in the jungle' for James."

10. Henry James, *A Small Boy and Others* (1913), in *Autobiography*, 123.

11. James, "To Rhoda Broughton," 10 August 1914, *Letters*, 4:713.

12. My references are to Robert Graves' autobiography *Good-bye to All That* (1929), Ford Madox Ford's tetralogy *Parade's End* (1924–8), and Vera Brittain's memoir *Testament to Youth* (1933).

13. James, *Within the Rim and Other Essays*, 31.

14. Bosanquet, *Original Diaries*, Friday, 30 October [1914], ts. 77–8.

15. See Eve Kosofsky Sedgwick, "The Beast in the Closet: James and the Writing of Homosexual Panic," in *Epistemology of the Closet* (Berkeley: U of California P, 1990), 182–212. In the terms suggested by Sedgwick, it may have been the "raw" Canadian who panicked in this homosocial situation.

16. Chronology is from Theodora Bosanquet's diaries.

17. Guided by Fredric Jameson's taxonomy of attitudes toward the past (antiquarianism, existential historicism, Nietzschean antihistoricism, and structural typology), Martha Banta gives a valuable analysis of the relationship between the past and art as it is described by Jameson as being characteristic of the existential historical position (of which he approves). This she takes to be an apt description of James's practice, which gives "the experience, rather, by which historicity as such is manifested, by means of the contact between the historian's mind in the present and a given synchronic cultural complex from the past" (Fredric Jameson, "Marxism and Historicism," *New Literary History* 11 [1979]: 50–1, quoted in Banta, "Beyond Post-Modernism," 99).

18. The typescripts for both versions are held by the Houghton Library at Harvard University, bMS Am 1237.8 boxes 1 and 2, and bMS Eng 1213 (73). Quoted by permission of the Houghton Library, Harvard University and Bay James, Literary Executor. Although James made numerous stylistic changes when he redictated the text in 1914–15, I think there would be little point in listing them all because they were not, in any case, final, as were, for example, the revisions to *The Portrait of a Lady* to which F. O. Matthiessen devoted such careful attention in his *The Major Phase* or the revisions of the whole New York Edition that Philip Horne has more recently and extensively studied in *Henry James and Revision: The New York Edition* (Oxford: Clarendon Press, 1990).

The changes that James made relating to the subject of the past are, however, significant, as is the first major change in the text, which is a long addition found on pages 8 and 9 of the New York Edition. Starting at the bottom of that page, "Strange he had always thought it . . ." and running to the end of the paragraph, this passage treats "the commonest wisdom of life," that secret that only "the given man and the given woman could possibly know the truth" of what it is that has brought them into "a relation of that intimacy, really of that obscurity, [of which] nothing was appreciable from outside." The conclusion of the paragraph changes significantly what we are told about Aurora's marriage, which otherwise could be imagined as happy: "if the future *did* owe her amends she probably saw them as numerous." James's emphasis on the mystery of "intimacy" is complicated by this last remark: it makes the attraction seem a very mixed blessing; the secret, one which is not without its price. Ralph stands very much in the relation of the child excluded from his parents's (sexual) secrets, competitive with the (faulty but still powerful) father figure, and wanting the immediate satisfaction of substituting a sexually experienced woman of his own age for his recently deceased mother. James's addition makes the Oedipal drama much more explicit in the 1915 version.

The most extensive changes between the 1900 and the 1914–15 typescripts are reproduced in the appendix.

19. T. S. Eliot, "On Henry James: In Memory" (1918), in *The Question of Henry James,* ed. F. W. Dupee (New York: Holt, 1945), 118.

Susan M. Griffin, in "Seeing Doubles: Reflections of the Self in James's *Sense of the Past,*" *Modern Language Quarterly* 45 (1984): 48–60, also argues that Ralph's initial way of reading the relation of past and present "as *un*connected" (52) leads him pathologically to attempt to master the past's knowledge in impossible ways. Her conclusion that he returns to Aurora "to become himself through conversation with others" (60) is more in line with my thinking about this process of transformation (see Part Three) than is the part of her analysis that is conducted in terms of self-mastery and autonomy.

For another reading of this relationship between James's and his hero's views of the past, see Susan L. Marshall, " 'Framed in Death': *The Sense of the Past* and the Limits of Revision," *Henry James Review* 10:3 (Fall 1989): 197–209. Marshall confuses the limitations of Ralph's initially false view of the past with James's. She blames James for his "inability to reconcile the two Ralphs" (207), the " 'masterful' Ralph of the Notes [and] the weakening artist of the text." In spite of her study of the 1900 and 1914 manuscripts for significant revisions, Marshall's reading of this text shows no awareness of the difference in historical circumstances, both personal and public, of these two undertakings. Indeed, the fact that one of the reasons that James did not finish the novel is that he died while he was working on it and other projects is not acknowledged.

Another recent essay on this novel also reads it as a failure of imagination because James leaves Ralph trapped in "the prison-house of the past." See Susan S. Williams, "The Tell-Tale Representation: James and *The Sense of the Past*," *Henry James Review* 14:1 (Winter 1993): 72–86.

20. Bosanquet, *Original Diaries*, 1 November [1915], ts. 78–9. The phrases she puts in quotation marks are ones James used frequently during this period of his correspondence, much of which he dictated to her.

Chapter 2. Genre Trouble

1. Henry James, *The Sense of the Past*, bMs Eng 1213 (73) and bMs Am 1237.8 box 1 and 2 ts. (1900) Houghton Library, Harvard University, 114. Quoted by permission of the Houghton Library, Harvard University and Bay James, Literary Executor.

2. Henry James, *The Notebooks of Henry James*, ed. F. O. Matthiessen and Kenneth B. Murdock (Chicago: Chicago UP, 1947), 362.

3. William Dean Howells, "To Henry James," 15 July 1900, in *The Life in Letters of William Dean Howells*, ed. Mildred Howells, 2 vols. (Garden City, N.Y.: Doubleday, 1928), 2:132.

4. Henry James, "To William Dean Howells," 9 August 1900, in *Henry James Letters*, ed. Leon Edel, 4 vols. (Cambridge: Belknap Press of Harvard UP, 1974–84), 4:159–60.

5. Henry James, *The Sense of the Past*, vol. 26 of *The Novels and Tales of Henry James*, 27 vols. (New York: Scribner's, 1917), 294. All further references to this edition are noted parenthetically.

6. Henry James, preface to *The Aspern Papers*, in *Literary Criticism: French Writers, Other European Writers, Prefaces to the New York Edition*, ed. Leon Edel (1907; New York: Library of America, 1984), 1183–4, 1181, 1185.

7. Herbert Butterfield, *The Whig Interpretation of History* (1931; London: G. Bell & Sons, 1951), 101–2.

8. There are several different kinds of allusions in the text, as well as one explicit reference – namely when Ralph thinks that his inheriting the house as the unforeseen result of writing his book makes it like a "fairytale" (45). There are repeated uses of the magic number three: Aurora says to Ralph "You're beautiful" (12); she shakes her head three times (8); she says that if he spent even three days, three hours in Europe, he would be spoiled for her purposes; the Midmores had been tenants three times (56); the house number is nine. The house itself is referred to as "an animated home" (1915 edition) which Ralph dreams of making speak (47); later he recalls that he had thought of testing the house, and now it seems to be testing him (84); Ralph's prevision of Mrs. Midmore in her black hood with a crutch reveals her to be a witch (71); Aurora refers to "Nick o' the Woods" who apparently likes to "beat out [the] brains" of people who annoy him (23). Perhaps most important, however, are Aurora's conditions, meaning both her state of being enchanted and her preposterous scheme. The transgression of law, as Tzvetan

Todorov points out in *The Fantastic: A Structural Approach to a Literary Genre*, trans. Richard Howard (1970; Ithaca: Cornell UP, 1975), 166, defines the social and literary functions of the fantastic: "Whether it is in social life or in narrative, the intervention of the supernatural element always constitutes a break in the system of pre-established rules, and in doing so finds its justification." The difference between the fantastic and the fairy tale in these terms is that in the latter a new and better law is established when the hero or heroine successfully overcomes the (usually three) trials he or she is faced with.

9. Bruno Bettelheim, *The Uses of Enchantment: The Meaning and Importance of Fairy Tales* (New York: Vintage, 1977), 10. See especially the chapter "Fairy Tale versus Myth: Optimism versus Pessimism." In her study *Problems of the Feminine in Fairy Tales* (Zurich: Spring Publications, 1976), the Jungian analyst Marie-Louise von Franz makes a similar distinction between the relations of the fairy tale and myth to the unconscious.

10. James, "To Bernard Shaw," 20 January 1909, *Letters*, 4:513.

11. Paul B. Armstrong, "Reading James's Prefaces and Reading James," in *Henry James's New York Edition: The Construction of Authorship*, ed. David McWhirter (Stanford: Stanford UP, 1995), 135.

12. Vladimir Propp, *Morphology of the Folk Tale*, trans. L. Scott (Bloomington: Indiana UP, 1958).

13. James, *Notebooks*, 369.

14. Northrop Frye, in *Anatomy of Criticism: Four Essays* (1957; Princeton: Princeton UP, 1971), 190, treats *The Sense of the Past* as an instance of the quest-romance. The labyrinthine underworld from which the hero returns is the past, and his savior is an Ariadne, who is (typically) sacrificed.

15. Jonathan Freedman, *Professions of Taste: Henry James, British Aestheticism, and Commodity Culture* (Stanford: Stanford UP, 1990). This deep and thick study replaces decades of discussion about the "aesthetic" and James, and Freedman's acute sense of the way the cultural and artistic issues raised under this term will reemerge in other terms is particularly valuable for what it suggests about the complex relations of critical fashions and social reality.

16. James Senior says that those who have produced paintings or poetry or music have "monopolized the name of Artist . . . simply because [they], . . . more than any other men, have thrown off the tyranny of nature and custom, and followed the inspiration of genius, the inspirations of beauty, in their own souls." In fact, "no painter, no poet, no sculptor has succeeded in snatching the inmost secret of Art and so making his name immortal . . . because the inmost secret of Art does not lie within the sphere of Art, but belongs only to Life. Art or doing . . . is itself but a shadow of the external fact which is life, or action." See *Henry James, Senior: A Selection of His Writings*, ed. and introd. Giles Gunn (Chicago: American Library Association, 1974), 130, 142.

17. Henry James, "Daniel Deronda: A Conversation" (1876), in *Literary Criticism: Essays on Literature, American Writers, English Writers*, 92.

18. Paul B. Armstrong, "The Politics of Reading," in *Culture and the Imagination*, ed. Heide Ziegler (Stuttgart: Metzler and Poeschel, 1995), 117–45.

19. Alan Bellringer, "Henry James's *The Sense of the Past*: The Backward Vision," *Forum for Modern Language Studies* 17:3 (July 1981): 213.

20. Anders Nygren, *Agape and Eros*, trans. Philip S. Watson (1932; 1938; 1939; rpt. Chicago: U of Chicago P, 1982).

21. Sister M. Corona Sharp's treatment of this figure in *The Confidante in Henry James: Evolution and Moral Value of a Fictive Character* (Notre Dame: U of Notre Dame P, 1963) records the prevalence of this device in James's fiction, but her emphasis on the "friendship" between characters without the need for erotic expression in some relationship limits her analysis. Her survey of the (older) women in James's life with whom he had friendships and on whom he relied for comfort, particularly Grace Norton, is valuable for what it shows about a possible unresolved conflict in James's own life.

22. Jacques Derrida, "The Law of Genre," in *Acts of Literature*, ed. Derek Attridge (New York: Routledge, 1992), 227.

23. Ibid., 238, 225.

24. Henry James, preface to *The American*, in *Literary Criticism: French Writers, Other European Writers, Prefaces to the New York Edition*, 1065.

25. Ibid., 1062–3

26. Paul B. Armstrong, "History, Epistemology, and the Example of *The Turn of the Screw*," in *Conflicting Readings: Variety and Validity in Interpretation* (Chapel Hill: U of North Carolina P, 1990), 105–6.

27. James, preface to *The American*, 1067.

28. See the discussion of Butterfield's critique of the whig interpretation of history in the Introduction of this book.

29. Willard Van Orman Quine addresses this issue in terms relevant to the truth claims of empiricism, terms that resonate with the distinctions made by Derrida and James – and with the acknowledgment of the impossibility of making those distinctions absolutely: "If this view is right, it is misleading to speak of the empirical content of an individual statement – especially if it is a statement at all remote from the experiential periphery of the field. Furthermore it becomes folly to seek a boundary between synthetic statements, which hold contingently on experience, and analytic statements, which hold come what may. Any statement can be held true come what may, if we make drastic adjustments elsewhere in the system. Even a statement very close to the periphery can be held true in the face of recalcitrant experience by pleading hallucination or by amending certain statements of the kind called logical laws. Conversely, by the same token, no statement is immune to revision." See "Two Dogmas of Empiricism," in *From a Logical Point of View: Nine Logico-philosophical Essays*, 2nd ed. rev. (Cambridge: Harvard UP, 1980), 43.

30. Sigmund Freud, "Further Recommendations in the Technique of Psychoanalysis: Observations on Transference-Love" (1915), in *Therapy and Technique*, ed. Philip Rieff (New York: Collier, 1963), 167–80.

31. Freud, "Further Recommendations in the Technique of Psychoanalysis: Recollection, Repetition and Working Through" (1914), in *Therapy and Technique*, 165.

32. Ibid., 164. This insight has been borne out by the practice of psychoanalysis, even if the understanding of what exactly does and should happen has changed back and forth over the years. For a good summary of the history of theories of transference, see Arnold M. Cooper, "Changes in Psychoanalytic Ideas: Transference Interpretation," *Journal of the American Psychoanalytic Association* 35:1 (1987): 77–98.

33. Freud, "The Dynamics of the Transference" (1912), in *Therapy and Technique*, 107.

34. Ibid.

35. Freud, "Observations on Transference-Love," 176.

36. Ibid., 177–8.

37. John Forrester, "Who Is in Analysis with Whom?" in *The Seductions of Psychoanalysis: Freud, Lacan, and Derrida* (Cambridge: Cambridge UP, 1990), 235.

38. Freud, "Recollection, Repetition and Working Through," 161.

39. Ibid., 162.

40. Freud, "The Dynamics of the Transference."

41. Freud, "Recollection, Repetition and Working Through," 165.

Chapter 3. Making Signs of the Past

1. Henry James, "To William James," 24 May 1903, in *Henry James Letters*, ed. Leon Edel, 4 vols. (Cambridge: Belknap Press of Harvard UP, 1974–84), 4:271–2.

2. Leon Edel remarks that all of James's work "from this time on was intimately related to his American past." But what Edel means by James's focus on and valuation of the past clearly expresses the view against which I will be arguing. Edel quotes approvingly Santayana's characterization of "James's stance as 'classical' " and then explains what he (Edel) means by this term: "Civilization meant order, composition, restraint, moderation, beauty, duration. It meant creation of a way of life that ministered to man's finest qualities and potential." See *Henry James: The Master, 1901–1916* (New York: Avon, 1978), 5:316. I will be arguing that James's sense of the classical value of civilizations is not rigid or exclusionary in the way this definition implies but is semiotic and evolutionary.

3. See Philip Horne, *Henry James and Revision: The New York Edition* (Oxford: Clarendon Press 1990), for a detailed biographical and textual study of this process in which Horne shows how James ex-

plores in many registers the relation of his own past work to his present work of revising both in the texts and in the prefaces.

4. One could argue that the retrospective is the natural point of view for an artist in his or her late period but nevertheless the work of the elderly Picasso or the very mature Balanchine is not focused, as was James's, on the general problem of the culture's relationship to its past but rather on the fear of a loss of artistic/erotic power. I'm thinking in particular of Picasso's late drawings and Balanchine's "Robert Schumann's 'Davidsbündlertänze.' "

5. My chronology for these compositions is taken from Leon Edel's biography, *Henry James: The Master, 1901–1916*, vol. 5.

6. The letter to Pinker is quoted in ibid., 5:313. Edel writes that James was kept awake the night of 3–4 August 1906 by the germ of this story idea.

7. Henry James, "The Jolly Corner," in *Tales of Henry James*, ed. Christof Wegelin (New York: Norton, 1984), 339.

8. I say "foreshadowed" following Edel's suggestion that this may have been the dream from which James awoke on 21 July 1910 feeling "great relief," as he remarked in his notebook, and after the worst of his depression triggered by the failure of the New York Edition to fulfill his expectations. Edel, *Henry James: The Master, 1901–1906*, 5:444–5. Edel admits that this is speculation on his part – James dates the nightmare only saying he awoke from it "in a summer dawn many years later." This coincidence of the dream and the lifting of the depression seems a reasonable suggestion to me because of the tremendous psychic importance both in its representational role ("Style") and the catharsis that James attributes to it in *A Small Boy and Others*. He describes his "dream-adventure founded in the deepest, quickest, clearest act of cogitation and comparison, act indeed of life-saving energy, as well as in unutterable fear. . . . The lucidity, not to say the sublimity, of the crisis had consisted of the great thought that I, in my appalled state, was probably more appalling than the awful agent, creature or presence, whatever he was . . ." and calls his victory over the creature, "The triumph of my impulse. . . ." Henry James, *A Small Boy and Others* (1913), in *Autobiography*, ed. F. W. Dupee (1956; Princeton: Princeton UP, 1983), 196–7.

9. Henry James, *The Sense of the Past*, vol. 26 of *The Novels and Tales of Henry James*, 27 vols. (New York: Scribner's, 1917), 48. All further references to this edition are noted parenthetically.

10. Henry James, *Hawthorne*, English Men of Letters (London: Macmillian, 1879).

11. Henry James, *The American Scene*, introd. and notes by Leon Edel (1907; Bloomington: Indiana UP, 1968), 24. All further references to this edition are noted parenthetically.

12. This is one of the many locutions by which James refers to himself in *The American Scene;* see, e.g., 13, 179, 455.

13. Absence and silence are, of course, important in much of James's

fiction as Tzvetan Todorov argues in *The Fantastic: A Structural Approach to a Literary Genre,* trans. Richard Howard (Ithaca: Cornell UP, 1975), as does John Auchard in *Silence in Henry James: The Heritage of Symbolism and Decadence* (University Park: Pennsylvania State UP, 1986). Both of these studies, however different the value of their interpretations, rely on dualistic notions of signification that ally James with a transcendental tradition that I think is quite foreign to his way of making sense of things, as I argued in more detail in my analysis of *The Sense of the Past* and will attempt to show later in this chapter when I invoke Peirce's triadic semiotics.

14. John Carlos Rowe in *The Theoretical Dimensions of Henry James* (Madison: U of Wisconsin P, 1984), 215, quotes Paul de Man's definition: "Prosopopeia makes accessible to the sense, in this case the ear, a voice which is out of earshot because it is no longer alive. In its most inclusive and also its etymological sense, it designates the very process of figuration as giving face to what is devoid of it" ("Epistemology of Metaphor," *Critical Inquiry* 5 [Autumn 1978]: 26); he adds that the trope is "the *substantial* activity of metaphor" that can cross boundaries of time and space, although not "without repression, which functions by effacing this crossing for the sake of a presence or by condensing memory traces in the illusion of an 'object.'" This description seems to makes James's interpretative activity more metaphysical than historical.

15. Henry knew enough not to expect such "popularity" when he found in his brother one of his most resistant readers, even if he did, in the end, admit Henry's success. See "To Henry James" 4 May 1907, in *The Selected Letters of William James,* ed. and introd. Elizabeth Hardwick (1961; rpt. Boston: Godine, 1980), 233–5.

16. Susan M. Griffin, *The Historical Eye: The Texture of the Visual in Late James* (Boston: Northeastern UP, 1991), 119.

17. John Carlos Rowe notes James's sympathetic advocacy of the dispossessed Indians in his interesting discussion of Donald Barthelme's revisions of James in his collage "Henry James, Chief" (a photograph of James with feather headdress and warpaint) and his story "Presents" in which James appears in some wonderfully unlikely situations. *Theoretical Dimensions,* 10–12.

18. James regretted that the title *The Return of the Native* was not available for his finished work. See "To George Harvey," 21 October 1904, *Letters,* 4:328.

My use of psychoanalytic terminology and concepts is intended to suggest a way of understanding James's diagnostic and therapeutic roles without claiming that one can apply to a culture the same categories describing psychic life that Freud developed for the individual, notwithstanding that Freud did this himself, especially in *Civilization and Its Discontents* (1930) and *Moses and Monotheism* (1939). See the end of Chapter 2 on the value of transference in *The Sense of the Past.*

19. Laurence B. Holland, *The Expense of Vision: Essays on the Craft of Henry James,* rev. ed. (Baltimore: Johns Hopkins UP, 1982), notes the "apocalyptic fervor" of *The American Scene.* Sacvan Bercovitch's description of the jeremiad as "the official ritual of continuing revolution" emphasizes the form's capacity for reconciling theology and ideology, particularly for justifying the practices of capitalism by appealing to the tenets of faith. See *The American Jeremiad* (Madison: U of Wisconsin P, 1978), 181. As a critique of the effects of capitalism, James's sermon is perhaps then more in the tradition of Moses returning from Sinai and finding his people worshiping the golden calf. But one does not wish to claim too strong a parallel: the image of a wrathful James in flowing robes provokes more mirth than insight.

20. I have in mind two theoretical assumptions here: first, that technique always signifies: as Jean-Paul Sartre wrote, "On aurait tort de prendre ces anomalies pour des exercices gratuits de virtuosité: une technique romanesque renvoie toujours à la métaphysique du romancier" ("À propos de 'Le bruit et la fureur': La temporalité chez Faulkner" [1939], in *Critiques littéraires: Situations, I* [Paris: Gallimard, 1947], 86); second, the inherent drama of dialogue as understood by Bakhtin: "Responsive understanding is a fundamental force, one that participates in the formulation of the discourse, and is moreover an *active* understanding, one that discourse senses as resistance or support enriching the discourse" ("Discourse in the Novel," in *The Dialogic Imagination: Four Essays,* ed. Michael Holquist, trans. Caryl Emerson and Michael Holquist, U of Texas Press Slavic Studies, no. 1 [Austin: U of Texas P, 1981], 280–1.

21. See Edel's introduction to his edition of *The American Scene,* xxiii, and Rosalie Hewitt, "Henry James, the Harpers and *The American Scene,*" *American Literature* 55 (March 1983): 41–7. Hewitt lays the blame for this omission squarely at the Harper's door: not only did the press omit by accident or design the final chapter on Florida but, to save a few pages, repaginated the text and suppressed James's wonderful running heads. He was furious.

22. See John K. Sheriff, *The Fate of Meaning: Charles Peirce, Structuralism, and Literature* (Princeton: Princeton UP, 1989), for a well-made argument about the difference for our conception of human experience between the dyadic sign that Derrida inherits from Saussure and the triadic sign formulated by Peirce. See also Chapter 9.

23. Francis Haskell, "Art and the Language of Politics," in *Past and Present in Art and Taste* (New Haven: Yale UP, 1987), 65–74.

24. Henry James, "To William James," 3 December [1875], *Letters,* 2:13.

25. Henry James, "To Catherine Walsh," 3 December [1875], *Letters,* 2:11.

26. Henry James, "To William James," 14 March [1876], *Letters,* 2:32.

27. The most important of the many studies that address the relationship of William and Henry in various ways are Richard Hocks, *Henry*

James and Pragmatistic Thought: A Study in the Relationship between the Philosophy of William James and the Literary Art of Henry James (Chapel Hill: U of North Carolina P, 1974); Paul B. Armstrong, *The Phenomenology of Henry James* (Chapel Hill: U of North Carolina P, 1983); Howard M. Feinstein, *Becoming William James* (Ithaca: Cornell UP, 1986); Ross Posnock, *The Trial of Curiosity: Henry James, William James, and the Challenge of Modernity* (New York: Oxford UP, 1991); Merle A. Williams, *Henry James and the Philosophical Novel: Being and Seeing* (Cambridge: Cambridge UP, 1993).

Most of these critics make some reference to Peirce, and David Liss has systematically made use of his work in "The Fixation of Belief in 'The Figure in the Carpet': Henry James and Peircean Semiotics," *Henry James Review* 16:1 (Winter 1995): 36–47. He has more courage than I in venturing into the realm of the Legisign and the Rheme.

28. Henry James, "To William James," 17 October 1907, *Letters*, 4:466.
29. Peirce renamed his philosophy by the awkward term "pragmaticism" after William James adopted his term "pragmatism" in ways that Peirce felt distorted his meaning. He figured, correctly, that no one would want to appropriate so awkward a term as "pragmaticism."
30. An explication of Peirce's terms – Sign-Object-Interpretant – will be given later.
31. Charles S. Peirce, "Logic As Semiotic: The Theory of Signs," in *Philosophical Writings of Peirce*, ed. Justus Buchler (New York: Dover, 1955), 100.
32. Peirce, "The Law of Mind," in *Philosophical Writings of Peirce*, 340.
33. Ibid., 341.
34. Henry James, preface to *Roderick Hudson*, in *Literary Criticism: French Writers, Other European Writers, Prefaces to the New York Edition*, ed. Leon Edel (1907; New York: Library of America, 1984), 1041.
35. Henry James, preface to *The Aspern Papers*, in *Literary Criticism: French Writers, Other European Writers, Prefaces to the New York Edition*, 1177.
36. Peirce, "Logic As Semiotic," 99.
37. See Ruth Bernard Yeazell's chapter "Talking in James," in *Language and Knowledge in the Late Novels of Henry James* (Chicago: U of Chicago P, 1976), 75–99, for another analysis of the importance of conversation as a way of making meaning in James.
38. Strictly speaking it is always already a sign – in some context, but not yet in the particular triad in which it becomes meaningful to Maggie.
39. I am indebted for this analysis to the one offered by Armstrong in *The Phenomenology of Henry James*, 163–9, in which he reads this scene in the terms of hermeneutics, a vocabulary that is partially translatable into that of semiotics because of the centrality of interpretation to both. The hermeneutic circle and Peirce's evolving triads have, to simplify the matter, different shapes and different

ends, although Armstrong also invokes Peirce in connection with the inevitability of interpretation.

40. Peirce, "Some Consequences of Four Incapacities" (1868), in *The Essential Peirce: Selected Philosophical Writings*, vol. 1, *1867–1893*, ed. Nathan Houser and Christian Kloesel (Bloomington: Indiana UP, 1992), 54–5.

41. Peirce, "Logic As Semiotic," 114.

42. Henry James, *The Question of Our Speech; The Lesson of Balzac: Two Lectures* (Boston: Houghton Mifflin, 1905), 10.

43. Peirce, "Logic As Semiotic," 115.

44. Henry James, *The Golden Bowl*, vol. 24 of *The Novels and Tales of Henry James*, 27 vols. (New York: Scribner's, 1909), 167–8. All further references to this edition are noted parenthetically.

45. Although Mikhail Bakhtin uses this same term, "dialogism," to characterize the development of the novel rather than to describe a precise logical process, his sense of the connections between the meanings of the past and those of the present is very much in line with the process I am describing here. See Tzvetan Todorov, *Mikhail Bakhtin: The Dialogical Principle*, trans. Wlad Godzich, Theory and History of Literature, vol. 13 (Minneapolis: U of Minnesota P, 1984), and Gary Saul Morson and Caryl Emerson, *Mikhail Bakhtin: Creation of a Prosaics* (Stanford: Stanford UP, 1990).

46. Charles Sanders Peirce, *Collected Papers of Charles Sanders Peirce*, vol. 3, *Exact Logic: Published Papers*, ed. Charles Hartshorne and Paul Weiss (Cambridge: Belknap Press of Harvard UP, 1933), 3: par.623. All citations from this edition will follow this standard form of referring to the volume number and paragraph number.

47. Henry James, *The Ivory Tower*, vol. 27 of *The Novels and Tales of Henry James*, 27 vols. (New York: Scribner's, 1917), 243. All further references to this edition are noted parenthetically.

48. The "Third" term in the semiotic triad is the Interpretant; it brings the "First," the Representamen (or Sign), and the "Second," the Object, into relation and thus initiates the endless semiotic process. For my purposes, the most important of these terms to understand is "the Third," the Interpretant, because of its generative nature.

For one of Peirce's explanations of the relation of First, Second, and Third, see "Logic As Semiotic," 99.

For a useful diagram of the relations of First, Second, and Third in the semiotic triad, see Sheriff, *The Fate of Meaning*, 59–60. These relations are not to be confused with Firstness (the thing in itself); Secondess (its reactive relation to another); and Thirdness (the representational value among things) on their own terms.

49. Peirce, "Evolutionary Love," in *Philosophical Writings of Peirce*, 371.

50. Ibid., 365.

Gérard Deledalle explains that "The chance of tychism and the continuity of synechism are incapable on their own of accounting for evolution. They can do nothing without the power of love 'the

great evolutionary agency of the universe.' (vol. 6: par. 287) . . .
Agapastic evolution is manifested at the level of thought through
the way in which we may acquire a mental tendency. 1. To stray
slightly from habitual ideas, without reason or constraint, is tychasm.
2. To adopt new ideas without foreseeing their consequences, but
under the external constraint of circumstances or the internal constraint of the logic of ideas, is anancasm. 3. To adopt certain mental
tendencies out of sympathy for an idea by virtue of the continuity of
mind, is agapasm." See *Charles S. Peirce: An Intellectual Biography*,
trans. and introd. Susan Petrilli (Amsterdam: John Benjamins,
1990), 70–1.

51. Peirce, *Collected Papers of Charles Sanders Peirce*, vol. 5, *Pragmatism and
Pragmaticism*, ed. Charles Hartshorne and Paul Weiss (Cambridge:
Belknap Press of Harvard UP, 1934, 1935), 5: par. 311.

52. This is not to say that consideration of this social dimension is
completely absent from Eco's account of semiosis, but that the essays
that are well known to literary critics, especially "Logic As Semiotic:
The Theory of Signs," give less sense of this important aspect of
Peirce's thought than do the essays I am quoting. See Umberto Eco,
A Theory of Semiotics (Bloomington: Indiana UP, 1976). In *Semiotics
and the Philosophy of Language* (Bloomington: Indiana UP, 1984),
Eco also notes in the course of explaining what Peirce means by
"abduction" that the "semiotic plausibility is based on social habits."

53. Peirce, "Evolutionary Love," 364.

54. Ibid., 363.

55. Ibid., 362.

56. Ibid.

57. One reference is made in the likely place of a review of William
James's *The Principles of Psychology*, where Peirce writes: "Brought up
under the guidance of an eloquent apostle of a form of Swedenborgianism, which is materialism driven deep and clinched on the
inside, and educated to the materialist profession, it can only be by
great natural breadth of mind that he [William James] can know
what materialism is, by having experienced some thoughts that are
not materialistic." Originally reviewed in *Nation* 53 (9 July 1891):
32–3; reprinted in *Collected Papers of Charles Sanders Peirce*, vol. 8,
Reviews, Correspondence and Bibliography, ed. Arthur W. Burks (Cambridge: Belknap Press of Harvard UP, 1958), 8: par. 55–90.

Another less likely reference, which makes me think that there
may be more scattered through Peirce's work, is in a review of
Sidney Edward Mizes's *Ethics: Descriptive and Explanatory* (New York:
Macmillan, 1901). The negative review concludes: "As we rise from
the reading of the whole book, we find ourselves saying, if *this* is
what morality is, we are disposed to sympathize with Henry James,
the elder, in his very limited respect for morality." Originally reviewed in *Nation* 73 (24 October 1901): 325–6; reprinted in *Collected*

Papers of Charles Sanders Peirce, vol. 8, *Reviews, Correspondence and Bibliography,* 8: par. 125.

I do not mean to imply that Henry James Senior was a major influence on Peirce in the way that Kant, Hegel, and Duns Scotus were, but it seems worth remarking that he was a frequent point of reference for ethical concerns, which have not been the issues most interesting to Peirce scholars, however. Peirce's substantial review of *The Secret of Swedenborg* (in *North American Review* 110 [April 1870]: 463–8) is critical of James's effort to philosophize about that which will never lend itself to proof, namely, religious experience, and of James's "cryptic use of terms," but he concludes that, even to the man "who cannot fully understand it, it will afford, as it has to us, much spiritual nutriment." Perhaps a certain indulgence of James Senior's effort can be explained best by Peirce's introductory remark: "Though this book presents some very interesting and impressive religious views, and the spiritual tone of it is in general eminently healthy, it is altogether out of harmony with the spirit of this age." So much for the spiritual health of this age.

58. This correspondence is a splendid example of the way in which a sympathetic mind can draw out the meaning of another. Peirce's explanations of his semiotics to the inventor of "significs" are among the most lucid he offered. He was clearly delighted to have an interested interpreter. See *Semiotic and Significs: The Correspondence between Charles S. Peirce and Victoria Lady Welby,* ed. Charles S. Hardwick and James Cook (Bloomington: Indiana UP, 1977).

59. James, *Question of Our Speech,* 6.

Chapter 4. Waste Makes Taste

1. Henry James, *The American Scene,* introd. and notes by Leon Edel (1907; Bloomington: Indiana UP, 1968), 159. All further references to this edition are noted parenthetically.

2. Thorstein Veblen, *The Theory of the Leisure Class,* introd. Robert Lekachman (1899; New York: Penguin, 1979), 154. All further references to this edition are noted parenthetically.

3. Even so acute a critic as Fredric Jameson trivializes James's grasp of history; yet his analysis of the problem of the American past is strikingly similar on most points to that which James expressed in *The American Scene* as seen in an interview on the occasion of the publication of *The Political Unconscious.* See "Interview with Frederic Jameson," *Diacritics* 12 (1982): 74.

4. See Jonathan Freedman, *Professions of Taste: Henry James, British Aestheticism, and Commodity Culture* (Stanford: Stanford UP, 1990).

5. Karl Polyani, *The Great Transformation: The Poltical and Economic Origins of Our Time* (1944; Boston: Beacon, 1957), 76.

6. Thorstein Veblen, *Absentee Ownership and Business Enterprise in Recent*

Time: The Case of America (1923; New York: Kelley, 1964), 168. All further references to this edition are cited parenthetically.

7. Many readers of *The American Scene* have noted in passing the similarities between Veblen's and James's critiques of the leisure class, but the effect of such recognition has not been to destabilize or deconstruct or understand the received image of James as a defender of the privileges of that class.

The references in passing to Veblen may be the late and perpetual fruits of William Dean Howells's widely read review of *The Theory of a* [sic] *Leisure Class,* which helped Veblen's work reach a general audience but, by characterizing it as a satire, may have given the impression to literary folk that they need not take it too seriously. See "An Opportunity for American Fiction," *Literature,* n.s., 16 (28 April 1899): 361–2; n.s., 17 (5 May 1899): 385–6. Of course, Veblen's own pithiness also leads to his being reduced to a few catch phrases.

An example of the casual reference to Veblen is found in B. C. Lee, "A Felicity Gone Forever: Henry James's Last Visit to America," *British Association for American Studies Bulletin,* n.s., 5 (1962): 31–42, in which he notes that the barbarity of American culture would be more obvious to Veblen because it is otherwise thin (33). The thinness of American culture is not a criterion of Veblen's schema for distinguishing between "savage" and "barbarian" cultures.

A welcome exception to this trend is Ross Posnock's "Henry James, Veblen and Adorno: The Crisis of the Modern Self," *Journal of American Studies* 21 (1987): 31–54, and his book *The Trial of Curiosity: Henry James, William James, and the Challenge of Modernity* (New York: Oxford UP, 1991). He writes in his article (31–3) that he "hopes to overturn the remarkably durable image of [James] as a genteel formalist" by "taking [him] seriously as a social critic" and, consequently, I find much to agree with in his discussion of James's "semiological character of manners, their functioning as a network of relations, a differential structure that produces public signs."

8. The classic case of destruction as possession is found in the potlatches of the native American of the Pacific Northwest as described by Marcel Mauss in *The Gift: Forms and Functions of Exchange in Archaic Societies* (1925; New York: Norton, 1967).

9. Robert A. M. Stern, Gregory Gilmartin, and John Montague Massengale, *New York 1900: Metropolitan Architecture and Urbanism, 1890–1915* (New York: Rizzoli, 1983), 61–69.

10. It should be noted that there were at this time the beginnings of preservation societies of various kinds, two of the earliest, interestingly enough, having been founded in California: Charles Flecther Lummis's Landmarks Club (1895), which was devoted to the preservation of that state's Spanish heritage, and John Muir's Sierra Club (1892), devoted to the preservation of prehistoric California.

11. Frank Kermode has most recently clarified this distinction between

a mere style and the "surplus of signifier" that defines the classic. *The Classic: Literary Images of Permanence and Change* (Cambridge: Harvard UP, 1983). 139–140.

12. Henry James, "To Frances Rollins Morse," 7 June 1897, in *Henry James Letters*, ed. Leon Edel, 4 vols. (Cambridge: Belknap Press of Harvard UP, 1974–84), 4:47.

13. Henry James, "To Ellen Temple (Emmet) Hunter," 3 July 1897, *Letters*, 4:49.

14. "Gen. Sherman's Statue Unveiled," *New York Times*, Sunday, 31 May 1903.

15. Ibid.

16. Eric Foner has contested the received idea that Reconstruction was a failure, but this is the conception that would have been commonplace at the time of James's visit. See *Reconstruction: America's Unfinished Revolution, 1863–1877* (New York: HarperCollins, 1988).

17. The recent (1990) restoration and regilding of the statue was sponsored by many historical preservation groups, including the Metropolitan Chapter of the Victorian Society in America, at whose fundraising party there was no mention of the burning of Atlanta.

18. There was no winner in the first round of competition for the design of this memorial. John H. Duncan's entry, inspired by Napoleon's tomb at Les Invalides, was happily chosen over Carrère & Hastings's beaux-arts extravaganza. Although the funds for this memorial were raised by public subscription, the "Expert Committee" was composed of notable architects, including Napoleon LeBrun, William R. Ware, George B. Post, and James E. Ware (Stern et al., *New York 1900*, 121–2, n. 453). The monument works, nevertheless (James says he "distinctly 'liked' it") because all of its elements are "*carried far enough*" and "yet do not dispel the Presence" (145–6). In more contemporary terms, this problem of commemoration and representation is illustrated by the two monuments to the victims of the war in Vietnam: Maya Lin's black wall cut deep into the earth, with the name of every American service person who died in that war versus the symbolic group of soldiers that mars the entry to the memorial.

19. That "Mrs. Jack" was a likely source of inspiration for the character of Mrs. Gereth in *The Spoils of Poynton* is convincingly argued by Adeline R. Tintner, *The Museum World of Henry James* (Ann Arbor: UMI Research Press, 1986), in her history of the various relations between Mrs. Jack and her art and James and his. See 198–206.

20. Stuart Johnson, in "American Marginalia: James's *The American Scene*," *Texas Studies in Language and Literature* 24 (1982): 83–101, makes a similar point about James's pleasure in the Gardner collection.

21. Philip Hendy, *The Isabella Stewart Gardner Museum: Catalogue of the Exhibited Paintings and Drawings* (Boston: Printed for the Trustees,

1931), vi. Among the great treasures of Fenway Court is a portrait of Henry James by William (his nephew) and presented by him to Mrs. Gardner in 1910. See 194–5.

22. Tintner, *Museum World,* 198.

23. In his essay on "The Benjamin Altman Bequest," a bequest that stipulated its maintenance as a collection not to be dispersed into the body of the Metropolitan, Francis Haskell notes that the Gardner collection was "the one outstanding exception" to the general rule for American collections that their "great art" was not acquired until after the death of Altman in 1914. See *Past and Present in Art and Taste* (New Haven: Yale UP, 1987), 206.

24. My colleague Wendy Graham pointed out that James would be interested, in every sense, in the creation of a class of professional critics.

25. Posnock makes a similar point in Adorno's more theoretical terms where he discusses the embracing of nonidentity as a means of overcoming reification: "Thus non-identity sublates – cancels and preserves – identity, a logic in accord with James's and Adorno's immanent critique. In short, the way out of the reification of self-identity is the way through it, a move James exemplifies and Adorno articulated when he writes that 'only he . . . who would have used his own strength, which he owes to identity, to cast off the facade of identity – would truly be a subject.' This decentered subjectivity, Adorno implies, is itself rooted in an aporia, whose basis 'is to be found in the fact that the truth that lies beyond the compulsion to identity would not simply be different from it, but would be mediated through it.' " See "Henry James, Veblen, and Adorno," 48–9; Posnock cites as the source of the quotations from Adorno *Negative Dialectics,* trans. E. B. Ashton (New York: Continuum, 1973), 277, 299.

26. Hendy, *Gardner Catalogue,* 321.

27. Immutable, barring, of course, damages wrought by accident or design, such as the theft in 1990 of, among other works, Vermeer's *The Concert.*

28. Henry James, "To Paul Bourget," 21 December 1905, *Letters* 4:387. Martha Banta notes that Bourget had seen the Sargent portrait in 1888 when it was first exhibited at the St. Botolph Club without knowing who the model was. *Imaging American Women: Ideas and Ideals in Cultural History* (New York: Columbia UP, 1987), 308. Francis Haskell notes of Sargent's style in "Enemies of Modern Art" (*Past and Present in Art and Taste,* 210) that "the carefully arranged 'spontaneous' brushwork seems almost to be a deliberate and conscious metaphor for the spending rather than the saving of money,"

29. This is the realization of the social and creative dimension of the kind of love, of *agape,* that James learned of from his father, as I argued in my analysis of *The Sense of the Past* in Part One.

30. Where one might expect a conflict, one finds a chiasmus or "antago-

nistic whole." Adorno's term is quoted and used by Posnock in his dialectical analysis of the "antagonistic whole" of identity and nonidentity. Posnock refers to Adorno's use of this term in "Sociology and Psychology," *New Left Review* 47 (1968): 74.

31. A description of the power of habits of mind is a crucial part of Peirce's explanation of how semiosis occurs. See in particular his essay on "The Fixation of Belief," in *Philosophical Writings of Peirce*, ed. Justus Buchler (New York: Dover, 1955), 5–22. John P. Diggens discusses Veblen's philosophical work with Peirce and others at Johns Hopkins in *The Bard of Savagery: Thorstein Veblen and Modern Social Theory* (New York: Continuum, 1978), 27.

32. *Leisure*, 395. Translation courtesy of Ellen Finkelpearl.

33. Diggens, *The Bard of Savagery*, 199, 32.

34. Thorstein Veblen, *The Theory of Business Enterprise*, introd. Douglas Dowd (1904; New Brunswick, N.J.: Transaction, 1978), 399–400. All further references to this edition are cited parenthetically.

35. Martha Banta shows in *Taylored Lives: Narrative Productions in the Age of Taylor, Veblen, and Ford* (Chicago: U of Chicago Press, 1993) the extent to which the model of rationalized work infused American culture at the turn of the century.

36. Thorstein Veblen, *The Higher Learning in America: A Memorandum on the Conduct of Universities by Business Men* (1918; New York: Kelley, 1965), 9. All further references to this edition are cited parenthetically.

37. Sigmund Freud, *Civilization and Its Discontents*, trans. James Strachey (1930; New York: Norton, 1961), 29. All further references to this edition are cited parenthetically.

38. Sigmund Freud, *Beyond the Pleasure Principle*, trans. James Strachey (1920; New York: Norton, 1961) 31.

39. Henry James, *The Ambassadors*, vol. 22 of *The Novels and Tales of Henry James*, 27 vols. (New York: Scribner's, 1917), 22:326.

40. Henry James, preface to *Roderick Hudson*, in *Literary Criticism: French Writers, Other European Writers, Prefaces to the New York Edition*, ed. Leon Edel (1907; New York: Library of America, 1984), 1041.

41. Ross Posnock concludes, citing Adorno's phrase, that it is Veblen's " 'inability to think through the problem of mediation' " that "ultimately vitiates Veblen's critique" ("Henry James, Veblen and Adorno, 34).

42. Georges Bataille, *The Accursed Share: An Essay on General Economy*, vol. 1, *Consumption*, trans. Robert Hurley (1967; New York: Zone, 1991), 22. All further references to this edition are noted parenthetically.

43. Henry James, "Is There Life after Death?" in F. O. Matthiessen, *The James Family: Including Selections from the Writings of Henry James, Senior, William, Henry, and Alice James* (1947; New York: Vintage, 1980), 610. All further references to this edition are noted parenthetically.

44. Jonathan Freedman traces the tendency of "the spectacular ability

of an advanced consumer society to transform criticism of that society into objects of consumption themselves...." (*Professions of Taste*, 60). But he is obviously proceeding on assumptions contrary to those of Bataille with respect to the desirability of consumption as the ultimate end of social life.

45. Jaroslav Pelikan *The Vindication of Tradition* (New Haven: Yale UP, 1984), 54.

46. Kermode, *The Classic*, 140.

Chapter 5. "Psychic Mulatto"

1. Lewis P. Simpson traces the origins and variations of this difference in Northern and Southern attitudes toward tradition and the past in *The Man of Letters in New England and the South: Essays on the Literary Vocation in America* (Baton Rouge: Louisiana State UP, 1973).

   This reverence for continuity is somewhat ironic since, as C. Vann Woodward points out in his introduction to *The Strange Career of Jim Crow* (1955; New York: Oxford UP, 1966), the South's history has been much more radically disrupted than that of the North.

2. Henry James, *The American Scene*, introd. and notes by Leon Edel (1907; Bloomington: Indiana UP, 1968), 365–70. All further references to this edition are noted parenthetically.

3. Henry James, *Hawthorne*, in *Literary Criticism: Essays on Literature, American Writers, English Writers*, ed. Leon Edel (1879; New York: Library of America, 1984), 342.

4. Ibid., 351.

5. James's sense of the aesthetic impoverishment of the South may have been exaggerated by the fact that most of the attention of artists in the Old South had been commanded by the desires of the wealthy for decorative rather than fine arts, wherever one draws that line. The craftsmanship of Charleston cabinetmakers, for example, was second to none and the architecture of the great plantations (which he did not have time to visit), townhouses, and public buildings was more rich, varied, and coherent than the stereotype of the white-columned plantation house would suggest. There were also, of course, many fine portraits of the distinguished and wealthy citizens, but there was little in the way of a more "disinterested" portrayal of life in the South. Francis Blackwell Mayer (1827–99), a Baltimore artist, was unusual in his choice of scenes of everyday life, however conventional was the allegorical meaning carried by "Independence: Squire Jack Porter" (1858) and "Leisure and Labor" (1858). The best paintings of slave life were done by outsiders, often foreigners. Works by Alfred Boisseau (1823–1901), a Frenchman; Christian Mayr (1805?–51), a German; John Antrobus (1837–1907), an Englishman; and Eyre Crowe (1824–1910), another En-

glishman, who accompanied Thackeray on his 1852–3 tour of America, are the highlights of a section devoted to the painting of 1826–60 in Jessie Poesch's *The Art of the Old South: Painting, Sculpture, Architecture and the Products of Craftsmen, 1560–1860* (New York: Knopf, 1983), on which research and analyses I have based my interpretation of James's reaction to the aesthetic blankness of the Old South. It strikes me as significant that the best-known painter of those treated in this encyclopedic work is John James Audubon, whose earliest ornithological studies were undertaken in the 1820s in the Deep South. Audubon was a native of Haiti (1785–1851) and his portraits of birds were not, obviously, involved in any direct way with the social and political conflicts of the South, however much they may have illustrated the relations of the environment and its inhabitants.

6. Another writer also characterizes this intellectual style as somewhat "rococo": "At its crest, the proslavery argument was so vital, so dynamic that it reached out to anticipate, for its own peculiar purposes, evolutionary science and sociology. It was fantastically imaginative, informed by masses of research, and profoundly and intricately worked out. On the eve of conflict it was a weirdly beautiful flower, the black orchid of antebellum Southern intellectual culture." Joel Williamson, *The Rage for Order: Black/White Relations in the American South since Emancipation* (New York: Oxford UP, 1986), 15.

7. See the introduction to this book for a more detailed explanation of this tradition of discontinuity.

Writing of the conversion of John Foxe, whose *Acts and Monuments,* begun in the 1550s, articulated the version of history that had been developing since 1517, when Luther delivered his theses at Wittenberg, Anthony Kemp summarizes this crucial shift in perspective: "The reversal of historical vision, from union to difference, must have taken place in a decade at most for Foxe, and his experience must have been replicated by almost all who followed the movement for reform; the past changed its shape, revealed the beliefs held universally by the Western world for fifteen hundred years to have been a falsehood, in a single generation." See *The Estrangement of the Past: A Study in the Origins of Modern Historical Consciousness* (New York: Oxford UP, 1991), 85.

8. Elizabeth Fox-Genovese and Eugene D. Genovese, "The Cultural History of Southern Slave Society: Reflection on the Work of Lewis P. Simpson," in *American Letters and the Historical Consciousness: Essays in Honor of Lewis P. Simpson,* ed. J. Gerald Kennedy and Daniel Mark Fogel (Baton Rouge: Louisiana State UP, 1988), 27.

9. Eugene D. Genovese, "The Southern Slaveholder's View of the Middle Ages," in *Medievalism in American Culture: Papers of the Eighteenth Annual Conference of the Center for Medieval and Early Renaissance*

Studies, vol. 55, ed. Bernard Rosenthal and Paul E. Szarmach (Binghamton, N.Y.: Medieval and Renaissance Texts and Studies, 1989), 31.

10. Quoted in ibid., 35.

11. Ibid., 32.

12. Ibid., 34–5.

13. George Fitzhugh, *Cannibals All! or, Slaves without Masters* (Richmond: A. Morris, 1857).

14. Genovese, "Slaveholder's View," 37.

15. Williamson, "Rage for Order," 38.

16. These are the dates Williamson (*Rage for Order,* 118) assigns for the dominance of Southern Radical racist ideology (not to be confused with the pro–civil rights Radical Republicans of the North).

17. Woodward, *Jim Crow,* 69, 73, 94, 107.

18. Williamson, *Rage for Order,* 85.

19. Kenneth W. Warren, in *Black and White Strangers: Race and American Realism* (Chicago: University of Chicago P, 1993), also reads *The American Scene* in relation to *The Souls of Black Folk* and takes the social context of the South at this time into consideration.

20. George Harvey, "Some Fresh Suggestions about the New Negro Crime," *Harper's Weekly* 48, 23 January 1904, 120–1.

    Williamson refers to Harvey's article (*Rage for Order,* 86) in the context of the development of the intellectual foundations of Radical thought, particularly the belief in "retrogression" and its correlation, the uncontrollable sexuality of the black rapist, that gave rise to the wave of lynchings that crested in 1892 when 156 black men were summarily and violently executed by lawless mobs (84). From 1889 to 1918, 88 percent of the nation's lynchings took place in the South.

21. Thomas Dixon, *The Leopard's Spots: A Romance of the White Man's Burden (1865–1900)* (1902). The founding of the Ku Klux Klan is one of the dramatic climaxes of this novel, which repeats with impressively obsessive regularity the supposedly repulsive physical characteristics of the black.

22. See *Life Under The "Peculiar Institution": Selections from the Slave Narrative Collection,* ed. Norman R. Yetman (New York: Holt, 1970).

23. W. E. B. Du Bois, *The Souls of Black Folk,* in *Writings,* ed. Nathan Higgens (1903; New York: Library Of America, 1986). All further references to this edition are noted parenthetically.

24. Quoted in Arnold Rampersad, *The Art and Imagination of W. E. B. Du Bois* (Cambridge: Harvard UP, 1976), 12.

25. W. E. Burghardt Du Bois, review of *The Negro: The Southerner's Problem* by Thomas Nelson Page, *Dial,* 1 May 1905, 316.

26. Ibid.

27. Ibid., 315.

28. Ibid., 317.

29. The historical fact that the notion of double consciousness has remained a formulation important to African Americans for their self-definition even as Du Bois's status has risen and fallen among them testifies to its usefulness in describing a radical alienation from the American mainstream veneration of the monadic (imperial) self. For a subtle consideration of the play between the racist implications of transcendental individualism and Du Bois's racialist advocacy of the special gifts of the Negro, see Cornel West's *The American Evasion of Philosophy: A Genealogy of Pragmatism* (Madison: U of Wisconsin P, 1989), esp. 142–3.

30. This connection is suggested, and this passage is quoted by Rampersad, *Art and Imagination*, 74.

David Levering Lewis is more skeptical about any direct influence in Du Bois's choice of this term, although he does see the similarity between William James's use of the term in the case study of a schizophrenic in a text Du Bois is likely to have read and Du Bois's analysis of the alienated condition of African Americans. See *W. E. B. Du Bois: Biography of a Race, 1868–1919* (New York: Henry Holt, 1993), 96.

31. Henry James Senior, *The Secret of Swedenborg: Being an Elucidation of His Doctrine of the Divine Natural Humanity* (Boston: Houghton, Mifflin, 1869), chap. 2. James Senior's theory of the creation of consciousness is discussed in detail in Part Three, "Patrimony and Matrimony."

32. Henry James, *Notes of a Son and Brother* (1914), in *Autobiography*, ed. Frederick W. Dupee (1956; Princeton: Princeton UP, 1983), 373. When James describes Strether in *The Ambassadors*, vol. 21 of *The Novels and Tales of Henry James*, 27 vols.(New York: Scribner's, 1909), 5, as being "burdened . . . with the oddity of a double consciousness" he describes something more solipsistic and chiasmatic: "There was a detachment in his zeal and a curiosity in his indifference."

33. Rampersad, *Art and Imagination*, 14.

34. Quoted in ibid., 123. In his analysis of this novel, Arnold Rampersad notes that "Du Bois wrote in 1944, looking back on his beliefs at the start of the century . . . 'I was not at the time sufficiently Freudian to understand how little human action is based on reason'" (ibid., 127). Du Bois later dramatized these conflicts again in his historical novel *The Black Flame* (ibid., 274–81).

35. Quoted in Anthony Appiah, "The Uncompleted Argument: Du Bois and the Illusion of Race," in *"Race," Writing and Difference*, ed. Henry Louis Gates Jr. (Chicago: U of Chicago P, 1986), 24.

36. Henry Louis Gates Jr., "Writing 'Race' and the Difference It Makes," in *"Race," Writing and Difference*, 5.

37. J. G. A. Pocock, "Texts as Events: Reflections on the History of Political Thought," in *Politics and Discourse*, ed. K. Sharper and S. Zwicker (Berkeley: U of California P, 1987), 30.

38. Appiah, "Uncompleted Argument," 36. Appiah gives a very useful summary of the current state of genetic research in which the whole concept of race is brought into question.

   Other writers on ethnic and racial questions have, of course, addressed this issue of interpretation, but none, to my knowledge, so decisively as Appiah. Werner Sollors, for instance, writes that since the dominant culture makes definition one of its prerogatives, those who are disenfranchised must often engage in complex strategies of "defiant reinterpretation," but he wants to hold onto some redefined category of ethnicity, just as Du Bois held onto the category of "race." See *Beyond Ethnicity: Consent and Descent in American Culture* (New York: Oxford UP, 1986), 193.

39. James notes that he was reading James Ford Rhodes's *History of the United States from the Compromise of 1850 to the Final Restoration of Home Rule in the South in 1877*. My references are to the version abridged and edited by Allan Nevins (Chicago: U of Chicago P, 1966). This abridgment is of the first five volumes of the 1907 edition of Rhodes's seven-volume history. As the fifth volume appeared in 1904, James could have been reading any of these five, although his remark about the recounting of "the long preliminaries of the war" by "Rhoades [*sic*]" in his "admirable History" indicates that he was reading the earlier volumes. Rhodes's chapter, which Nevins titles "Southern Society," recounts the consequences of slavery, both good and evil, for Southern culture – namely benevolence and gentility on the one hand and brutality and closedmindedness on the other – that arise from the exercise of nearly absolute power over other human beings. Rhodes comments on the Englishman's pleasure in Southern society in this same chapter (78–9).

40. This designation for African Americans that is so offensive to our ears may have seemed to James appropriate to apply to these particular blacks because of their condition. Yet he is just as ready to take note of squalor among white people. He writes in *The American Scene* of its general absence in America, but refers to a few exceptions "also, below the Southern line, certain special, certain awful examples, in Black and White alike, of the last crudity of condition" (178).

   For the historical record, the term "darky" seems to have been used derogatorily, as in the instance cited in the *Oxford English Dictionary* from *Century Magazine* in 1883: "the manners of a cornfield darky," as well as descriptively, as in *Nineteenth Century* in 1884: "a coffin of curious darky workmanship."

41. Henry James, "The Beast in the Jungle," in vol. 17 of *The Novels and Tales of Henry James*, 27 vols. (New York: Scribner's, 1909), 126.

42. Probably James's only other encounter with a large group of blacks was during his visit in the spring of 1863 to his brother Garth Wilkinson James in Readville, where he was stationed at Camp Meigs

with the famous 54th Massachusetts, the first black regiment, led by Robert Gould Shaw and the sons of many other prominent Bostonians. For a more complete telling of this episode in the life of the James family, see Jane Maher, *Biography of Broken Fortunes: Wilkie and Bob, Brothers of William, Henry, and Alice James* (Hamden, Conn.: Archon, 1986), my source for the quotations from Wilkie's letters.

43. Williamson writes of the antebellum South: "It was a strung-out, tension-laden society where vast energies were spent simply holding one's self together. The tension was there because the blacks were there. In a real way, the Southern white was the person black people made simply by being in the South in such numbers and in such a manner as they were. That manner was recurrently rebellious—in the fields, in the kitchens, and in the cabins—and it made of Sambo's keepers a peculiar people" (*Rage for Order*, 24).

44. Warren suggests that James's "disparagement of black servants" is part of a critique of the general vulgarity of American life (*Black and White Strangers*, 123).

45. Warren suggests that "James's blindness is not surprising because the path to black subjectivity in *The American Scene* runs through their capacity for personal service" (ibid., 122). I would agree that James does not try to identify with the black's point of view, but that he is, nevertheless, displaced from his own racial position by his encounter with the Virginian (see subsequent discussion).

46. As Eugene Genovese writes in the first sentence of *Roll, Jordan, Roll: The World the Slaves Made* (1972; New York: Vintage, 1974), 3: "Cruel, unjust, exploitative, oppressive, slavery bound two peoples together in bitter antagonism while creating an organic relationship so complex and ambivalent that neither could express the simplest human feelings without reference to the other."

47. If nowhere else, James had encountered a very critical firsthand view of conditions in the "slave state" from the "Journal of a Residence on a Georgia Planation," written by his longtime friend, the famous actress Fanny Kemble. He considers this "strong, insistent, one-sided" work the best among her prose writings, and in 1893 remarked that he thought it a useful corrective to the "impressions begotten by that old Southern life which we are too apt to see to-day as through a haze of Indian summer." See Henry James, "Frances Anne Kemble," in *Literary Criticism: Essays on Literature, American Writers, English Writers*, 1089.

48. L. Moody Simms Jr., "Henry James and the Negro Question," *American Notes and Queries* 10 (1972): 127–28.

49. Maxwell Geismar, *Henry James and the Jacobites* (1962; New York: Hill and Wang, 1965) 352.
    I treat the negative characterizations of James – Geismar accuses him of anti-Semitism and proto-Nazism (350) – in the introduction.

50. Henry James Senior, "The Social Significance of Our Institutions,"

in *Henry James, Senior: A Selection of His Writings,* ed. and introd. Giles Gunn (Chicago: American Library Association, 1974), 116.

51. An interesting light is thrown on James's earlier attitude toward slavery and contemporary theories of racial characteristics in his 1875 review of Sir Samuel Baker's *Ismailïa: A Narrative of the Expeditions to Central Africa for the Suppression of the Slave Trade, Organized by Ismail, Khedive of Egypt.* James's irony about this benevolent mission should not, of course, be mistaken for advocacy of slavery. James, in *Literary Criticism: Essays on Literature, American Writers, English Writers,* 732–6.

   See also Sara Blair, *Henry James and the Writing of Race and Nation* (Cambridge: Cambridge UP, 1996), chap. 1.

52. In his analysis of James's evasive explanation of his "obscure hurt" in *Notes of a Son and Brother,* Leon Edel concludes that the injury was not the castration some had imagined, was something nevertheless physically painful, but not so severe as to keep James from feeling guilty (and possibly thereby aggravating his injury as was the custom of the psychosomatically inclined James family) about not enlisting. See *Henry James: The Untried Years, 1843–1870* (1953; New York: Avon, 1978), 167–83.

53. In "Jim Crow Henry James," Walter Benn Michaels offers a subtle and persuasive reading of another instance in which James transvalues the racial dichotomies of turn-of-the-century America in his characterization of the "brown lady" in *What Maisie Knew* (1897), by which he declines to subscribe to the racial categories Jim Crow. *Henry James Review* 16:3 (1995): 286–91.

54. Sigmund Freud, "Recommendations for Physicians on the Psychoanalytic Method of Treatment" (1912), in *Therapy and Technique* (New York: Collier, 1963), 122.

55. See Henry James, *The Sense of the Past,* vol. 26 of *The Novels and Tales of Henry James,* 27 vols. (New York: Scribner's, 1917), 48–9.

56. The Virginian's reverence for the past is what Jaroslav Pelikan calls traditionalism, "the dead faith of the living," which is distinguished from tradition, "the living faith of the dead." It is, he adds, "traditionalism that gives tradition such a bad name." Jaroslav Pelikan, *The Vindication of Tradition* (New Haven: Yale UP, 1984), 65.

57. For a more detailed description of the ambivalence of the transference relationship, see the conclusion of Part One, "Making the Last Romance," where I discuss it in relation to *The Sense of the Past.*

58. Warren notes that James's allegiance to the North and to the present South with its poverty of whites and blacks is also shaken when he catches a romantic glimpse of a Charleston garden, only to have the "elderly mulatress" shut the door in his face (121).

59. "Make [the reader] think the evil," James says of his method in *The Turn of the Screw,* "make him think it for himself, and you are released from weak specifications." Henry James, preface to *The*

Aspern Papers, in *Literary Criticism: French Writers, Other European Writers, Prefaces to the New York Edition*, ed. Leon Edel (1907; New York: Library of America, 1984), 1188.

60. Henry James, *The Bostonians*, in *Novels 1881–1886*, ed. William T. Stafford (1886; New York: Library of America, 1985), 1023, 1027. Thanks to my colleague Wendy Graham for suggesting that I take this scene into consideration.

61. David Levering Lewis describes the positive potential of double consciousness in similar terms: "Henceforth, the destiny of the race could be conceived as leading neither to assimilation nor separatism but to proud, enduring hyphenation." *W. E. B. Du Bois*, 281.

62. Some of these forms of culture would surely come in forms James would not be able to appreciate. Where he heard only "the weird chants of the emancipated blacks" (which is, nevertheless, the only Southern music he finds it worth his while to mention) (387), Du Bois sees the unique and invaluable contribution of the blacks to the "ideal of human brotherhood": "there is no true American music but the wild sweet melodies of the Negro slave; the American fairy tales and folklore are Indian and African." Du Bois, *Souls*, 52.

63. Henry James, "To Bernard Shaw," 20 January 1909, in *Henry James Letters*, ed. Leon Edel, 4 vols. (Cambridge: Belknap Press of Harvard UP, 1974–84), 4:513.

64. The conflation between semiotics and fellowship that occurs at this point in my argument is justified by C. S. Peirce himself in his less popular essays on, for example, "Evolutionary Love," in *Philosophical Writings of Peirce*, ed. Justus Buchler (New York: Dover, 1955), chap. 27. He is, I think, quite clear about his Christian hopes for a meaningful life, although he might not subscribe to the erotic element I am suggesting is also part of this desire to interpret.

65. James's sympathetic union with this representation of General Lee makes a companion piece to his rebellion against the duplicity of Saint Gaudens's Sherman. See Chapter 4.

Chapter 6. Return of the Alien

1. Henry James, *The American Scene*, introd. and notes by Leon Edel (1907; Bloomington: Indiana UP, 1968), 136. All further references to this edition are noted parenthetically.

2. Henry James, *The Portrait of a Lady*, vol. 4 of *The Novels and Tales of Henry James*, 27 vols. (New York: Scribner's, 1908), 415.

3. For a reading of the figure of "the margin" as a value in *The American Scene*, and the way in which the alien threatens the distinction between the insider and the outsider, see Stuart Johnson, "American Marginalia: James's *The American Scene*," *Texas Studies in Literature and Language* 24 (1982): 83–101, esp. 89.

4. This is the distinction that Werner Sollors makes between "descent"

and "consent" in his analysis of ethnicity. See *Beyond Ethnicity: Consent and Descent in American Culture* (New York: Oxford UP, 1986). In *The World, the Text and the Critic* (Cambridge: Harvard UP, 1983), Edward Said describes this doubleness of national identity as "filiation" and "affiliation," namely, connections to one's place of birth and connections to various other groups. The two aspects of national identity may coincide or be at odds with one another (24).

5. Jacob A. Riis, *How the Other Half Lives* (New York: Charles Scribners's Sons, 1890), 97.

6. Ibid., 102.

7. Ibid., 122, 126.

8. Ibid., 106–7.

9. Ibid., 154.

10. Alexander Alland Sr., *Jacob A. Riis: Photographer and Citizen* (New York: Aperture, 1974), 6–7.

11. Ibid., 34.

12. Alan Trachtenberg, "The American Scene: Versions of the City," *Massachusetts Review* 8:2 (1967): 293; Jonathan Freedman, "Trilling, James, and the Uses of Cultural Criticism," *Henry James Review* 14:2 (Spring 1993): 145.

13. See my introduction for an explanation of what Butterfield means by the "whig interpretation of history."

14. Riis, *Other Half*, 207.

15. Jacob A. Riis, *The Battle with the Slum* (New York: Macmillan, 1902), 233.

16. Ibid., 138–9.

17. Ibid., 168.

18. Pelikan, *The Vindication of Tradition* (New Haven: Yale UP, 1984),65.

19. Werner Sollors, "Immigrants and Other Americans," in *Columbia Literary History of the United States*, ed. Emory Elliott (New York: Columbia UP, 1988), 573. Sollors writes that Cahan made this remark in a review of *How the Other Half Lives* in the *Commerical Advertiser*.

20. The rural (and urban) Christian Danes, however, turned themselves into "Jews" when, following the example of their king, they donned the yellow star of David that marked the chosen victims of the Nazi regime.

21. Riis, *Other Half*, 136–47.

22. Maxwell Geismar, *Henry James and the Jacobites* (1962; New York: Hill and Wang, 1965), 350.

23. Peter Buitenhuis, *The Grasping Imagination: The American Writings of Henry James* (Toronto: U of Toronto P, 1970), 189–90.

24. Leon Edel, *Henry James: The Master, 1901–1916* (New York: Avon, 1978), 5:291.

25. Freedman, "Trilling, James and the Uses of Cultural Criticism," 145.

26. Edel, *Henry James: The Master, 1901–1916*, 5:291.

27. Riis, *Other Half* 56.

28. Ibid., 301–2.

29. Ibid., 208, 80, 122, 133.

30. Frank Kermode, *The Classic: Literary Images of Permanence and Change* (Cambridge: Harvard UP, 1983), 139–40.

31. For a fuller treatment of the dubious biological grounding of "race," see my chapter on James's visit to the South, "Psychic Mulatto."

32. Buitenhuis also catches this reference to Henry Senior (see *The Grasping Imagination*, 190).

33. Henry James, "Daniel Deronda: A Conversation," in *Literary Criticism: Essays on Literature, American Writers, English Writers,* ed. Leon Edel (1876; New York: Library of America, 1984), 981.

34. Thorstein Veblen, "The Intellectual Pre-Eminence of Jews," in *Essays in Our Changing Order* (1919; New York: Kelley, 1964), 226.

35. Ibid.

36. For two informative historical surveys of the prevalence of anti-Semitism and the racist grounds on which it was perpetuated in turn-of-the-century America, see Michael N. Dobkoski, "American Anti-Semitism: A Reinterpretation," *American Quarterly* 29 (Summer 1977): 166–81; Robert Singerman, "The Jew As Radical Alien: The Genetic Component of American Anti-Semitism," in *Anti-Semitism in American History,* ed. David A. Gerber (Urbana: U of Illinois P, 1987), 103–28.

37. Daniel Boyarin and Jonathan Boyarin, "Diaspora: Generational Ground of Jewish Identity," *Critical Inquiry* 19:4 (1993): 721.

38. Henry James, "The Saint's Afternoon and Others," in *Italian Hours* (1909: New York: Grove, 1959), 363.

39. Henry James, "To William James," 29 October 1888, in *Henry James Letters,* ed. Leon Edel, 4 vols. (Cambridge: Belknap Press of Harvard UP, 1974–84), 3:244.

40. Ibid., 3:242.

41. Freedman, in "Trilling, James, and the Uses of Cultural Criticism," makes the argument that Trilling "brings James and the Jew together under the sign of a notion that resonated in the experience of both: that of the alien," especially in the sense of the urban cosmopolite (148).

42. These essays are discussed in greater detail in the context of my discussion of gender in Part Three, "Patrimony and Matrimony."

43. Henry James, "The Speech of American Women" *Harper's Bazar* 40, 4 parts, November 1906–February 1907, reprinted in *French Writers and American Women,* ed. and introd. Peter Buitenhuis (Branford, Conn: Compass, 1960), 47.

44. T. S. Eliot, *Notes towards the Definition of Culture* (London: Faber and Faber, 1948), 59.

45. Edel, *Henry James: The Master, 1901–1916,* 5:528.

Chapter 7. Heterosocial Acts

1. Henry James, *The American Scene*, introd. and notes by Leon Edel (1907; Bloomington: Indiana UP, 1968), 164. All further references to this edition are noted parenthetically.

2. Joseph Allen Boone, in *Tradition Counter Tradition: Love and the Form of Fiction*, (Chicago: U of Chicago P, 1987), 187–201, alert to the play between gender and genre as shifts in social relations affect the shapes of stories, reads the ambiguous "happy ending" of *The Golden Bowl* as a complex negotiation between James's open ending and the closure of certain romantic possibilities between Maggie and her Prince.

3. As Martha Banta has written in "Men Women, and The American Way" (*The Cambridge Companion to Henry James*, ed. Jonathan Freedman, forthcoming): "There is little or nothing going on in Henry James's mind that is *not* about social relations between men and women; every issue is ultimately gendered. Thus to think about gender in James is to think of just about everything he said and wrote." Banta shows in this essay how flexible James's construction of gender is compared with that of his contemporary, Theodore Roosevelt, defender of "masculinity." In his essay "In the Closet with Frederick Douglass: Reconstructing Masculinity in *The Bostonians*," *Henry James Review* 16:3 (Fall 1995): 292–8, Leland S. Person traces the conflict in that novel between Basil's attempt to construct an "unreconstructed manhood" – and James's consistent subversion of that attempt.

I point to these few recent works because the critical literature on James and gender is too vast to pretend to survey in a footnote. Disagreements about James's views of women and marriage abound in this rich body of scholarship. I would also point, however, to Susan L. Mizruchi, in "Reproducing Women in *The Awkward Age*," *Representations* 38 (1992): 101–30, because she analyzes James's critique of the contradictions of marriage at this time with reference to the various contemporary social science theories and concludes that James's "reinvention of femininity in the modern era will result in a different form of subordination" (117).

Placing James's critique of marriage in an American literary tradition, Douglas Anderson, in *A House Undivided: Domesticity and Community in American Literature* (Cambridge: Cambridge UP, 1990), argues for the continuous centrality of the topos of marriage as a model for social relations, seeing James as the heir to the patrimony of Winthrop's and Hawthorne's models of Christian charity.

John Carlos Rowe in *The Theoretical Dimensions of Henry James* (Madison: U of Wisconsin P, 1984), 89, claims that the incomplete analysis of alternatives to contemporary gender relations is typical of James: "In another sense, it is fair to conclude that all too often James's feminine characters end up achieving *only* the awareness of their contradictory relationship to social institutions. James's novels and stories are centrally concerned with marriage as a primary social institution; as critical as James is of marriage, his characters remain trapped by its values to the very end."

4. Henry James, "The Death of the Lion," vol. 15 of *The Novels and Tales of Henry James*, 27 vols. (New York: Scribner's, 1909), 115–16.

5. Henry James, *The Ivory Tower*, vol. 27 of *The Novels and Tales of Henry James*, 27 vols. (New York: Scribner's, 1917), 205. All further references to this edition are noted parenthetically.

6. I derive this term from Eve Kosofsky Sedgwick's "homosocial" but acknowledge Philip Horne's further elaboration (in "Henry James: The Master and the 'Queer Affair' of 'The Pupil,' " *Critical Quarterly* 37:3 [1995] 75–92) of the spectrum of social/sexual/erotic relations to which he adds another useful term: "heteroerotic" (77).

7. See Eve Kosofsky Sedgwick, "The Beast in the Closet: James and the Writing of Homosexual Panic," in *The Epistemology of the Closet* (Berkeley: U of California P, 1990), 207, for a reading of a similar potential relation between May Bartram and John Marcher.

8. Adrienne Rich, "Compulsory Heterosexuality and the Lesbian Existence," in *The Signs Reader: Women, Gender and Scholarship*, ed. Elizabeth Abel and Emily K. Abel (1980; Chicago: U of Chicago P, 1983), 139–68.

   There are also, of course, autobiographical reasons for James taking an interest in the reconfiguration of sexual and social identities and roles but this is not my present concern. See Sedgwick, "The Beast in the Closet"; Fred Kaplan, *Henry James: The Imagination of Genius: A Biography* (New York: Morrow, 1992); Wendy Graham, "Henry James's Subterranean Blues: A Rereading of *The Princess Casamassima*," *Modern Fiction Studies* 40:1 (Spring 1994): 51–84; Sheldon Novick, *Henry James: The Young Master* (New York: Random House, 1996), for recent studies of James and homosexuality.

9. For two different readings of the social and juridical origins of the nineteenth century's various Married Women's Property Acts, see Peggy A. Rabkin, *Fathers to Daughter: The Legal Foundations of Female Emancipation* (Westport, Conn.: Greenwood Press, 1980), and Norma Basch, *In the Eyes of the Law: Women, Marriage and Property in Nineteenth-Century New York* (Ithaca: Cornell UP, 1982).

10. John Carlos Rowe notes the ambiguity of gender references in the central images of the novel: "Simply put, the tower and the letter both share and confuse masculine and feminine characteristics that encourage us to view them as doubles." See *The Theoretical Dimensions of Henry James* 4.

11. Eve Kosofsky Sedgwick, *Between Men: English Literature and Male Homosocial Desire* (New York: Columbia UP, 1985), esp. 207, on various ways in which women are excluded from the homosocial.

12. In this connection, we might refer to Julia Kristeva's remark in the interview known as "Why the United States?" in which she entertains

the possibility of something quite interesting but definitely different from psychoanalysis emerging in America because of its nonverbal culture. In *The Kristeva Reader,* ed. Toril Moi (New York: Columbia UP, 1986), 279. The interview was originally published in 1977 in *Tel Quel.*

In the "Postscript: Notes on Psychoanalysis Today," of his book *Freud and the Culture of Psychoanalysis: Studies in the Transition from Victorian Humanism to Modernity* (New York: Norton, 1984), Steven Marcus discusses the shift in cultural values from those – such as the belief in hard work and rationality – which characterized the bourgeois culture in which psychoanalysis arose to other values that characterize contemporary American culture – such as the demand for immediate gratification – and he also speculates that in such a cultural context psychoanalysis may find its value as a heuristic and as a therapeutic instrument increasingly marginalized and problematical.

13. Henry James, *The Question of Our Speech; The Lesson of Balzac: Two Lectures* (Boston: Houghton Mifflin 1905), 21. All further references to this edition are noted parenthetically.

14. Ferdinand de Saussure, *Course in General Linguistics,* ed. Charles Bally, Albert Sechehaye, and Albert Reidlinger, trans. Wade Baskin (1915; New York: McGraw-Hill, 1966). See in particular the chapter on "Immutability and Mutability of the Sign."

15. *Nation,* October 1868, 332–4.

16. Henry James, "The Speech of American Women," *Harper's Bazar* 40, 4 parts, November 1906–February 1907; "The Manners of American Women," *Harper's Bazar* 41, 4 parts, April–July 1907. These essays are reprinted in the collection *French Writers and American Women,* ed. and introd. Peter Buitenhuis (Branford, Conn.: Compass, 1960), and it is to this edition that I will refer parenthetically in the text.

17. For works by critics who take this position see Jean Strouse, *Alice James: A Biography* (Boston: Houghton-Mifflin, 1980); Alfred Habegger, *Henry James and the "Woman Business"* (Cambridge: Cambridge UP, 1989).

Chapter 8. Odd Couples

1. His son William noted his father's predilection both in his introduction to *The Literary Remains of the Late Henry James,* ed. and introd. William James (Boston: Houghton-Mifflin, 1884), 9, when he said that "[p]robably few authors have so devoted their entire lives to the monotonous elaboration of a single bundle of truths"; and in an illustration he did in his youth for his father's forthcoming *Substance and Shadow:* "a small woodcut to be put on the title-page, representing a man beating a dead horse." The paterfamilias was amused. Quoting an anecdote told by Thomas Sergeant Perry in Percy Lub-

bock's preface to *The Letters of Henry James*, 2 vols. (1920; New York: Octogon, 1970), 1:9.

2. Henry James, *Notes of a Son and Brother* (1914), in *Autobiography*, ed. Frederick W. Dupee (1956; Princeton: Princeton UP, 1983), 337.

3. C. S. Peirce, review of "James's Secret of Swedenborg," *North American Review* 110 (April 1870): 463–8. See his comments on the confusion between real and symbolic women (467).

4. I would include among the readers who miss James Senior's theological foundation (as well as his irony) Alfred Habegger in "The Lessons of the Father: Henry James, Sr. on Sexual Difference," in *Henry James and the "Woman Business"* (Cambridge: Cambridge UP, 1989), 27–62. Habegger's unfortunately hostile biography of Henry James Senior, *The Father* (New York: Farrar Straus and Giroux, 1995), continues and compounds this error.

5. Henry James Senior, *The Social Significance of Our Institutions* (1861), in *Henry James Senior: A Selection of His Writings*, ed. and introd. Giles Gunn (Chicago: American Library Association, 1974), 118. See also "Socialism and Civilization" (1849) when James says, "We degrade and disesteem every person we own absolutely, every person bound to us by any other tenure than his own spontaneous affection" (Gunn, 89).

6. James Senior, " 'The Woman Thou gavest with me,' " *Atlantic Monthly* 25 (January 1870): 71.

7. *Oeuvres complètes de Charles Fourier*, ed. Simone Debout Oleszkiewicz, 12 vols. (Paris: Edition Anthropos, 1966–8), 7:150. Quoted in Jonathan Beecher, *Charles Fourier: The Visionary and His World* (Berkeley: U of California P, 1987), 207. James knew Fourier's work from numerous sources and was the translator of Victor Hennequin's *Les amours au phalanstère* in 1848. Fourier's magnum opus on this topic *Le nouveax monde amoureux* was not publicly available until 1967 when published as volume 7 of *Oeuvres complètes*.

8. According to Fourier, the twelve radical passions fall into three groups: the luxurious passions of the five senses; the four affective passions: friendship, love, ambition, and parenthood; and three distributive passions. It is this last category that is Fourier's most original psychological contribution and needs to be explained in a little more detail than the other more self-evident passions. Fourier believed that the repression of these distributive passions was responsible for many of the evils in society and that recognizing them and incorporating them into the social scheme of "Harmony," the proper name of his projected phalanx, would insure it proper functioning.

He called the first of these "the Cabalistic or intriguing passion, the penchant for conspiring, calculating, forming combinations" and saw it at work in the "real intrigues" of markets and courts as well in the "artificial ones like games, the theatre, or novels."

The alternating passion, or the "Butterfly," was the need for variety and contrast. This passion, when left unsatisfied or thwarted as it was in monogamous marriage, activated the Cabalistic passion to achieve its ends and thence came much of the suffering of human society.

The "Composite" passion is, wrote Fourier, "the most beautiful of the passions, the one that enhances the value of all the others." It dominates in the realm of love but "A love is only beautiful if it is a composite love that engages both the senses and the soul."

The basic 810 personality types were formed by variously combining the twelve radical passions.

For a review, see Beecher, *Fourier*, 227–9. I've drawn extensively on Beecher's formulations of Fourier's theory of the passions because his reading is informed by *Le nouveau monde amoureux* as earlier summaries of Fourier's work, such as that found in Austin Warren's *The Elder Henry James* (New York: Macmillan, 1934), were not.

9. "But in every marriage contract, there are three inevitable parties; a particular man and woman, professing mutual affection for each other, on one hand, and the society of which they are members, on the other." James Senior, " 'The Woman Thou gavest with me,' " 69.

10. Ibid., 71.

11. Henry James Senior, "The Logic of Marriage and Murder," *Atlantic Monthly* 25 (June 1870): 747.

12. James, Henry Senior. "Is Marriage Holy?" *Atlantic Monthly* 25 (March 1870): 363.

13. Ibid., 364.

14. James Senior, " 'The Woman Thou gavest with me,' " 70.

15. Ibid., 67–8.

16. Ibid., 66, 69.

17. Ibid., 71.

See Thomas Laqueur, *Making Sex: Body and Gender from the Greeks to Freud* (Cambridge: Harvard UP, 1990), for the most detailed recent history of this fundamental shift from the one-sex to the two-sex model. Of particular interest for our purposes is his charting of the ways in which the one-sex model continued to exert considerable influence on cultural conceptions of gender even as the description of the two incommensurate sexes became biological orthodoxy. See Chapters 5 and 6. This theoretical inconsistency is possible, he argues, because sexual knowledge is no more factual than is that concerning gender:

No discovery or group of discoveries dictated the rise of a two-sex model, for precisely the same reasons that the anatomical discoveries of the Renaissance did not unseat the one-sex model: the nature of sexual difference is not susceptible to empirical testing. It is logically independent of biological facts because already embedded in the language of science, at least when applied to any culturally resonant construal of sexual difference, is the language of gender. In other words, all but the most circumscribed statements about sex are, from their inception, burdened with the cultural work done by these propositions. Despite the new epistemological status of nature as the bedrock of distinctions, and despite the accumulation of facts about sex, sexual difference in the centuries after the scientific revolution was no more stable than it had been before. Two incommensurable sexes were, and are, as much the products of culture as was, and is, the one-sex model. (153)

James Senior's comment shows an awareness that both of these theories were shaping reactionary resistance to what he took to be progress for society in general.

Laqueur locates the general shift from the one-sex to the two-sex model in the eighteenth century, although other scholars dispute this late a date.

18. *The Anchor Genesis,* ed. and trans. E. A. Speiser (New York: Doubleday, 1964), 16. Speiser suggests this analogy and emphasizes that it was not puns but symbolic, magical connections that were of interest to ancient writers.

19. Henry James Senior, *The Secret of Swedenborg: Being an Elucidation of His Doctrine of the Divine Natural Humanity* (Boston: Houghton Mifflin, 1869), 137. All further references to this edition are noted parenthetically.

20. Henry James, *A Small Boy* (1913), in *Autobiography,* 123–4.

21. James Senior, "The Logic of Marriage and Murder," 745–6.

22. Ibid., 746.

23. *Feminine Sexuality: Jacques Lacan and the* école freudienne, ed. Juliet Mitchell and Jacqueline Rose, trans. Jacqueline Rose (New York: Norton, Pantheon, 1983). All further references to this edition are noted parenthetically.

Mitchell chooses as the epigraph to her introductory essay in this volume a passage from a letter written in 1935 from Freud to Carl Müller-Braunschweig in which he declares his opposition – "I object to all of you (Horney, Jones, Rado, etc.)" – to the confusions perpetrated by his followers and his dissidents of the psychic and the biological. This distinction was at the center of the "great debate" about female sexuality that raged among analysts during the twenties and thirties. Lacan's charge that theories of female sexuality that try to define it in positive, naturalistic terms are ideologies and not psychoanalysis refers to the same insistence by the "ideologues" that it is the body (or the real), and not the symbolic, that creates sexual difference (3, 17). As Mitchell charts the history of the contradictions and developments of Freud's theorizing of sexual difference, she shows how he came to realize that his rendering of the girl's experience of the Oedipus complex *assumed* heterosexuality as natural instead of explaining how it came about. Thus the focus of his interest in explaining sexual difference shifted from the Oedipus complex to the castration complex. With many questions unresolved at the time of his death, he clearly had the sense that this was *the* key to *the* mystery: "The *castration complex* is of the profoundest importance in the formation alike of character and of neurosis." Quoted in Mitchell (13) from *The Standard Edition of the Complete Psychological Works of Sigmund Freud,* ed. and trans. James Strachey in collaboration with Anna Freud, Alix Strachey, and Alan Tyson, 24 vols. (London: Hogarth, 1953–74), 20:37 (1925).

24. Freud, *Standard Edition,* vol. 23 (1940).
25. Samuel Weber, *Return to Freud: Jacques Lacan's Dislocation of Psychoanalysis,* trans. Michael Levine (Cambridge: Cambridge UP, 1991) 149.
26. Quoted by Mitchell. Freud, *Standard Edition,* 11:188–9 (1912).
27. Jacques Lacan, "The Signification of the Phallus," *Écrits: A Selection,* trans. Alan Sheridan (New York: Norton, 1977), 287.
28. The wives that Swedenborg encounters during his celestial travels tell him how misrepresenting their desire for their husbands is the only way in which the "ultimate delights" of "conjugial love" may be fully experienced by both of them. Of course, the wives cannot reveal to him, a man, all of the ways in which this misrepresentation proceeds, but he accepts the difference in the ways the genders relate to each other: "But that these outbursts of anger, and these dissimulations, have wisdom for an end, and thence the reception of love with the husband, is plain from the fact that in a moment she can be reconciled. Moreover, wives have such means of concealing the love inherent in their heart and marrow, to the end that conjugial cold may not break forth with the man, and extinguish the fire of his scortatory heat also, and thus from green wood make him a dry stick." Emanuel Swedenborg, *The Delights of Wisdom pertaining to Conjugial Love after which follow the Pleasures of Insanity pertaining to Scortatory Love,* trans. Samuel M. Warren, rev. Louis H. Tafel (1856; New York: Swedenborg Foundation, 1980), par. 294, par. 299.

   Unfortunately, Henry James Senior's copy of *Conjugial Love* is no longer (July 1993) to be found among his papers and books in the trunk of his belongings that was given to the Swedenborg School of Religion in Newton, Massachusetts. It is listed as being in this collection.

29. Weber, *Return to Freud,* 148.
30. For a clinically based explanation in Lacanian terms of the necessity of male and female genders in the formation of the imaginary, see Wilfried Ver Eecke, "Gender and Sexuality: Some Unconscious Articulations" in *Psychoanalysis, Feminism, and the Future of Gender,* Psychiatry and the Humanities, vol. 14, ed. Joseph H. Smith and Afaf M. Mahfouz (Baltimore: Johns Hopkins UP, 1994), 121–36.
31. Mitchell and Rose, *Feminine Sexuality,* 40.

Chapter 9. Irony Makes Love

1. *Oeuvres complètes de Charles Fourier,* ed. Simone Debout Oleszkiewicz, 12 vols. (Paris: Edition Anthropos, 1966–8), 5:157. Quoted in Jonathan Beecher, *Charles Fourier: The Visionary and His World* (Berkeley: U of California P, 1987), 193.
2. Beecher, *Fourier,* 302.
3. Henry James, *A Small Boy and Others* (1913), in *Autobiography,* ed. Frederick W. Dupee (1956; Princeton: Princeton UP, 1983), 124.
4. Henry James, *Notes of a Son and Brother* (1914), in *Autobiography,* 331. All further references to this edition are noted parenthetically.
5. "To Henry James [Senior]," 14 March 1870, in *Henry James Letters,* ed. Leon Edel, 4 vols. (Cambridge: Belknap Press of Harvard UP, 1974–84), 1:187.
6. Ibid., 188.
7. Henry James Senior, "To Henry James," 9 May 1882, in *Henry James Senior: A Selection of His Writings,* ed. and introd. Giles Gunn (Chicago: American Library Association, 1974), 286.
8. Irony is a trope that can do many different kinds of things, and my use of it here as a figure that unifies the differentiated, as a trope that brings speakers together in a complex act of understanding differences, develops from James's examples rather than from a textbook definition. An important contemporary attempt to theorize the relation between irony and community has been made by Richard Rorty in *Contingency, irony, and solidarity* (Cambridge: Cambridge UP, 1989), but the limitations of his understanding of the way that irony involves the reader in necessary contradictions rather than allowing her to maintain a safe distance have been lucidly analyzed by Paul B. Armstrong in "The Politics of Irony in Reading Conrad," *Conradiana* 26:2–3 (1994): 85–101.
9. Juliet Mitchell, "Introduction-I," in *Feminine Sexuality: Jacques Lacan and the école freudienne,* ed. Juliet Mitchell and Jacqueline Rose, trans. Jacqueline Rose (New York: Norton, Pantheon, 1983), 23.
10. Mitchell and Rose, *Feminine Sexuality,* 7.
11. One different reading of James's formation of his sexual identity is offered by Eve Kosofsky Sedgwick in "The Beast in the Closet," in *Epistemology of the Closet* (Berkeley: U of California P, 1990), 182–212.

   Another reading of this scene is offered by Ross Posnock in *The Trial of Curiosity: Henry James, William James, and the Challenge of Modernity* (New York: Oxford UP, 1991), 202–5. Although I'm in sympathy with his valorization of difference, I think that his use of object-relations theory leads to an oversimplification of what he takes to be the classic psychoanalytic position of identification with the parent of the same gender.
12. John K. Sheriff, *The Fate of Meaning: Charles Peirce, Structuralism and Literature* (Princeton: Princeton UP, 1989), 140, 130, 116.

13. Henry James, *The American Scene,* introd. and notes by Leon Edel (1907; Bloomington: Indiana UP, 1968), 334, 336. All further references to this edition are noted parenthetically.

14. For a more detailed analysis of this passages on the fate of the leisure class woman, see the section on Mrs. Gardner in Chapter 4.

15. James, *A Small Boy,* 122–3.

16. James Senior, " 'The Woman Thou gavest with me,' " *Atlantic Monthly* 25 (January 1870): 66, 17. Henry James, *The Sense of the Past,* vol. 26 of *The Novels and Tales of Henry James,* 27 vols. (New York: Scribner's, 1917), 35. This transformation in the hero's understanding is the subject of Part One of my book.

18. Henry James, *The Ivory Tower,* vol. 27 of *The Novels and Tales of Henry James,* 27 vols. (New York: Scribner's, 1917), 61–2.

INDEX

Bettleheim, Bruno, 29–30
binary opposition, *see* polarization
Björnson, Björnstjerne, 16–17
Blair, Sara, 223 n2
Boone, Joseph Allen, 258 n2
Bosanquet, Theodora, xiv, 23–4, 26, 35, 233 n20
Bourget, Paul, 246 n28
Boyarin, Daniel and Jonathan, 156–7
Braudel, Fernand, 7
Broughton, Rhoda, 22–3
Budick, Emily, 224 n6
Buitenhuis, Peter, 148
Bushnell, Horace, 194
business culture, 95, 108, 167, 203, 204; *see also* barbarian; capitalism; leisure class
Butterfield, Herbert, 6–10, 29, 39

Cahan, Abraham, 147
capitalism, 78–9, 113, 136; *see also* business culture
Carroll, Charles, 123
Carroll, Lewis, 29–30
castration complex, 189–93, 198, 207, 209, 264 n23
causality, contingency, 8, 9, 31, 39, 107, 184, 187; necessity, 7, 9, 184; Peirce's categories of, 69, 241 n50
Chase, Richard, 224 n6
Chinese, 141, 143
Christ, Jesus, 184
Civil War, 127–30, 252 n42, 254 n42, 254 n52; *see also* Grant, Ulysses S.; Lee, Robert E.; Lincoln, Abraham; Massachusetts 54th Regiment; Shaw, Robert Gould; Sherman, William Tecumseh; South
class, 14, 16; *see also* leisure class
classic value, 75, 84, 105, 153, 157, 236 n2; *see also* taste
community, 113, 116, 126, 130, 145, 158, 255 n64; *see also* heterosociality

conservative, xiii, 8, 13, 16, 176, 180, 213, 225 n17
conspicuous waste, 79, 89, 92
contingency, *see* causality
conversation, xiii, 60, 70, 76, 203, 215, 240 n37; female art of, 179, 193, 195; between genders, 167, 173, 178–9, 208, 211; development of, 65, 84; gaps in, 165, 168, 214; lack of, 33, 53, 82, 259 n12; social value of, 33, 72, 84, 173–4, 178–9, 204, 209, 214; *see also* irony; language
Cooper, James Fenimore, 2
cultural property, 78, 79, 91

Daniel Deronda, review of, *see* James, Henry, works by
Davis, Natalie Zemon, 7
De Man, Paul, 4, 238 n14
Dekker, George, 224 n6
Deledalle, Gérard, 241 n50
Denmark, 146, 256 n20
Derrida, Jacques, 11, 36–7, 42, 95, 201, 239 n22
dialogism, 68, 241 n45
Dickens, Charles, 148
difference, 10, 30; and castration complex, 190–3, 198; Derridian, 11, 95; effacement of, 53–4, 56–7, 137, 141, 154, 165–6, 168, 172, 174, 208; ethnic, 135, 137–8, 141, 143; in fiction, 13; of gender, 166, 168, 172, 185–9, 202, 205, 207; Jamesian, 11, 71; of Jews, 148–50, 152–7; necessity of, 92, 186, 197, 204, 208, 264 n30; Peircean, 11, 71, 176; play of, 50, 55, 169, 211; social value of, 100–1, 188–9, 211
Diggins, John P., 247 n31
discrimination, *see* difference
divine-natural-humanity, *see* genesis, of gender; heterosociality